Making It Up
As I Go Along

Making It Up As I Go Along

MARIAN KEYES

MICHAEL JOSEPH
an imprint of
PENGUIN BOOKS

MICHAEL JOSEPH

UK | USA | Canada | Ireland | Australia
India | New Zealand | South Africa

Michael Joseph is part of the Penguin Random House group of companies
whose addresses can be found at global.penguinrandomhouse.com.

First published 2016

001

Text copyright © Marian Keyes, 2016

The moral right of the author has been asserted

Set in New Caledonia LT Std
Typeset by Palimpsest Book Production
Falkirk, Stirlingshire
Printed in Great Britain by Clays Ltd, St Ives plc

A CIP catalogue record for this book is available from the British Library

HARDBACK ISBN: 978–0–718–18252–6
TPB ISBN: 978–0–718–18173–4

www.greenpenguin.co.uk

MIX
Paper from
responsible sources
FSC® C018179

Penguin Random House is committed to a
sustainable future for our business, our readers
and our planet. This book is made from Forest
Stewardship Council® certified paper.

For Jonathan

Contents

Contents

Contents

Contents

Introduction

Hello, and welcome to *Making It Up As I Go Along* (tales from an eejit who was off buying shoes the day Life's Rulebook was given out).

It's a collection of autobiographical articles that I have written over the last nine years. Some have already been published in magazines or newspapers, such as *Irish Tatler* and *Marie Claire*. I'd like to offer special thanks to the *Sunday Times Style* magazine, who've given me a regular column called 'Mind Your Head'. Other pieces have been cherry-picked from the monthly newsletters I used to write for my website, and some have – gasp! – never been seen before!

I have grouped the pieces into sections like 'Friends and Family', 'On My Travels', 'A Year in the Life' and that sort of thing. They're not always in chronological order; I've arranged them so that you can dip in and out and read them any way you like. You could even start reading from the back, if that's the kind of daredivil you are. Feel free to break the rules. Either way, I very much hope you enjoy the articles.

My publisher Louise Moore and my editors Maxine Hitchcock and Celine Kelly worked very hard with me, sifting through TONS of raw material to come up with this collection, and I'm very grateful to them.

I'd also like to thank Himself, who is always my first reader, the voice of reason, a stalwart support and the best colleague in the whole world.

And now, off we go!

Cast of Characters

I thought it would be a good idea to compile a cast list, because I mention many, many people in this book and you won't have a rasher's who half of them are. Many people I've described in terms of their relationship to someone else (for example, 'X: Y's husband'.) This is not to imply that X is not a viable person in their own right. I am only trying to keep things simple and easy to refer to. But of course, I am afeerd of offending people, because that is the way of life, is it not? Despite our best intentions, someone is always bound to be offended.

Anyway! Here's the list, which I hope will be helpful. I should mention that I come from a family of five children (shamefully small by Irish standards) and I'm the eldest and as a result I feel responsible for everyone's happiness and that's a scourge of a burden and I'd have much preferred to be the youngest, but what can you do?

Anne Marie Scanlon: very old friend. Also mother of Jack Scanlon.
Bruce: husband of Laura, who is a long-time, beloved friend. (So when you come to Laura, you can refer back to Bruce and then you'll know who she is. Do you see? This is how it works.)
Bubs: Tadhg and Susan's youngest dog. (They have two.)
Caitríona: my sister. (I've two.) She's four and a half years younger than me and is the funniest person alive. She lives in Brooklyn and is married to Seán, who is a tremenjuss musician and a tremenjuss cook.

Cast of Characters

Caron: my sister-in-law and a hugely talented writer (Caron Freeborn is her full name). Partner of Himself's brother Chris and mother of Jude and Gabe.

Cathy Kelly: my soul sister. A wonderful writer (yes, she's *that* Cathy Kelly), a warm, wise friend and a great souce of comfort.

Chris: Himself's brother, partner of Caron and father of Jude and Gabe.

Claudia Winkleman: ah, lookit, you must know who she is.

Dad: my father. He used to be a 'Traditional Irish Father', by which I mean he was a right cranky-arse who would come home from work and say, 'Right! Which one of you am I to shout at first?' But in recent years, he has mellowed. Is it okay to say he has dementia? But mercifully he has a nice version where he is very loved up and often asks Mam to marry him.

Davina McCall: I refer you to **Claudia Winkleman**.

Dermot O'Leary: I refer you to **Davina McCall**.

Dylan: eldest son of Rita-Anne and Jimmy. Also known as Redzer the Elder. As I write, he's seven, but you might be reading it 'further down the line', so my apologies for any confusion.

Eileen: aka Eilers. Old friend.

Elizabeth: aka Beth, friend to the entire Keyes family – cleans our house and minds it when Himself and I are away, drives Mam and Dad to Mass every Sunday, and is always obliging and cheerful and a stalwart support.

Ema: daughter of Niall and Ljiljana. My beloved niece. Currently aged fifteen. I love her with all my heart. I have plans to pitch a TV show called *My Niece Is the Best*, which she would DEFINITELY win.

Fergal: great friend, and husband of Judy.

Gabe: youngest son of Chris and Caron.

Gwen: very good friend, partner of Ken and mother of Edward.

Cast of Characters

Hilly: very good friend, and part of our walking club.

Himself: the fabliss man I'm lucky enough to be married to. He is the best, kindest, funniest, most clever person ever.

Jack Scanlon: son of my pal Anne Marie Scanlon.

Jenny: Australian friend who lives in London and is the 'most good' person I've ever met.

Jimmy: husband of my sister Rita-Anne.

John: Himself's dad, aka my father-in-law.

Jonathan Lloyd: my literary agent. He's been my agent for more than twenty years, he's great fun, wholly supportive, and I owe my career to him and Louise Moore, my publisher.

Jude: eldest son of Chris and Caron.

Judy: very special friend. The woman I want to be when I grow up. She is married to an equally wonderful man called Fergal.

Katie: Tadhg and Susie's eldest dog. She's a boxer and named in honour of Katie Taylor (the boxer).

Laura: long-time, beloved friend. Married to Bruce.

Ljiljana: wife of my brother Niall. From Serbia. (Note: Ljiljana is pronounced 'Lilly-anna'.)

Louise Moore: my publisher. She is WILDLY fabliss, has published me for twenty years, and I owe my career to her. See also **Jonathan Lloyd**.

Luka: son of Niall and Ljiljana. Currently aged fourteen. Very handsome, although he goes mad when I say it, so maybe I shouldn't . . .

Mam: aka Mammy Keyes. Mother of all the Keyesez. A living legend.

Mark: good friend, and part of the walking club.

Milenko: Ljiljana's dad, who very sadly died three years ago.

Niall: my brother. (I've two.) He's two and a half years younger than me, is married to Ljiljana, and is the father of Ema and

Luka. Currently living in Dublin, but they used to live in Prague and are still known as the Praguers.

Oscar: youngest son of Rita-Anne and Jimmy. Also known as Redzer the Younger. As I write, he is five.

Posh Kate: aka Kate Beaufoy. Wife of Posh Malcolm. Beloved friend of mine and Himself's.

Posh Malcolm: aka Malcolm Douglas. Husband of Posh Kate. Beloved friend of mine and Himself's.

Praguers: see **Niall**.

Rita-Anne: my youngest sister. (I've two.) She's eight and a half years younger than me, and she and Tadhg are twins. She's married to Jimmy and is Mother of the Redzers (Dylan and Oscar).

Seán: husband of my sister Caitríona.

Shirley: Himself's mammy, aka my mother-in-law, and I couldn't have wished for a better one. I love her dearly.

Siobhán: aka Shivers. Old friend.

Susan: wife of my brother Tadhg. Also referred to as 'Susie'.

Suzanne: my sister from another mister. Her mam and my mam worked together in Limerick 4,000 years ago. She was in Caitríona's class at school, and she and I were flatmates for years and years in London. Bonded for life.

Tadhg: my youngest brother. (I've two.) He's eight and a half years younger than me, and he and Rita-Anne are twins. He's married to Susan and they have a little boy, baby Teddy, and two dogs – Katie and Bubs. (Note: Tadhg is pronounced 'Thigh-ge'.)

Tania: sister of Seán, who is married to Caitríona.

Teddy: son of Tadhg and Susan. As I write, the 'newest' Keyes.

Tom Dunne: lead singer in Something Happens, radio presenter, and owner of a beautiful voice and a charming personality. We share a bin night.

Vilma: naturopath from Lithuania and a beautiful human being.

Zaga: mother of Ljiljana, she lives in Belgrade and if feeding people was an Olympic sport, she would take home the gold.

Zoë Ball: I refer you to **Dermot O'Leary**.

Lexicon

Just in case you don't speak Hiberno-English fluently – and there's no shame in that, no shame at all! – I thought I'd do a little dictionary for you.

agin: a derivative of 'against', it means 'counter to'. For example, to 'take agin' a person means one has developed an antipathy towards a certain person and wishes them ill. One of my favourite words. Taking agin people can count as a hobby, to be listed on job applications along with keeping fit and cooking, except it doesn't have to be a lie.

banjaxed: broken. For example, 'That fecking IKEA chest of drawers is banjaxed' means 'That item of furniture I purchased from a well-known Scandinavian retailer no longer functions.'

banjoed: same as **banjaxed**. Unless one is talking about furniture, in which case it means 'upcycled'.

bayshte: beast. As in 'I made a bayshte of meself, ayting them four Easter eggs.' Can also refer to animals ('bayshtes of the field').

be the Janeys: an expression of astonishment.

bet-down: burdened by life. Having endured a lot of disappointment and looking every inch of it.

bolloxed: Can mean broken or inebriated. Context is key. 'My hairdryer is bolloxed' means one's hairdryer is *hors de combat*. But 'Cripes, you were bolloxed last night' means a person was extremely inebriated on the previous evening.

bould: comes from the word 'bold', but does not mean 'daring' or 'courageous'. Rather it means very badly behaved. 'Bould as bras' is as bad as it gets.

by the hokey: an expression of astonishment, very similar to **be the Janeys**.

cliothar: I'm guessing, but I think it's related to 'clatter'. It means a short, sharp blow. Often used in reference to a child who has just drawn all over your lovely Designers Guild wallpaper: 'What that little fecker needs is a good hard cliothar.' A word that Mammy Keyes seems particularly fond of.

clob: face, as in, 'I stuffed me clob.' Confusingly it can also mean 'mouth'.

craythur: a derivative of 'creature'. A term of compassion, as in, 'Ah shur, the poor oul' craythur, he was never right after he drove the combine harvester over the postman.'

divil: a derivative of 'devil', but does not refer to Satan/Lucifer/ the man below. It's usually a term of compassion and often accompanied by a sigh. 'Ah, the poor oul' divil . . .'

eejit: a foolish person. For example, 'The fecking eejit's after leaving his jacket on the bus. Again!'

enjoying the day: inebriated.

feck: the most misunderstood, falsely maligned word ever. It is NOT a swear word. Anyone, even the Pope, could say 'feck' and no one would look askance. It is nothing like the other 'F' word. Feel free to use it liberally.

gawk: enjoys two usages. One is 'to look at or view'. The other is 'to vomit'. Context is key. 'The gawks', or worse still 'a desperate dose of the gawks', is when one cannot stop vomiting – often the morning after one has been **enjoying the day**. This is also when 'the dry gawks' may occur.

gobshite: a powerfully disparaging term of abuse. Mildly sweary.

gom: I refer you to **eejit**.

grand: a fascinating word, which does not mean 'swanky', 'excellent' or 'awe-inspiring'. Mostly it means 'just okay' or 'barely adequate'; however, an entire (very funny) book has been written on the word by Tara Flynn. I urge you to read it.

in top form: usually means 'inebriated'. But – confusingly – it can sometimes mean simply 'in top form'.

jar: drink, alcohol, Babycham, aquavit, grappa and whatever you're having yourself.

JohnEamonChippyBill: the wonderful pundit-men on the panel for Ireland's football games.

lad: can mean 'a teenage boy', but when I use it I tend to be referring to a penis. For example, 'Well, if he thinks he can arrive around here, with his lad in his hand, he can think again!'

lads: a greeting, which can apply to both sexes, even those who are not lads or who don't *have* lads. Always accompanied by an exclamation mark, for example, 'Lads! How's it going?'

lock-hard: specifically 'lock-hard men' – famous creatures in Dublin who appear from nowhere while you're trying to parallel-park on the street. They will stand and shout instructions, always urging you to 'lock hard' on the steering wheel. They will invariably make the job of parking your car far more fraught than it would otherwise have been and will expect a couple of yoyos for this.

looderamaun: I refer you to **eejit**.

lungeon: the meal you 'take' in the middle of the day, if you are posh. See **sangwidge** if you are not posh.

now: means anything *but* the present time. For example, 'I'll do that now in a minute' means 'I'll do it as soon as I feel like getting round to it. Now feck off and leave me be.'

oul': a derivative of the word 'old', but does not mean 'aged'. It's a fascinating word that enjoys many usages. It can be disparaging, for example: 'He never rang me, the thick oul' eejit.' But it can also be compassionate: 'Ah shur, the poor oul' divil, and the guttering after falling down on his head.' However, sometimes 'oul'' adds nothing to a sentence, except to perfect the rhythm, which matters a lot in conversational Hiberno-English. If this is the case, there is no need to ascribe meaning to it.

oxter: armpit.

praties: potatoes, spuds, the staple diet of the Irish.

press: a cupboard.

quare: unusual, distinctive, astonishing, special.

ride: a very attractive person, often used by women to describe men, but these days women say it to each other, in this manner: 'Look at you, you great big ride, you.' This is a compliment of the highest order. 'Ride' can also mean 'an act of sexual congress'.

ridey: an adjective derived from **ride**, it means 'very sexually attractive'.

sangwidge: a casual lungeon, consisting of two slices of bread bracketing cheese or ham or similar.

scuttered: inebriated.

shite: like 'shit' but marginally less bad.

skaw-ways: crooked.

spannered: inebriated.

stotious: inebriated.

sure: pronounced 'shur', it has no meaning. It's most definitely *not* a term of agreement (as in '*Sure!*'). It's simply an extra word added to the start of a sentence, in the way 'so' is used in the modern global lingo. Except it's not annoying.

tay: comes from the word 'tea', and it can mean a hot drink in a mug or one's evening meal.

togs: a bathing suit, a swimming costume, trunks, those sorts of things.

thrun: comes from the word 'thrown' but hints at unhappiness – to be 'thrun in the bed' implies a bout of depression.

tool: a foolish man.

yoke: a catch-all word that seems to defy translation. Basically it can mean *anything*. Some people have said that 'whatjama-callit' or 'thingummyjig' is the same as 'yoke', and certainly 'Where's the yoke?' can mean (and frequently does) 'Where's the remote control?' Or 'I broke the little yoke on the yoke' can mean 'I've broken the small attachment on my spiralizer.' But 'yoke' means much more and can also be used to disparage a person. For example, if a man with whom you shared sexual relations does not seek to repeat the experience, you could call him, in very bitter tones, 'a hairy-arsed oul' yoke'. Or if an acquaintance has recently lost weight and is making much of it, you could say, 'Look at her there, the skraggy-arsed oul' yoke, swanking around in her size 6 jeans, thinking she's it.'

yoyos: the currency of Ireland. Sometimes known as euros.

(BAD) HEALTH
AND BEAUTY

Over the years I've written various beauty columns, and many of you who folley me on Twitter will know about my great love for chemists. And you will also know that I 'enjoy' bad health. That's what this bit is all about.

Where It All Began

My love of cosmetics goes back decades and I blame Mammy Keyes – well, like all mammies, the poor woman has (entirely unfairly) got the blame for many of her daughter's woes over the years, so why shouldn't she get the blame for my deep and abiding love of cosmetics? One of my earliest memories is of her sitting at her dressing table, patting some funny liquid in the palm of her hand until it eventually emulsified into a white cream, which she then spread over her face. 'Take care of your skin,' she often told me, 'and some day it will take care of you.'

The strange thing was, this was Ireland in the 1960s and 70s, when the Catholic Church controlled everything and the message it gave was that women were meant to be baby factories who entirely neglected themselves in order to boil massive pots of praties and say round-the-clock novenas while kneeling on frozen peas. A weekend away with the girls consisted of forty-eight hours in Lough Derg, eating burnt toast and singing 'Hail, Holy Queen' and walking on pointy stones in their bare feet.

Vanity was a total no-go area and my mammy was – and is – a devout holy type. But still, she couldn't resist the lure of the beauty counter. Like, she didn't go mad or anything, she wasn't an eyelashed glamour-puss who showered me with perfumed kisses and called me 'Darlink', but she had the basic products, and one day when I was about twelve I smothered my face in her foundation and I was stunned – I looked . . . well, FABULOUS!

My whey-white Celtic skin was bright orange – I think it was actually the law at the time that all foundation sold in Ireland be that colour – and the chic way to apply it was to cut it off at the jawline so that the face looked like an orange lollipop, balanced on a white neck.

Mesmerized by my own orange loveliness, I gazed at myself in the mirror, seeing that the white bits of my eyes looked extra-white and the green bits looked extra-green and my shameful freckles had been banished entirely. The transformative effects of make-up were never so obvious, and because I'd always felt like an ugly little yoke I vowed that this magic gear would be part of my life for evermore.

Funds, of course, were initially a problem. But mercifully my new love of cosmetics coincided very neatly with the traditional early-teenage shoplifting years and I was down in Woolworths in Dún Laoghaire most Saturdays, relieving them of the odd kohl pencil or lipstick. (I've since repented and am very sorry for that carry-on. If I could go back and change things I would, but that's life, isn't it? We all do things we subsequently regret and the guilt is our punishment.)

But enough of the philosophizing and on with the make-up! I got my first job when I was seventeen, and from the day I got my first pay cheque to one morning about three months ago I quite literally NEVER left the house without wearing foundation. I really mean it. No matter how tired I felt, no matter how poor I was, foundation was my bridge to the outside world. I genuinely felt I wouldn't be able to look someone in the eye without it. My desert-island product would have been foundation, because if I hadn't any, I wouldn't have been able to jump around on the beach, waving my T-shirt and shouting at a rare passing ship to please rescue me. Instead I'd have to hide behind a coconut tree, to protect the pirates from getting a shocking gawk at my freckly clob. (What happened about three months ago was I had IPL on my face which did some quare business where my freckles all disappeared and my skin became – and forgive me for sounding like a boasty boaster – very fresh and even. Apparently the trauma of the IPL (which stands for Intense Pulsed Light) stimulated bow-coo de collagen. I was told that this would happen, but in my heart I think that anyone who makes a promise like this is a liar and no one was more surprised than me that it actually really did work. I mean, it won't last, I'll have to go back and get it done again at some stage, and it's a) spendy and b) painful beyond description. But still!

In my twenties I moved to London and shared a flat with two other girls and lipstick became our non-negotiable product. Chanel lipstick, no less. We lurched from pay cheque to pay cheque, borrowing and bartering, barely able to keep ourselves in Jacob's Creek, and yet we prioritized Chanel lipstick. Red, of course. Because it was empowering, so we were told. We'd get promotions if we wore red lipstick. We'd run the world if we wore red lipstick. We'd get on the property ladder and learn to drive and get married if we wore red lipstick. Anyway . . .

Despite the red Chanel lipstick, my life hit the skids in spectacular fashion when it transpired that I'd become a little too fond of the Jacob's Creek and I ended up in rehab. (Even there, I wore foundation every single day.) After six weeks I emerged and at high speed my life changed course and I started writing a book and got a publishing deal and met a lovely man and got married – so maybe, in a roundabout way, the red lipstick *did* work!

Then I got a gig doing a make-up column, and to this very day I still say it's the nicest thing that's ever happened to me. I swear to God, you have no idea! Free make-up began arriving at the house in the PEOLs (Padded Envelopes of Loveliness). My first batch was from Lancôme, and this was around the time when women were trampling over each other in beauty halls to get their paws on Juicy Tubes, and I got three – THREE! – of the new colours in the envelope. It was so thrilling that a family conference was called, and all my brothers and sisters and Mam and Dad came to admire the free make-up, and we sat around the kitchen table staring at it, and no one could really believe it, and Dad, who used to be an accountant, totted up how much it would have cost if I'd paid for it, and we MARVELLED at the figure, and my mammy became quite anxious because she was sure there had to be a catch, but all in all, it was *bloody fabulous*!

Overnight, the arrival of the postman flipped from being something to dread – bills and strange requests and that sort of thing – to something to anticipate. If he rang the bell, it was a really good day – it meant that he had a Padded Envelope of Loveliness that was too big to be shoved through the letter box. No matter how early he arrived, it was with a joyous heart that I skipped down the stairs to open the door to him. Soon he began to realize that I was causing him more work than the rest of the road put together, and all I could do was apologize and give him a decent tip at Christmas time.

I hit a rough patch when I worried that loving make-up was incompatible with being a feminist, but I've eventually made my peace with it.

However, as we know, all good things come to an end and eventually the magazine I was writing for folded and the Padded Envelopes of Loveliness stopped arriving. (Ten years on, thinking about it still gives me a stabbing pain of loss in my sternum.) However, I stayed passionately interested in all aspects of beauty, getting particularly animated by anything officially 'New and Exciting'.

Where It All Began

Now the thing is that I wasn't (and I'm still not) a beautician or a trained make-up artist, I'm simply an enthusiastic amateur – a very, *very* enthusiastic amateur. But I do have my moments of insight. Like, you've heard of the 'Lipstick Index'? It's the theory that during a recession, sales of lipsticks increase as women shift their spending habits from expensive fripperies like shoes and handbags to more affordable things like lipsticks. Well, it's been overtaken by the Nail Varnish Index, and what kills me is that I predicted it! I knew it was happening because I could see it in my own behaviour – I was haunting Rimmel counters and buying two or three nail varnishes in super-bright colours, bagging the whole lot for under a tenner. But the only person I shared my theory with was Himself, and I'm *raging* that I didn't do a David McWilliams and write a scholarly paper on the topic for the *Sunday Business Post*, and be hailed as the new Irish economic sage, but shur, there we are.

First published in *Irish Tatler*, November 2014.

Eyelash Extensions

Eyelashes. Such lovely things. The more the merrier, thanks. Over the years, when I'd had my make-up done, I'd seen the dramatic effect of false eyelashes, but I never got the hang of doing them myself.

Then I heard about eyelash extensions: false eyelashes that are glued, one by one, to a person's own lashes and last until the lashes fall out naturally. No more mascara. Just constant, round-the-clock, dark-lashed loveliness. It sounded like something from a fantasy.

So I went and lay on a bed and – this was a few years back – to my great dismay, the extensions were so heavy they pulled my eyelids down and, in the following days, I was told, more than once, that I looked like Salman Rushdie.

Also, I felt very 'blinky'. Every time I blinked (and I discovered that I blink an awful lot) it was as if it was happening in slow motion. Worse still, the lashes were rigid and sort of crunchy, so at night I was kept awake by them scritchy-scratching against my pillow and if I slept on them funny I awoke to find them bent into strange geometric contortions.

Next thing – within days – they started to fall out, taking my own eyelashes with them, and very soon my eyelids were bald. It was a bad experience and I thought, 'Ah well, we live and learn.'

But about nine months later, I decided to give it another go. I went to a different saloon where they used lovely lightweight lashes – so I didn't feel heavy-lidded or blinky and no one looked like Salman Rushdie. Except Salman Rushdie.

And I cannot tell you how *fabulous* I felt. The effect was dramatic: the long dark lashes changed the shape of my face and made my eyes 'burst'. (In a good way.)

The long and the short of it is, you look GREAT with eyelash extensions. You wake up looking fantastic. You go to bed looking fantastic. You can go swimming and look fantastic. It doesn't look like you're wearing false lashes – especially if you go for the more expensive silk extensions – it just seems like you've got gorgeous long, natural eyelashes, with more va-va-voom than even the fonciest mascara could ever give you.

However, with great power comes great responsibility, and it's no joke having semi-permanent eyelashes in your care: they are highly strung, nervy beasts. Basically you have to avoid touching them at all because they're easy to upset, and when they're upset they leave you, and that is more unpleasant than I know how to describe.

So it's tricky putting on eye make-up. And it's even trickier taking it off. To do my eyeliner I had to use a very, very long make-up brush and use tiny, exquisitely delicate stokes.

You know that game where you have to move an object on a loop along an electrified wire, without touching the wire? (Would it be called Operation?) That's what it's like. My concentration was *intense*.

Taking the make-up off was even more nerve-racking. I used a cotton bud soaked in oil-free remover, and if I ever accidentally touched the lashes, I had to shout, 'Sorry, sorry! I'm really sorry!'

To be frank, living with eyelash extensions was like being in a dysfunctional relationship.

After a few rounds of acrylic lashes, I upgraded to silk ones –

more expensive, but even more lightweight and dark and clustery. I fell even deeper in love.

'They' say that extensions are supposed to last about six weeks, but that, of course, is a lie. Even with the gentlest care, at around the three-week mark they would start to fall out, usually taking my own real lash with them. And every lost lash felt like a mini-death.

I'd start filling in the gaps with mascara, which needed to be removed every night, which interfered with the extensions, making them fall out faster and faster – and long before the six-week mark I'd arrive back at the saloon, looking for a refill.

The few days before the appointment were always the worst. I'd feel utterly naked and lived in dread of being taunted, 'Baldy lids, baldy lids!'

In I'd go, looking all meek and blinky and baldy-eyed – and two hours later I'd swagger out, batting my fabulous lashes left, right and centre, interfering with the flight paths of planes, sending wheelie bins racing along the road and crashing into each other, and generally feeling like the most powerful woman on earth.

I was utterly addicted to the extensions and couldn't contemplate going back to a life without them. But the thing is, you're only supposed to get them for about six months and then you have to stop because you're depriving your natural lashes of sunlight and oxygen and all that other blah.

But when the six-month time limit arrived, there was NO WAY ON EARTH I was stopping. So – like the true addict I am – I began to lie and cheat. I started going to different beauticians, the way I used to go to different off-licences when I was drinking, so no one would know the full extent of my habit.

When the beauticians would ask me how long I'd been getting

the extensions, I'd say, with elaborate vagueness, 'Let's seeeee, hmmm, maybe about . . . God, I don't know, four months?' When the reality was, I'd been getting them for *a year and a half.*

However, when I hit the two-year mark, it all came crashing down. I'd gone to a beautician who was basically my enabler – she knew that I was lying and she still went along with it. However, on this particular day she was away, and in her place was what you might call a locum – and this new one was on to me immediately!

She removed my mascara and the last few extensions that were still clinging on, and made me take a good hard look at my own lashes – and I was horrified. They were pale brown stumps. 'You've got to stop,' she said. Basically she refused to serve me!

Then she cast me out on to the street with a tube of some RapidLash yoke and instructions to apply it twice daily, and told me that I was now in Eyelash Rehab.

It was a low, low moment: I'd hit rock bottom and the game was up. No more eyelash extensions for me for a very long time.

I consoled myself by thinking bitter thoughts about her and nursing elaborate plans to start again as soon as possible; but after some time passed and I got used to having normal-style eyelashes again, I began to feel as if a burden had been lifted from me. It had been hard, *hard* work maintaining the lifestyle of an eyelash addict – and I'd been freed from it. I hadn't wanted to be free, but now that I was, I kind of liked it.

So, as things stand, I have no immediate plans to resume the habit.

First published in *Irish Tatler*, November 2014.

Fake Tan

Oh God, it's that time of year again. Sooner or later every year, the snows of winter melt and the daffodils bloom and the weather gets warmer and before we know it, it's fake-tan time. Or self-tan time. Or sunless-tan time. Call it what you want, the smell is the same.

At first glance, self-tan is a godsend for the likes of me, because I never enjoyed sunbathing. It was so boring, lying still, while sweat ran into my hair, and I never had anyone to talk to because I always went on holiday with devoted sun-lovers who believed that conversation cancelled out the efficacy of the sun's rays. Besides, sunbathing never worked for me because (am I the only one?) I have entirely different types of skin on different parts of my body. This is how I tan: feet – golden. Stomach – mahogany. Shins – Germolene pink. Face – bluey-white, offset with a massive, red, peeling, Bozo-the-clown nose. At the end of two weeks in the sun I look like a patchwork quilt.

And yet I refuse to bow to the inevitable and remain my natural milk-bottle pallor, so you'd think I'd be thrilled with fake tans. However, everything has a price and I can't decide which is the worst:

1) The horrific smell
2) The curse of the orange paw
3) The tie-dyed heels
4) The hour of naked freestyle dancing, as I wait to dry

5) The indelible amber-coloured stains on my sheets
6) All of the above

If I may come back to the horrific smell. The first time I ever 'did' myself, I went to bed, only to wake in terror in the middle of the night, wondering what the unspeakable stink was. The devil? Wasn't he supposed to be preceded by dreadful, poo-type smells? Quaking with fear, I peeped over the covers, expecting to see coal-red eyes and a forked tail, only to discover that the choking stench was none other than my freshly tanned self. In recent years, cosmetic companies have been working hard on diluting the ferocious pong, and now some brands even claim to have 'a pleasant fragrance'. Yes, indeed they *do* have a pleasant fragrance. But mark me well here, that's *as well as*, that's *in addition to*, the extremely *un*pleasant fragrance that is the hallmark of all self-tanners.

I have made every fake-tan mistake in the book.

Mistake number one: I was in a mad hurry for a colour and decided that one thick layer would do just as well as several thin layers. The result? My entire body looked like it had been tie-dyed and I couldn't leave the house for a week.

Mistake number two: forgetting to wash my hands after 'applying', so that I ended up with the orangest palms on earth; if I'd held them upwards, they could have been seen from outer space. However, I learnt one important thing from this tragic omission: surgical gloves. Not only do they save me from the curse of the orange paw, but I enjoy a delicious little ER moment whenever I snap them on – Nurse Keyes to the rescue.

Mistake number three: I decided to do it properly. I'd do wafer-thin layers and leave plenty of time to dry between applications. But the thing is, I got a little obsessive about it and it took over my life. I'd apply a layer, then do some freestyle dancing as I waited for it to dry, then I'd apply another layer and do some more dancing, and when the colour still hadn't come, I'd apply another layer. I'd even enlisted a floaty red scarf to waft about over my head during the dancing. At some point, the end product of a tan no longer seemed to matter: it was the *doing* that was the important thing (which, in fairness, is how self-help gurus are always telling us to live our lives).

Then Himself walked into the room and yelped, 'Jesus Christ!' I thought it was the freestyle dancing and stopped abruptly, more than a little mortified by the scarf. 'Look at yourself,' he urged. 'Look!'

So I looked, and instead of the radiant golden hue I'd been expecting, I was a nasty Eurotrash mahogany which probably went all the way down to my internal organs. Again I couldn't leave the house for a week. I mean, no one wants to be humiliated in the street by strangers shouting, 'Who's been drinking the fake tan, then?'

Mistake number four: the mud, administered in a saloon by a professional. My first time, it was only when I was covered in the smelly muck that I discovered I couldn't wash it off until the following morning.

'Obviously you'll look manky this evening,' the girl said, 'but tomorrow you'll have a fabulous tan.'

'Fine, fine,' I said, in a high, tight voice.

She seemed to pick up on my anxiety. 'You hadn't planned to go out tonight, had you?'

'No, not really.' Just for my mammy's birthday.

At the restaurant I caused a bit of a stir. As if the smell wasn't bad enough, bits of the mud were going black and green and falling off my face into my dinner.

So I'm asking myself, Is it worth it? Will this be the year I embrace my blue-white Irish skin? Maybe . . .

Previously unpublished.

Skincare

For the first time in years, I'm on a strict skincare 'diet' – that is to say, I'm using one brand and *one brand only* for every single thing: make-up remover, toner, night serum, eye cream, day serum and day cream. It's a French brand called Payot. I was persuaded to do the whole-hog thing by lovely Mihaela at my local saloon, Pretty Nails Pretty Face, because for many years I've been cherry-picking from a variety of brands that have caught my fancy.

Anyway, the Payot is perfectly lovely and I would recommend it – my skin looks nice, it feels fine, and although the price isn't low, it's not extortionate either. However, amigos, I cannot do this. I cannot do skincare monogamy.

When my Payot stuff runs out – and I'm hoping it will be soon because I am *bored out of my skull* – I will be moving on. Because that is my way.

If I were a man and skincare brands were women, I would growl sexily at each new one I meet, 'Don't fall in love with me, baby, because I'll only break your heart.'

I cannot be faithful. I will never be faithful. My head is turned by each new brand I encounter – and there are so, so many. The market is absolutely saturated with them, all fighting for my attention and my money, and I want every single one of them.

The whole matter is very tricky and I'll try to articulate how I feel.

Okay, the biggest promise from most skincare brands is young-looking-ness. As a feminist I have deep-seated objections to the 'You ladies must stay young for ever' message, but in the last few years the message has started being foisted on to men too. And I don't think that makes things fairer or easier; it means that the burden to keep looking young is becoming heavier on everyone.

The point is, how can the efficacy of a face cream ever be proved? I know most brands say stuff like '81 per cent of users noticed a reduction in fine lines' and '78 per cent noticed an increase in resilience' and so forth. But the only way the claims can ever really be proved is when I die, right? If God wheels out a far younger-looking version of me and says, 'This is the face you *would* have had, if you had used Brand such-and-such every day of your life. But no! Despite all the ads featuring lovely luminous ladies splashing themselves with slow-motion water, you chose the inferior brand and you ended up looking like *this*. You big eejit!'

I know that expensive skincare will not save me from ageing and dying, but I still have a powerful emotional response to it. I love it. Like, I LOVE it. Sometimes in the beauty halls in department stores, I get a funny taste in my mouth and I feel really thirsty and like I'm going to pass out.

All those bottles and jars get me on some primal level which short-circuits the rational part of my brain – because if it was simply about a face cream's efficacy, why would I be affected by the packaging, the colour, the smell and the 'story'? What does it matter if it comes with a little ceramic spoon or a silver space-agey lid or a laboratory-style pipette? Or if it's made from ingredients that are only picked at midnight under a full moon by naked people who do the Lindy Hop as they work?

Here's how bad I am: when I went to Florence, I got far more excited about a jar of night cream from Profumo-Farmaceutica di Santa Maria Novella than from seeing Michelangelo's *David*. In the Farmaceutica, all they had to do was bandy around words like 'friars', 'medicinal herbs', 'balms' and 'oldest chemist in the world' and I was utterly enchanted.

So here I am, stuck with a quarter-jar of the Payot cream (which really is excellent). But I'm champing at the bit, dying to move on to something new, while feeling terribly guilty. Which then makes me defensive, so every time I have to engage with it, I'm taking more and more out of the jar and shouting, 'Stop looking at me in that mournful way and hurry up and be finished!'

First published in *Daily Mail Plus*, August 2013.

Nails

May I speak freely and frankly with you about nails? Okay! Thank you! Well, for my whole life I've had very ugly hands. My fingers are short and stumpy, my knuckles always remind me of ET's face, and as for my nails – don't be talking to me! I'm not being self-deprecating here in the hope that you'll like me, I really do have horrible nails and for my entire life they've made a show of me.

It's not just that they're short and break the minute they grow a millimetre, it's that they're all different shapes. I'm like a variety pack of nails, where you get one of each of ten types. The nail on my index finger on my right hand is *definitely* my best: it looks normal and nail-shaped and it grows and doesn't always break; I still remember the Summer of the Good Nail with wistful longing. (I was twelve at the time.)

To strengthen my nails I tried doing that thing of eating a cube of jelly a day, but a) I think it might be an old wives' tale, and b) I couldn't stick to just one cube a day; instead I ate the whole packet every time.

So basically I disengaged from my fingernails for most of my life. I didn't even – gasp! – get a manicure for my wedding day! I just showed up with my bare, crooked-shaped nails, and although I try not to have regrets in life, that would definitely be one.

The thing is, I love colour and I love nail varnish, so I've always painted my toenails. But I would punish my fingernails by showing them the varnish and saying, 'Lovely, isn't it? Well, NONE for you!'

Then I started getting pedicures from my lovely friend Helen Cosgrove. She'd paint my toenails some gorgeous colour and then she'd insist on also painting my fingernails, even though I'd be shouting, 'No, Helen, no! They don't deserve it. Don't encourage them.'

However, I quickly grew to love having colouredy fingernails. I'm a divil for bright colours. They have a huge effect on my mood. They cheer me up enormously. When my nails are painted, it's like having fruity hard-boiled sweets sellotaped on to the ends of my fingers. Nice nails make me deeply happy. (When I can force myself to do my gratitude list – I'm supposed to do it every night, but to be honest I only do it about once a week – coloured nails always feature. Hey, you take your pleasures where you can.)

Then Helen gave me a present of a bottle of lilac nail varnish and, amigos, that was my gateway drug . . .

I started buying nail varnishes. Left, right and centre, as is my way, when I'm in the grip of an obsession. I was – and still am – extremely attracted to Rimmel ones. They have a massive range of colours, and as well as having all the pinks and reds they also have edgy, directional colours – I've just bought a yellow one from them. And the thing about Rimmel is, their nail varnishes cost half nothing.

Then I found an *even cheaper brand*. In my local chemist, where I spend a goodly portion of my life with my various ailments, I found a brand called Essence and I got the cutest glittery mauve one the other day for one euro, seventy-nine cents!

Now I must veer off slightly to another story here, if you'll bear with me. About a year ago, I started getting the Shellac and/or

Gelish nails (they're much the same). I'm sure you know about them, but just in case you don't, they are sometimes called the 'two-week manicure'. And sometimes they are even called the 'three-week manicure', and I can personally vouch for that. And in a world that's full of marketing spake followed by crushing disappointment, this was a THRILLING success for me.

I go to Elena and Mihaela in Pretty Nails Pretty Face in Stillorgan, where they paint some chemical on my nails, stick my hand under an LED light for thirty seconds, then paint on some lovely colouredy varnish and stick my hand under the yoke again, then once more. The nails are dry instantly!

So I'm spared all that awful time hanging around, being underfoot in a saloon, waiting for them to dry. (It's not so bad with hands, but my idea of hell is the time spent waiting for painted toenails to dry so that I can put my socks and boots back on and continue with my life. It is a purgatory of a time. I get more and more panicky as the minutes elapse – twenty minutes, thirty minutes – and I'm still not allowed to leave, and often I jump up and grab my socks and cry, 'It's fine! All dry! Please let me through. Leaving, goodbye, thank you! See you in three weeks, but I must leave now because I just must. No need to check the nails are dry, I am a woman of my word. Goodbye.' Of course the nails are NOT dry and I am NOT a woman of my word and I get the pattern of my socks imprinted on to my still-wet toenails, but if I'd waited one second longer, I would have gone bananas. And I know I should get flipflops, but I live in Ireland. For much of the year I'd get trenchfoot if I started sporting flipflops.)

So yes, Gelish or Shellac or Artistic Colour Gloss and their ilk are wonders. They don't chip (except sometimes you can be unlucky and bang your hand off the corner of something and a piece of your Shellac-iness will choose to leave you). They come in a range of colours that is growing all the time, and they are getting blues and purples and turquoises and other lovely shades. And the best bit is that my own nails grow underneath – the hard cover of the Gelish/Shellac protects them from breaking – and for the first time ever my nails are long and my fingers feel slender and elegant. (Long nails are like high heels for the hands.)

Naturally I wondered where the catch was – because there's always a catch. Sure enough, dire warnings began to circulate that my natural nails would be ruined. But my natural nails were horrible anyway – they couldn't BE any more ruined. I had nothing to lose!

However! When you have your nails Gelished, you are stuck with that selfsame colour for two to three weeks, and I must whisper something to you . . . I started to get bored. All around me were delightful nail varnishes whispering, 'Buy me, wear me,' and I had to lift the palm of my hand and shove it at them, like Wonder Woman repelling something, and say, 'I cannot. I am on a different path in life now. I am a Gelish-stroke-Shellac girl. Please stop tempting me, for I am weak . . .'

But then! I came up with a WONDERFUL solution, which is all my own invention, if you will permit me to be a boasty boaster. What I do now is I get Gelished in clear varnish! Yes, so I get the strength and length and non-ridginess – and the chance to change my colour myself every two or three days. That is to say, I myself, not a manicure person, paint my nails and although I do an imperfect job it's good enough for me. And so long as I use a remover that is acetone-free, it doesn't damage my Gelish nails underneath.

So I've mentioned Rimmel and Essence, and may I talk to you about Barry M? Everyone in the UK knows about Barry M, but I don't think we get it in Ireland because when I discovered it in a

Superdrug in Saffron Walden (land of my parents-in-law) I nearly took a weakness and keeled over in the shop. The colours! The glittery over-coats! The low cost!

Then there's Illamasqua! Be the Janeys, they really are 'out there' regarding the nails; they even have ones which promise a 'rubberized' finish, which I am desperately curious about. Anyway, I finally got my Speckle in lilac – I don't know what went wrong with the post, but it took a month to get to me – and it is strange and beautiful and I love it.

And please may I mention one more nail varnish. It's called Vapor and is by the ever-fabulous Tom Ford. It's a pearlescent *white* – yes! White! Which at times looks almost silvery and will be 'straordinarily striking on tanned hands and feet. It's so . . . different. It blew my mind when I saw it and then I thought, 'But of *course*. How come no one else thought of it!'

I brought six nail varnishes over to my mammy the other evening, to paint her nails. She was baffled by the Rimmel yellow, utterly *baffled*. She couldn't BELIEVE that people would wear yellow nail varnish. 'But I am ould,' she said. 'What would I know?' She lingered a while on the Illamasqua Speckle, obviously very drawn to it. But in the end, didn't she go for the Tom Ford! 'You have great taste,' I told her. 'Magazine editors and famous people will be wearing this colour this summer.'

'Are oo in airnesht?' she asked, evidently extremely pleased. (Translation: 'Are you in earnest?' aka, 'Are you telling me the truth?') 'Say his name again for me,' she says, 'so I can tell them at bridge.' So she wrote 'Tim Vard, nail varnish' on a little piece of paper and put it in her handbag, ready to do a bit of swanking around the bridge tables. I told her that she'd written the name wrong and she said she didn't care, that her bridge players would still be impressed.

Nails

So thank you, my amigos. It was all there in my heart, bursting to be let out. I really needed to 'talk' about all of this and thank you for indulging me. Just a few things I feel I should say. Item 1) Loving colourful nails is not incompatible with being a feminist. Item 2) PLEASE don't ever spend money you haven't got, on nail varnish or indeed any beauty product. Item 3) I am in the pay of no one. If I rave on to you about a product I love, it's because I really do. What I'm trying to say is that you can trust me.

mariankeyes.com, April 2013.

My Chanel Nail Varnish Museum

Let me tell you about my Chanel nail varnish museum. For as long as I can remember I've had a thing for Chanel – not the suits and the couture gowns, I hasten to add; sadly I'll never be that woman – but the cosmetics. Even in my twenties (as I've already told you), when I was totally skint, my lipstick was always Chanel. Something about the sleek cylinder with the iconic interlocking Cs elevated my life beyond its shabby reality, where I spent my rent money on wine, my wardrobe was missing a door and every night at 2 a.m. my upstairs neighbour strapped woks to his feet and tap-danced loudly enough to wake the dead.

Eventually my circumstances improved and I was able to embrace other products from the Chanel oeuvre, particularly the foundations, but their nail varnishes didn't feature on my radar because of my very disappointing nails. (Short, weak and a bizarre selection of shapes, as I mentioned in the previous piece.)

However, one November I was in Henri Bendel's in New York, in the throes of a bout of MITHness (mad in the head-ness), where the world seemed like a smoking, post-apocalyptic landscape.

Suddenly I saw something so exquisite I thought my eyes would burst – it was a nail varnish. It stood alone on a plinth, radiating a greeny-blue beauty powerful enough to light up the planet.

You know when people use the phrase 'I fell on it' to imply that they were extremely keen to get the thing? Well, I *literally* fell on it. I threw my body over it, like I was shielding a baby from gunfire, because I was so afraid that someone else might get there before me.

A chat with the salesperson established that it was a limited edition Chanel nail varnish called Nouvelle Vague, and Himself was so relieved to see me excited about something that he bought it for me. And right away I was in the grip of another addiction.

I've no end of addictions: alcohol, sugar, Twitter, sleep, box sets, spending money . . . I could probably get addicted to paper bags if I put a bit of effort into it (white? Manila? Patterned? With handles? Without? Flat? Or with a fold-out base?).

Addiction is often called the disease of More – because when we experience something pleasurable our brain produces dopamine ('the happy hormone'). So if you're an addict like me and you find something you like, you'll keep replicating the experience in the hope of generating fresh hits of delightful dopamine.

The long and the short of it was, I needed more Chanel varnishes, and mercifully family and friends helped out. Each little bottle marked an occasion: my mammy gave me Vendetta as reimbursement for paying her milkman while she was in hospital with pneumonia; Rita-Anne handed over Azure as thanks for minding the Redzers; and Caitríona bought me Atmosphere in Rome airport because she was flying back to New York and I was going home to Dublin and who knew when we'd see each other again?

I spent (and still do) an unholy amount of time on eBay, yearning after discontinued limited editions as rare as gold dust. However, I was badly bruised by my first – and only – auction, where I battled for Skyline (from the Bleu Illusion collection, but hey, you probably knew that). I live-tweeted the bidding and frankly I thought I had it in the bag – but I was outbid at the very last second (and it was literally the very last second: people explained to me later about Sniper and other such fiendish jiggery-pokery). So I limped away and now I simply hint heavily to my loved ones about which discontinued varnishes I crave.

Of course, there are always the new ones arriving 'on counter'. And something incredibly amazing happened to me in May 2015. I'd been doing a beauty column for nearly a year for *Irish Tatler* and I'd been sent a lot of athlete's foot ointment and acne-banishing face washes, but nothing at all from Chanel. One morning I was working away when the doorbell rang and Himself dealt with it. Then I heard him coming up the stairs and I assumed he'd taken delivery of a dandruff-banishing shampoo or something equally unthrilling. But when he came into the room he looked ashen, and when I enquired as to what was making him seem so shocked, he silently held up a small black cardboard bag, with little rope handles. A small black cardboard bag, with the word CHANEL written in white.

'. . . no . . .' I uttered through bloodless lips.

'Yes,' he said. 'Yes.'

'Quick!' I commanded, my lips rubbery and disobedient. 'Quick, show me!'

Together we tore at the bag and out tumbled FOUR CHANEL NAIL VARNISHES!!!!! Yes! The Summer 2015 Méditerranée Collection, and even now, remembering the beauty of the colours makes me feel warm and happy! We shrieked with excitement and jumped around the room and I shouted, 'I EXIST!!!' (I'm not exactly sure what I meant, something to do with Chanel acknowledging that I was worthy of their nail varnishes meant I felt endorsed as a human being.)

Then! The bell rang again! And Himself and I exchanged haunted looks.

'Is it the Chanel man?' I asked. 'Back to take the nail varnishes off me?'

'Feck,' Himself uttered. 'Maybe they were meant for Liz-next-door?!'

You see, in a bizarre coincidence, Liz-next-door is also a beauty editor, and she's a full-time real one, instead of an enthusiastic amateur like me, and she gets LOTS of fabliss stuff and I know this because sometimes we take in deliveries for her.

'Don't answer,' I said.

'I *won't* answer,' he said.

'I'm not giving them back,' I said. 'I can't.'

'You're *not* giving them back,' sez he. 'Possession is nine-tenths of the law. We'll just barricade ourselves in here and refuse to surrender.'

As it transpired, the varnishes really *were* intended for me, but the fact that I was willing to break the law is a sign of how the Chanel-lust sends me insane.

Over time, by all these different means, I've built up a fairly sizeable collection but – this is where I might lose you – I rarely wear them: they're far too precious and I'm afraid of using them up. I get my pleasure simply from looking at them.

But I was embarrassed by my carry-on. Until Himself suggested I turn my thinking on its head and regard them as precious *objets* (French word) and not as nail-pigmenting workhorses. It was a eureka moment and shortly afterwards came the first mention of the word 'museum'.

The museum is housed in a handbag (not a Chanel one – I've never owned one; like I said, I'll never be that woman) which lives in the bottom of my wardrobe, and I now have about forty exhibits. (Actually, I'm lying. The number is closer to sixty, but an addict always tries to downplay the full extent of the problem.)

In my more whimsical moments I suggest taking the museum on the road and displaying it in parish halls around the country, so that everyone can get to marvel at its beauty. Each varnish would stand alone on a tastefully lit column, bearing a short description of its provenance. And of course, on my deathbed, I will bequeath the collection to the Irish people. Or the V&A. I'm still deciding.

When my friends bring their little girls over, there's always a great clamour to see the museum, so I take out The Handbag and delicately unveil selected bottles and in a hushed voice say curatory-sounding things like, 'Here's a very rare blue, dated Summer 2013, which I think you'll appreciate.' But their eager little hands start grabbing the exhibits and pulling them from their boxes and then – then! – they sometimes have the audacity to *try them on*!

Before I know it bottles are upended and boxes are being stood on and I start snatching the varnishes back from reluctant little hands and I snap, 'Thank *you*.' In a high, tight voice, I say, 'Stop crying, Felicity. That's enough of the museum for today, girls. Let's move on to the home bingo kit.'

Some people go to art galleries to receive an infusion of beauty, for other people it's elaborate gardens, but I can't tell you the happy, *happy* hours I've had, lining my varnishes up on my bed, sometimes colour-coding them, sometimes acting out *West Side Story* where a pink falls in love with an orange, and on those joyous occasions when I receive a new varnish, instagramming a David Attenborough-style documentary as it seeks to integrate into the herd.

Yes, we take our pleasures where we can.

First published in the *Sunday Times Style*, April 2015.

Hairy Legs

Bad hair days. And I'm not talking about my head, I'm talking about my shins. Bad, oh yes, bad. How bad? Well, the fact of the hirsute matter is that if I'd been born in a warm country, like Australia, I'd have had to emigrate at the first opportunity. How could I survive in a country where people have to wear shorts on a regular basis? If I couldn't wear opaque tights, thereby covering the shame – yes, *shame* – of my hairy legs, I wouldn't be able to leave the house. I am so fortunate to have been born in a cold, rainy country.

But sometimes – like if it's the two days that constitute the Irish summer, or if I have the misfortune to be going away to a balmy clime – I'm forced to engage with my hairiness.

Which brings me to waxing. Yes. Wonderful stuff. It hurts but it's wonderful. Whenever I have it done, I return home with a skip in my step, feeling light and liberated and prone to twirling in circles, a joyous look on my face.

But a conspiracy of misinformation surrounds waxing. Ask *anyone* how long it lasts and they'll assure you that you're looking at six glorious weeks of super-smooth legs. But this is a blatant lie! It doesn't last six weeks. Not on me. From the moment I get it done, I watch my legs like a hawk, I actually *patrol* them, and I'm lucky if I get a week out of it before the pesky little blighters start poking their hairy heads up again. Sometimes I swear I can actually *see* them growing – like that cute moment when the chicken breaks his shell. And then what can I do? I'm *semi-hairy*. Enough hairs to have to return to the opaque tights, but not enough hairs to make another waxing worthwhile.

And while we're at it, here's another lie: the hairs get weaker and softer the more you get waxed. On no, they don't. Not on me. I've been having it done for twenty years and my leg hairs are as hardy and lush now as they were the first time I had it done.

And shaving? Strictly forbidden! Shaving undoes all the 'good work' of waxing, and there are beauty therapists out there who'll say it's no wonder my hairs never get weaker if I alternate waxing with shaving. But at times I've had no choice! I've wanted to be waxed – indeed pleaded to be – but was told that my hairs were 'too short' and was turned out, mildly hairy, on to the street. What could I do?

However, even when I have a close, close shave, my shins look like a sexy man's jaw . . . sort of blue . . . the stubble lurking beneath the skin just waiting for their chance. Which begins approximately half an hour later. Nasty black little bristles start poking their pushy way out into the world, like something from a horror film, penetrating through the tight-knit shield of my opaque tights. At times, with lower deniers, even laddering them . . .

A close friend (she agreed to speak to me only on the condition that she not be identified) had her leg hairs lasered. 'Lasered' is a nice word. It sounds modern and clean and sort of *Star Trek*ky. But what it really means is *burnt*, and by all accounts is more excruciating than childbirth.

My anonymous friend said she nearly puked from the pain, despite having managed to lay her hands on some anaesthetic cream. Not only that but they lasered her knee with such enthusiasm that it left a permanent scar, which then had to be microdermabrasioned away.

Lasering is also very expensive. And time-consuming: they

pretend you only need one session (liars, liars, they're all liars!), but it's like therapy, you've to make a commitment for months and months and months and months.

Now, what if I was to admit that I was worried about more than the hair on my legs? What if I were to . . . let's see . . . admit I was worried about, ooh . . . the hair on the small of my back? For example. Just theoretically. Would other women be grateful? Would they say, 'Thank you for articulating our secret shame, Hairy-Backed Girl'?

But even if they did, would they mean it? I suspect it would be like Tom Cruise in *Jerry Maguire* when he wrote his manifesto slagging off his job. Yes, everyone applauded him and said, 'Nice one, mate! Thanks for saying the unsayable.' But then what happens? Yes! Next day he gets the sack.

The thing is that girls aren't meant to be hairy – apart, of course, from the hairs on our heads and eyes, which are meant to be long and lustrous and luscious. We are meant to be *very* hairy in these departments, but otherwise entirely bald (a concession can be made for eyebrows, so long as they are well behaved and know their place).

Why? Why is hair good in one place and very, very bad in another? (Because upkeep on both keeps women exhausted and demoralized and without energy to get promoted? Do men expend time and money and anxiety combatting bad hair days? Just a thought . . .)

Wouldn't it be great if we didn't have to worry about any of this? If we all decided that we were going to stride forth together, hairy and proud? Look at all the time we'd save. And money. And energy. And worry. Wouldn't it be great?

First published in *Marie Claire*, August 2006.

Lasering

I had my hairy legs lasered and it was a resounding success! Previous to this I have had the hairiest legs in Christendom. Loads of times I've met people and they've said, 'Oh no, I bet my legs are hairier than yours, mine are REALLY hairy,' then I unveil my furry limbs and they usually swallow hard and step back and say, 'Riiiight, I see what you mean . . .'

I've had them waxed for decades, but the upkeep has always been a full-time job – about twenty minutes after I've had them waxed, they start to grow back.

So I went to have them lasered, and in all fairness they did warn me that one go wouldn't cure me, but even after one go there has been a DRAMATIC lessening, a great deforestation. I can't tell you just how astonished I was, because NOTHING works for me, not fake tan, not Restylane, not even automatic doors. (I often have to jump around on the pad in front of the door for some time before it finally notices me.)

But this worked. Christ, though, the PAIN. I admit I'm a whinger, but I've never found leg waxing to be painful – in fact I find it quite relaxing, and I really unsettle beauticians, who say I'm an oddball, which I am, but not in the way they mean. So I was feeling quite cocky before my laser patch test – and within moments I was beaten. It was incredibly unpleasant, like being burnt over and over again, and I was trembly and nauseous for ages after it ended.

Lasering

So I went on the interwebs, oh yes I did, and found a dodgy site willing to sell me Emla (local-anaesthetic cream) without a prescription. I put in my details and gave them my credit card number and wondered if I'd just been royally swizzed.

Then maybe ten days later, this massive box, a veritable CRATE, amigos, arrived, laden with jumbo-sized tubes of Emla, and joy abounded.

Except for Himself. Joy didn't abound for him, because he is naturally cautious. 'Tubes, I grant you,' he said. 'Big ones, yes, I admit they're big ones, and lots of them, and they DO say Emla on the outside, but it mightn't be Emla on the inside, it might be some useless stuff that does nothing.'

But I had faith. Also, a little bit of trepidation. Because there's a reason Emla's only given on prescription. Caitríona, who is a nurse, told me that people have DIED from overdosing on Emla, because it shuts down blood circulation.

But anyway! I was willing to take the risk, to walk on the wild side a little, and when the day of my second go of lasering dawned, I closeted myself in my bedroom, with a new tube of cling film, and started glooping the Emla on to my legs and it went fecking everywhere, on to the carpet and then – disaster! – I was squeezing the last bit out of a tube and a big lump shot straight into my right eye and started stinging like bejaysis, which is very wrong when you think about it, because it's meant to ANAESTHETIZE me, not sting me.

I rushed to the bathroom, trying not to spill any more of the cream off my leg, and started splashing cold water like mad into my eye, and I was worried because later that day I was going to London, for a big photo shoot the following day, with hair and make-up and stylists and art directors, and what if my right eye was like a tomato? I'd have to incorporate a wink into my look. And, *mes amies*, I am NOT a winker.

I splashed cold water into my eye and splashed cold water into my eye and wondered which saint was the one you prayed to, to banish bloodshot eyes. Mam would know, but I couldn't get hold of her, so I went back to glooping the gear on my legs, then – and this was tremendously satisfying – wound loads and loads of cling film around my legs, thus sealing the cream and letting it take full effect.

For about two hours I crinkled around the house, then I had to try to get my jeans on over the cling film without dislodging it, which was harder than it sounds; then, after splashing one last handful of water at my eye, I went to the lasering place.

Well, it was FECKEN FANTASTIC. I felt NOTHING – compared to the last time, which had been utter torture. Then I went straight to the airport, and Himself accused me of behaving oddly and he was right, I WAS feeling somewhat spacey, and then we realized that the Emla must have entered my bloodstream, because, addict that I am, I'm extremely sensitive to any kind of drug, and things that wouldn't bother the normal person at all have a profound effect on me. Like, I get high from the local-anaesthetic injections you get at the dentist, that's how bad I am.

So there I was, wandering around Dublin airport, with a bloodshot eye, banging into things and knocking over displays of Butlers chocolates and making people stare hard at me, and poor Himself was trying to reconstruct pyramids of boxes and chocolates and generally keep a lid on things.

When we got on the plane I sort of went to sleep, but it was better than sleep, I was utterly EUPHORIC. I felt warm and whole and at peace, but a wonderful euphoric kind of at peace, not a boring kind of at peace. It was probably the happiest I've ever been in my whole life, and when the pilot said, 'Twenty minutes to landing,' I felt a great sense of loss because I knew I had only twenty more minutes of this lovely bliss and then it would all be over, and I wondered if I'd become addicted to Emla cream.

Anyway, the plane landed and the euphoria abated and my eye cleared up and the photo shoot went grand and I haven't been tempted to smear myself with Emla cream since, so I think I'm in the clear. (Please don't do as I did. Please! I got told off by concerned medical types that what I'd done was very dangerous and that I was lucky to be alive.)

However – baldy legs! I mean, they'll grow back, the hairs, lots of them will, Rome wasn't built in a day and when you've legs as hairy as mine, you're in it for the long haul, but for the moment I'm slippery and smooth and yes! Baldy!

The only drawback is that I no longer get ingrowing hairs, which I've always thought was Mother Nature's consolation prize for the hairy-legged woman. The HOURS of fun I've had, equipped with just a pair of simple tweezers. All gone now.

mariankeyes.com, September 2007.

Perfume

You know Christmas is on its way when the mad perfume ads start. A five-second flash of spooky, long-limbed beauties running through a black-and-white forest while a voiceover whispers nonsense like, 'I am flat-footed . . . I am prone to colds. I am . . . *Incorrigible.*'

Perfume is funny stuff and lives in a peculiar place in our consciousness. It's 'glamorous', it's a way of connecting with a luxury brand – we might not be able to afford a couture coat, but we can afford a little bottle of fragrant water. Which is why it's the default purchase of every unwashed boyfriend lurching through the duty-free before his flight home from a stag weekend, having spent the previous forty-eight hours drinking heavily, and realizing, almost too late, that his girlfriend will be expecting a gift in exchange for letting him go, and having the presence of mind to appreciate that a Toblerone just might not cut it.

In recent times, we show the love for our celebrity of choice by buying their perfume. I had a recent entanglement with a gang of adolescent girls, and I don't know whether they were Directioners or Beliebers, but they were drenched in some bouquet of chemicals that caught me in the back of the throat and was so sweet, my teeth felt loose in my gums. I extricated myself from the encounter, feeling deeply unhappy. One of the ingredients in the perfume – who knows what it was? – had conjured up the awful confusion of being twelve years of age. For me – for most people, it seems – the sense of smell is linked inextricably with memories, and one whiff of something can kick off a cascade of complex recollections.

Which means no matter how well you think you know someone, you can't predict what fragrance they'll like. You can't even depend on a classic, as I discovered last year on my birthday. Suzanne always gets me a present that I really want – because I take the precaution of hinting heavily. (She does the same to me. Her birthday is a day after mine, and as she says, 'Why waste the money on crap that we don't want?') But last year she decided to freestyle and clearly she thought she'd done pretty well, because she was all smiles as I tore off the paper. 'You can't go wrong,' she said, 'with Chanel No 5.'

I have news: you *can* go wrong with Chanel No 5. To millions of people it smells of timeless glamour, but to me it smelt of suffocation, as though my head was trapped inside a musty, talc-filled polo neck.

Although that is *nothing* compared to the effect some aftershaves have on me. There are a few whose names I can't even utter because they trigger such an avalanche of awful memories, of certain men and bad times. These nameless man-colognes are filed in a locked room in my brain under 'TERRIBLE MISTAKES' and I never go there.

But there's a positive side to being a person who can be poleaxed by a perfume: I dot nice smells throughout my life, especially at the trickier junctures. I find mornings particularly difficult, but it felt wrong to ask Himself to come into the bedroom and stick an oar under me and oust me on to the floor. Surely there was a more dignified way of getting out of bed? So I embraced alluring shower gels.

In fact, I now have a . . . well, a sort of *library* of shower gels.

Yes, decadent as it sounds, I have an *array*. To match my mood. Like, there are days when the bracing smell of ginger is what I need. But on other mornings ginger seems like a drill sergeant and I gravitate to something pink and sappy, like rose, or something sunny and cheerful, like orange.

I'm partial to a French brand called Roger & Gallet. They do lots of pretty smells and they're not too spendy. You used to be able to buy them only in France, so whenever I visited I'd ferry home several shower gels and swank around, feeling like the owner of rare and exotic beasts.

Then the chemist up in Stillorgan started selling them and I was *quite put out*.

I'm fonder still of the shower gels from Espa – do you know the brand? Oh God, it's lovely! It uses essential oils and natural, sustainable ingredients but it's not REMOTELY earnest or Goop-y. They do an Energizing Shower Gel, but because the price tag is fairly hefty I use it only on the mornings I need the heavy guns. But a little goes a long way and it changes my mood for the better and makes the whole house smell lovely.

Then I grapple with the vexed area of body lotion. Sometimes it's one job too many, but when I do manage to throw some on I'm always glad, because throughout the day I catch an occasional hint of fragrance and it's like a little present to myself.

However, I'm not a fan of perfume itself – I find it too concentrated and 'sudden'. It's a bit like being hit on the head with a mallet. Nevertheless, I get endless enjoyment from the ads and pass many a happy hour 'doing' my own versions. Indeed, it is a game that could be played by all the family. '*I am hirsute . . . I am verboten . . . I am certifiable.* Certifiable. *The new perfume from Marian Keyes.*'

First published in *Daily Mail Plus*, October 2013.

Chemists

Once a month I go to my local chemist to pick up my anti-mad tablets and each visit gives me so much pleasure that frankly I wish I had to go every day. I hand over my prescription to my lovely pharmacist – we'll call him Edward (although his name is Ronan) – and while he assembles my Madness-Be-Gone kit, I have the option of sitting peacefully on the Chemist Chair.

I'm such a connoisseur of chemist shops that I schedule visits on foreign holidays (in the same way that other people go to the market looking for knock-off handbags), and I have strong opinions about what makes a place perfect: every well-appointed emporium should have one chair. Two would also be acceptable in case you get a crock-off – two equally infirm people both looking for a sit-down. But three chairs are too many; three would encourage chat, and above all I value the peace and quiet of chemists, where the only sound, like the soothing babble of a distant stream, is the whisper of a worried man disclosing details of his strange rash to Edward.

So I eschew the chair and I browse the shelves with great pleasure and discover all kinds of things I hadn't realized I needed. It's like being in a glittering Aladdin's Cave. The feet section is a particular delight. Blister plasters always make the cut, because a blister can happen at any time, right? And are you familiar with the tubey things for bunions? Sadly, I don't have bunions myself, but perhaps I might have a visitor to my home who would say, 'Listen, any chance you'd have a tubey thing for a bunion? I've been caught short.' *It could happen.*

The bandages section also holds particular allure for me. Whenever I gaze upon those rolls of stretchy salmon-coloured stuff that could be used to strap up a sprained ankle, I vow for the millionth time that this will be the year I do a first-aid course, so I can be an Emergency First Responder should anyone 'take a tumble' with me in the vicinity.

But perhaps it's best I don't do one of those courses, because there's a serious chance that I might start impersonating a doctor.

If I may speak philosophically, I find that some products in a chemist connect me with the suffering in my fellow man. I mean, what goes on in a person's life that they need a latex finger coverer? Never mind walking a mile in a person's shoes – wear their latex finger coverer for ten minutes and see how it feels.

Moving on, I throw some cotton buds into my basket – everyone needs cotton buds, they'll always come in handy. And cotton-wool discs are another staple. And fizzy vitamin C is a great cure-all – you'd pity the home that doesn't have any. And a couple of make-up sponges. And a bottle of nail-varnish remover. And some eyebrow dye . . .

It's always a particular thrill when something that's been advertised on telly actually appears in the shop. The day Voltarol pain-relieving gel arrived was a great one, and immediately I snapped up three tubes, fearful that they'd sell out, like a limited edition nail colour from Chanel.

Some chemists stock fancy cosmetic brands like Clinique, but mine has the cheapest range I've ever encountered. It's called Essence and someone told me (it might even be true) that it's Rimmel's diffusion line, and seeing as Rimmel isn't exactly spendy itself, that will give you some idea of the prices. Rock bottom. I can never stop myself from picking up a nail varnish from Essence. Or two.

Lovely colours, they have.

The skincare section features LaRoche-Posay, which really is very good and not at all spendy, so I always convince myself I need something from it. I mean, sun protection is an essential, isn't it? All year round.

Then I arrive at the strange perfumes, clearly left over from Christmas – peculiar acrid smells by Kylie and Justin Bieber. They never fail to get me in the back of the throat, which serves to remind me to buy some Strepsils.

At the counter, the perfect chemist must feature tins of Fisherman's Friends, little boxes of strawberry-and-cream diabetic sweets and rolls of Panda liquorice. I don't buy them, but I do appreciate them being there.

A little chat about my purchases always enhances my experience.

Edward says, in surprise, 'You have a bunion now?'

Blushing slightly, I admit that I'm simply anticipating the needs of some future, as-yet-unknown guest to my home.

'It's good to plan ahead,' he agrees. 'Anything else I can get you?'

'Rennies, please. And Panadol ActiFast. And Imogas. And Zovirax – the pump, not the tube. And you might as well throw in some Clarityn – I know it's only March, but summer will be here at some stage. Is there anything you think I've missed? Anything new and exciting?'

With pride he produces a little bottle of eye drops. 'It's to combat the itchy eyes people often get with hay fever. Just out this week.'

'Well,' I say, all excited, 'in that case I'll take it!'

So I pay for my purchases and leave with my bulging bag, and I'm already looking forward to next month.

First published in *Red*, May 2013.

Teeth

There I was, minding my own business, bothering no one, and while I was being so blameless, eating a bar of chocolate, I took a bite, which was just like all the previous bites I took – except the next thing I heard this unmerciful cracking noise. I'd fecking broken the bridge on my teeth.

I swear to God, my teeth cause me nothing but misery and it's entirely my own fault: I didn't go to the dentist for ten years, from the age of twenty to thirty. I mean, I was drinking alcoholically, and if you think you're worthless and deserve nothing and you're contemplating killing yourself, you're hardly going to go to the dentist, now, are you? So I didn't, and although sometimes I used to wake up in the middle of the night in the total horrors, wondering if the day was coming when I'd wake up with a mouthful of rotten teeth, I did my best to ignore it.

Then I ended up in rehab and one of my teeth kicked off and honestly I haven't had a moment's peace from it ever since. I had to have a root-canal thing WHILE I WAS IN REHAB.

But on the upside, because my life was such an epic shambles, having to go to the dentist seemed like nothing at all. All my fear had gone. Which is just as well, because I have been a very regular visitor since. Not by choice, either.

I'd had some sort of cap put on that root-canally tooth, and one day when I was back at work I was eating a Toffo and the next thing out the entire tooth came, attached to the Toffo.

So I shoved it back in again, and a while later I got published and was sent off to Bath to visit Waterstones, and I was having a cup of tea and a scone with a girl who worked there, and I was as nervous as billy-o – her name was Cordelia, I still remember, because the incident had such an impact on me – and the next thing my tooth was rattling around in my mouth. Yip. Rattling around. In my mouth.

And I was trying to suck up to Cordelia, so I didn't know what to do. I was terrified to swallow my bite of scone in case I swallowed the tooth, and I was terrified to open my mouth because she'd see the enormous, draughty, echoey black hole of a gap. So I spent the rest of my time with her nodding silently and giving enthusiastic, clamped-mouth smiles and gesturing expansively until I was finally able to leave, some centuries later, and spit the half-chewed mouthful of scone and the runaway tooth into my hand.

Awful! Eventually it became so unstable that I had to have a bridge put in. And for those of you who don't know what a bridge entails, the dentist files down the two healthy teeth on either side of the gammy one, so that when your bridge cracks and falls out, it looks like you're missing not one but – yes! – three teeth.

A delightful look. Especially if you're – as I was – due to have your photo taken the coming Monday morning with the gorgeous Cathy Kelly, for *Woman and Home*. And especially if you're – as I was – making a television ad the following Wednesday. And especially if you're – as I was – going to New York in two weeks for a lunch with the glossy magazines.

Mercifully I got an emergency appointment with the dentist and he fitted a temporary yoke. Then I got home and had my lunch, which happened to be chickpea curry, and a while later I was passing a mirror and glanced in only to see that the teeth in my new temporary bridge had gone BRIGHT YELLOW. The yellow of jaundice. The yellow of fever. The yellow of cowardice. It was the fecking turmeric in the chickpea curry!

Too late I remembered what the dentist had said the last time I'd had a temporary bridge put it – that the bridge was made of very porous acrylic, so to stay away from foods that could stain. E.g. Ribena, Diet Coke – and curry!

So I scrubbed and scrubbed. I scrubbed till my gums bled. I scrubbed till I'd nearly dislodged the fecking thing, and mercifully most of the yellowness faded.

mariankeyes.com, July 2009.

Sweets

Sweets. Twirls, limited edition Magnums, Percy Pig and Pals: I love them as much as I love shoes and handbags, and my specialist subject on *Mastermind* could be Confectionery of Our Times.

Subsisting on a diet of Chunky KitKats and Cornettos did me no harm whatsoever! Because I was as healthy as a very healthy thing.

Apart from all the times I was sick. Yes, okay, apart from all the times I was sick. About once a month I succumbed to a high temperature, swollen glands, ear infections, achy limbs and a muzzy head.

I was perpetually up at the doctor's, whingeing about my gammy health, and eventually he sent me for a load of tests, which, to my extreme surprise, all came back normal. At the very least, I'd been expecting ME (even though I'm told it doesn't exist), an overactive thyroid and some mild form of diabetes. It was a crushing blow, and that was when I decided to go the alternative route, kicking off with acupuncture.

I explained my symptoms to the acupuncturist and lay back, waiting for her to stick a couple of needles in me and effect a miracle cure. But no. She asked many, many questions about my lifestyle and diet and suggested that it might be an idea to knock the sugar on the head. I said, 'Mmmm, yes, maybe,' humouring her, like. It was *inconceivable*.

But a few days later my temperature shot up again, my energy

plummeted and suddenly I got an overview of the past year: I'd
been sick every three weeks, I was constantly exhausted and I had
a box of Max Strength Lemsip about my person at all times. With
that, something happened . . .

I had a flashback to this really horrible, humourless woman I'd
once met in Los Angeles who used to bore on about how the
manufacturers of processed sugar should be sued for destroying
health, in the same way that cigarette companies were being
sued. At the time I'd despised her, thinking she was a no-fun
body-fascist, but – unthinkable thought – what if she'd been
right? What if refined sugar really *was* Satan's dandruff?

And why was it all right for me to nod along knowingly with
Jamie's Dinners and to shake my head sadly at all the children
subsisting on white sugar in all its wondrous forms, but to eat so
much of it myself and not expect to get fat/hyper/sick?

I still don't know what exactly happened to me, but suddenly I
was just sick of being sick and I thought, 'If there's a chance that
I might feel well occasionally, I'll give this no-sugar thing a go.'

It was the most unlikely thing ever. I was so fiercely bonded to
sweets, I had planned that, on my death, I'd be buried with a
selection box and my coffin would leave the church while the
organist played the Flake theme. I loved sugar as much as I had
ever loved alcohol – actually maybe even more so, because a bag
of M&S fruit gums (the very best kind, connoisseurs will agree,
because of their soft texture) had never made me puke on my
new shoes or go home with a man I'd just met.

Being the kind of person I am, I couldn't just cut down. If I
had even one square of Fruit & Nut (still a classic, I think you'll
agree, despite so many upstart pretenders), it would trigger a
chocolate-based orgy and there was no knowing where it might
end. It was all or nothing, and unfortunately it had to be nothing.

Sweets

This might sound self-indulgent, but giving up sugar was a bit like a death. The thought of never eating cheesecake again made me jackknife with grief and I actually dreamt about chocolate, the way you might dream about an old boyfriend who'd broken your heart.

Without sugar, I felt naked and bare, all alone in a hostile world; it had calmed me when I was anxious, cheered me when I was upset and fired me full of energy when I was knackered (mind you, I'd crash far worse, half an hour later).

Some kind soul suggested that I attack my cravings with a handful of almonds. Great. Thanks.

But almonds it is, and I've had three straight months without falling sick. Also, I look different – everyone says. They study my face and ask, 'What is it?' and I say, 'I've shaved off my moustache.'

'No, no,' they say. 'It's not just that . . .' My skin, they say, is glowing and my eyes are clear and bright. Which makes me wonder what I looked like before – from the sounds of things, like something out of *Night of the Living Dead*.

However, another massive change awaited me. To be continued . . .

First published in *Marie Claire*, September 2005.

Learning to Cook

... Right, you know about the terrible tragedy that befell me when I had to give up sugar on account of my atrocious health? It was horrific – like having to walk away from the love of my life because his mother had put a contract out on me or because he'd decided to join the priesthood.

Bad and all as that was – and let me make no bones about it, my heart was broken – there was worse to come: it wasn't just as simple as not eating chocolate, Krispy Kreme doughnuts, Bounty ice creams, cheesecakes, summer puddings, custard . . . I made the shock discovery that sugar is lurking in just about all processed food. Even savoury stuff. Yes, even *dinners*. The stark truth was staring me in the face: I'd have to start cooking.

I didn't cook. I didn't know how and I didn't want to learn. The thought of having to have meat ready at the same time as potatoes at the same time as two veg made me want to crouch in a corner, whimpering and rocking. I literally couldn't boil an egg. Worse, I was quite proud of it (because it subverted men's expectations of women).

Preparing dinner for Himself consisted of piercing the cellophane on two plastic trays of ready-made meals and slinging them into the microwave.

To ensure we stayed healthy (although we didn't), I made us take a daily vitamin pill the size of a horse tablet. And every Thursday we went to my mammy's for dinner, ensuring that we got at least one hot, home-cooked meal a week. One Thursday she'd give us spaghetti bolognese, the next chicken casserole, the next spaghetti bolognese, the next chicken casserole. Even when we went away the spaghetti/casserole two-hander would continue and when we returned we'd slot smoothly back in, as if we'd never been gone. Very comforting. A fixed point in an uncertain world.

I was so disconnected from all culinary business that when Siobhán visited with her toddler and needed to open a tin of baby food, I spent many fruitless minutes hunting through drawers and cupboards before I realized that, actually, I didn't have a tin-opener. I mean, who doesn't have a tin-opener?!

Then Siobhán dropped her glass (probably from the tin-opener shock), and when I went to sweep up the broken bits I discovered I hadn't a clue where the dustpan and brush lived. I was pretty sure I had one, but for the life of me . . . Again, I must admit I was quite proud of this.

I scorned domestic goddesses. Cooking for others? Making a rod for your own back, more like. But I was too beaten to resist – I was on day four of my Percy Pig cold turkey (the worst day; I kept hallucinating that I could see bags of Penny Pigs, when everyone knows Penny Pigs were discontinued over two years ago) – and I surrendered to the inevitable.

Overnight, I booked lessons, bought cookbooks and invested in some Le Creuset.

The classes were a revelation. Instead of making shank of lamb and loin of pork and other pompous, terrifying stuff, the teacher made Thai curries and things *I actually liked*.

Once I started, I found cooking to be the most charming thing ever: I was mesmerized that you can take all these separate, disparate things, put them together in a certain way and suddenly you have this delicious dinner. It was like magic!

Because I'm such an all-or-nothing person, I went overboard to embrace the new me. I bought a folder and started tearing out recipes from magazines; it now contains three recipes.

The real sign that I'd undergone a profound change happened on a recent mini-break: instead of scouting out the nearest chemist, I went to a kitchen shop and bought a slotted spoon, a Y-shaped peeler and a pastry brush. (I haven't a notion what to do with the pastry brush, but I'm hopeful it'll come in handy at some stage.)

I can hardly believe it's me, and yet I always flirted with a soft-focus vision of myself, pottering about my kitchen in a kaftan and gold flipflops; when glamorous friends dropped in unexpectedly, I'd throw together a delicious four-course banquet from three mouldy tomatoes at the bottom of the fridge.

However, it's not all fun and games. In the first financial quarter since the new me, M&S's shares have dropped by 19 per cent and I'm sure it's all my fault. I used to have a kitchen that gleamed with cleanliness but now it's a spattered shambles. And what about cooking smells in your hair? Am I the only person who cooks wearing a shower cap?

I've also made the painful discovery that not everyone loves a gourmet-swot. When I told a friend that, for dinner, I'd made pork and apple sausages with lentils in a red wine reduction (she asked, I wasn't boasting, simply answering a question), she said, 'Christ, you can't do anything by halves, can you?' This was not meant as a compliment.

And then, of course, there's the farmers' market. At my local one I buy spices and swotty multi-grain bread and manky-looking organic vegetables and chat about recipes and stuff to the stall-holders and it's all very nice.

The problem is that music is provided by pan-pipe-playing,

poncho-wearing types, and family groups sway about to them, sipping at their freshly squeezed organic apple juice, and frankly the whole hippy-dippy carry-on makes my scalp sweat with embarrassment. But what can I do? These are my people now.

mariankeyes.com, October 2007.

How to Break Up
with Your Hairdresser

It's the old story. Girl meets hairdresser. Girl falls in love with hairdresser. Girl falls out of love with hairdresser and in love with another hairdresser who works at the same saloon. Girl is doomed to a lifetime of yearning and bad hair. The end.

Here's my story. I had a hairdresser, we'll call him Eric. He was competent but unimaginative, even a little surly, but I'd previously been through the Hairdresser Wars, so I was grateful for someone who didn't try to 'challenge' me and who didn't push me out of my comfort zone with high-maintenance cuts and edgy new products that I didn't know how to use. (Salt spray, anyone?) Also, I liked that he spoke very little, as I believe that excessive small talk damages the immune system. Eric suited me.

However, when Eric went on holiday I was shunted on to Sabrina (not her real name). I told her what I wanted, knowing that she would completely ignore me and give me Blowdry of the Week, the strange combover-from-the-back they were sending everyone else out with, and I consoled myself with the fact that at least my hair would be clean. But when she switched off her dryer I was astonished and humbled. She had done exactly what I had asked for. This Sabrina 'got' me in a way Eric never had. A happier future unfurled ahead of me. I saw myself running in slow motion down a hill, with my really, really nice hair bouncing behind me. I wanted Sabrina to be my hairdresser for ever. Then the cold truth hit me. There was no way I could have her. I was sworn to another. Everyone, from the top down – i.e. the terrifying receptionist – knew I was Eric's client.

There was nothing I could do. There's no protocol for breaking up with your hairdresser. If I had wanted to end my marriage it would have been easier. I'd say, 'We need to talk.' Then, 'It's not you, it's me.' Or, 'I just can't do this any more' (the current favourite phrase from relationship-enders), and that would be it. I'd be free!

The same problem applies to same-sex friendships. I had a friend and we used to see each other a lot, then we didn't see each other so often, then when I did see her I found myself thinking, 'Was she . . . *always* so stingy?' And, 'God, I wish she'd stop "weighing" me' (checking me out not-very-discreetly to see how much fatter I'd got since the last time we'd met). Quite simply we had – yes! – drifted apart. But until the end of time we'll have to meet up three times a year and squeeze out enough conversation to fill two miserable hours and go home sapped of the will to live, knowing we'll have to do it all again in four months' time.

But back to Eric and Sabrina. I embarked on a course of subterfuge, like having an affair. 'Secret' appointments – Eric's day off was Thursday, so I started booking all my appointments for Thursdays and faking disappointment when I heard that Eric wasn't in, then very, very quickly, in a high, tight voice, suggesting that perhaps Sabrina could do me instead. But it didn't always suit me to come on Thursdays, so more imaginative manipulation was called for. I'd ring and ask what times Eric was available and would murmur, 'Oh dear, no, I can't do nine. Or ten. Or eleven. Isn't that a bummer?' Only when I'd established the one hour of the day when Eric *wasn't* available, would I be able to say, 'But sadly, that's the very time I want to come in.'

The thing is – and you might find this hard to believe if you've had as many hair disasters as I have – that hairdressers are not stupid. They have a low territorial cunning and hair saloons are snakepits, hotbeds of bitchiness, where each stylist regards all the others as mortal rivals and clients are jealously guarded. Eric noticed my absence but he couldn't front me up and tearfully accuse me of playing away. He had to content himself with giving me wounded passive-aggressive smiles whenever I took my place at Sabrina's station.

Then! Everything changed! Eric got a job at another saloon! He invited me to jump ship with him, and as I stuttered my excuses his eyes locked with mine in the mirror and he said silkily, 'Unless you'd prefer to stay with Sabrina.' Having delivered his killer blow, he turned on his heel and stalked away with dignity, and although I was now free to openly love Sabrina, the whole thing felt a little sour.

It's all very tricky. At the moment I want to break up with my dentist. His waiting room has a very poor magazine selection and he's mingy with his post-surgery painkillers. (My friend's dentist gives out Vicodin like they're Smarties.) But I can't just abruptly abandon my dentist for Vicodin-man, he has all my notes; somehow I'll have to get them off him.

It seems that the only time you can properly break up with someone is if you've slept with them, and am I being unreasonable in not wanting to have sex with my dentist in order that I can go elsewhere?

But what else am I to do?

First published in *You*, April 2008.

How to Deal with
Hostile Hairdressers

As we established in the previous piece, I'm very lucky because I have a lovely hairdresser and I've gone to her for a long time and I really like her and she never keeps me waiting and she does exactly as I ask and she never suggests that it might be 'Time for a change', and when I ask her to take half an inch off the ends, she takes half an inch off the ends and not half a foot, and when I took a notion and wanted colouredy extensions, she didn't shriek, 'What?! At your age?!' She simply calmly went and organized the colouredy extensions. And when I said to her recently, 'I'd like to change my colour,' she changed my colour. And when I didn't like it, I was able to say, 'I don't know about this . . . could we try something else?' And she calmly complied and she didn't take offence and I knew she wouldn't take offence and I am very lucky.

However, recently (I'll be vague about dates because I don't want the poor chap to be identifiable) I was away from home and wanted to have my hair blow-dried and so I went to a hairdresser's that I'd never been to before. This hairdresser's is part of a chain and I think that always make things worse because they have rigid and elaborate customer-humiliating protocols in place. Anyway, the second I stepped through the doors, it all came rushing back to me! The power struggle for ownership of your spirit that goes on in most hairdresser's.

The idea is that they break you, break your spirit entirely, and when they've reduced you to a nothing with no sense of self, with no voice of your own, then they will rebuild you in their image and you will do exactly what they tell you to do and use the products that they sell you, and perhaps even buy a hairdryer and maybe even a house from them. They *own* you – soul, hair, everything.

But I can help you. I have a guide right here to help you!

Step One: The Arrival. When you arrive, the receptionist will ignore you – they will be on the phone or pretend to be checking something in their book or on their screen. They are not bad people, they are simply doing what they've been trained to do. In the past I used to stand there like an anxious sap, staring miserably, trying to catch their eye, thinking, 'Please look at me, please don't make me feel invisible.' But you don't have to be like me. Oh no! Instead, take out your phone! Call a good friend, someone you haven't seen for a while, and commence a warm and lengthy catch-up!

Step Two: The Coat Removal. When you have finished your call – and take your time about it, *enjoy* your chat – the receptionist will offer to take your coat. Be vigilant! This is where the second blow to your self-esteem will be struck. Some 'friendly' comment will be made on your appearance. On my visit a few days ago the person said, 'Well! You're very colourful today!' Then he exchanged a look with his colleague and a silent snigger passed between them.

There was one time when a hairdresser's receptionist stared at my handbag and said, 'Is that Prada?' And when I said it was, he said, 'From the cheap range?' (This is an honest-to-God, swear-on-my-nephew's-life fact. I could actually tell you this man's name, but of course I won't.) Do not think that you will avoid this essential part of the humiliation process by having no coat to give. 'No coat?' they will say, all wide-eyed and scornful. 'Well! Let's hope it doesn't rain.'

There are a couple of ways of dealing with Step Two. You can fight fire with fire and respond in kind with some comment on *their* appearance. For example, 'I love your spots. They're so . . .' cough, snigger '. . . *youthful.*' Or you can do something totally different. You can stare at them, hold their gaze and think the words, 'I feel boundless compassion for you.' Hold the gaze for a couple of seconds longer than is considered mannerly and force love out from behind your eyes. This will badly rattle them.

Step Three: The Wait. 'Elijah will be down in a moment,' the receptionist will tell you. But as we all know, Elijah will NOT be down in a moment. Elijah will be down when it suits him. Elijah is on Twitter, trolling his ex. Or Elijah is out the back having a cigarette. Or indeed Elijah may be doing nothing and may be keen to see you. But he cannot! Alas, he cannot! Because rules are rules and The Wait is vital – it says to the client, 'Your time is as nothing. You are blessed to be in here and it's important that you know it.'

There are a couple of ways to address The Wait. You could walk out – I've done it once or twice. Or you could decide to draw up a list of everyone you've ever slept with. Take out a pen and notebook that you've brought specially for this purpose and start. Be rigorous. One-night stands, everything. Don't forget people you 'met' on holiday. Rack your brains good and proper. At some point Elijah will appear and you will be expected to jump to your feet. My orders to you are DO NOT! Finish your list. When you are finished – and I want you to do a thorough job – then and only then may you look up at him. If you feel you could manage to, I beg you to quirk an eyebrow at Elijah and say, 'Ready then?' Practise this at home if you don't feel confident you can do it for the first time in the saloon.

Step Four: The Gown. Elijah will hold it in a way that no matter how you try to get into it, it will be wrong. If you try to go in front-ways, it will be like a coat. If you approach it like a coat it will have to be put on over your head. Indeed, rumour has reached me that some hairdressers are inventing onesie gowns that you have to step into, feet first. I've discovered that I cannot out-think them in this matter. The only thing I can suggest is that you say, 'Okay, Elijah, you win round four.'

Step Five: The Consultation. Be alert: *this is the central part of the process.* This is when the real meat of the breaking happens. This is where you sit in front of the mirror and Elijah will lift a piece of your hair and contemptuously let it fall again. He will lift another strand and, in disgust, drop it. If everyone has done their job right, you will be close to tears at this point. Then Elijah will say, 'So what happened here?'

Usually I stammer, 'How do you mean?'

And Elijah will say, 'Well, it's a disaster. Did you get it cut like this for charity? Sort of like a Movember thing?'

'. . . but . . .'

'And the condition! It's so dry it's breaking off in my hands.'

Then he will ask the most leading question you will be asked in your visit. He will say, 'What do you use for your home care regime?' And this is where you need to have your answers ready, my amigos. The very best thing you can do is to lift your chin, meet his eye in the mirror and say scornfully, 'Home care? I *never* blow-dry my hair myself! My hairdresser comes to my house every morning at seven.'

However, if you feel you can't manage to pull this off, there are a couple of alternatives. You can say, 'I use Frédéric Fekkai.' (This is the most expensive hair range that I know of.) 'Admittedly, Elijah, it costs an arm and a leg but it's worth it, right? I've just started using that overnight conditioner, the one that costs 195 quid a bottle and I find it perrrr.ittty immmp.ressive. In fact, Elijah, your *own* hair is looking a bit banjoed, you could do with some yourself. I've got a bottle here in my bag. I can give it to you for . . . let's say . . . £220?'

OR you could say, 'I use Majestic Gold,' and Elijah will curl his lip and say 'What?' (Because you've just made it up.) And you will say, 'Oh yes. It's from the United Arab Emirates. Next-generation haircare. Miracle stuff. It's, like, literally the most expensive range on the planet.' Pause and give a little tinkle of a laugh. 'They use real gold in it. I hear they're starting to use it in —' And here you will mention their nearest rival.

OR you can say, 'Elijah, you know and I know that my hair is fine. I know you're going to try and sell me an expensive conditioner. But, Elijah, here's how it is. I have enough money to buy the conditioner or I have enough money to give you a tip. But I don't have enough money to do both. It's up to you. You decide.'

You must plump for one of these options. A stand *must* be taken. Else when you go to the till, you'll find a little bag with rope handles waiting for you.

Step Six: The Hairwash. You will be taken to a basin and a child who dreams of being on the minimum wage will ask if you would like a head massage. You will say yes. The child will place their thumbs on your skull and press twice. The massage is now over.

Step Seven: The Blow-dry. It all depends. It might go okay. Elijah might do what you ask. Or he might not. It depends on how bitter he is that you didn't buy the conditioner.

Step Eight: The Conversation. Elijah will fire an opening salvo by asking if you've been on holidays recently. You can shut things down fast by saying, 'I haven't been anywhere for a while. Not since they made me surrender my passport.'

Step Nine: The Hairspray. Be a good girl and take your medicine. Open your clob and let Elijah spray in a mouthful. Don't drag it out.

Step Ten: The Removal of the Gown. You will stand up and expect Elijah to start untying bows. He won't. You will have to do it yourself.

Step Eleven: The Stealthy Sell. When you go to the till to pay, the receptionist person will say in a sing-songy casual way, 'Did you want to take any products, at all?' And you will see the conditioner Elijah tried to flog you sitting there, gazing at you hopefully like a puppy in an abandoned dog's home. Just say no. Again.

Step Twelve: Your Next Appointment. Super-casually, the receptionist will ask, 'When will I book you in for your next appointment, at all?' Are you brave enough to say, 'When hell freezes over'? I confess I haven't yet been, but I hope one day I will be.

Step Thirteen: The Return of Your Coat. The receptionist will ask, 'What's your coat like?'

'It's blue.'

'Reeeeealllly?' A blue coat? How . . . well . . . hysterical!

They'll disappear into a little cubbyhole and while they're in there they'll eat a Twirl and check their texts. Some time later they'll re-emerge, swallowing down the last of their chocolate, and say, 'No blue coats.' They'll look at you like you're a halfwit who can't even remember what they put on that morning.

'But there must be. It has a hood –'

'A *hood*?!'

There will be a moment when you think, 'Why would I want a blue coat with a hood? Wouldn't I just be better leaving without it?'

Stand your ground, I urge you. Stand your ground. Make them go back in.

After a while they'll come out dragging a rag along the floor. It will be your coat. Feigning astonishment that anyone would wear such a thing, they'll ask, 'Is *this* it?'

Shame will have you teetering on a knife edge. You really will consider denying it and just running away. Don't. It is your coat. You bought it because you loved it. Don't abandon it.

Very accusingly the receptionist will say, 'It was under a pile of other coats.'

Do NOT apologize.

The Final Humiliation: Putting Your Coat On. The receptionist will go behind you and pretend to help you into your coat, but in reality they will be pinching the armholes closed so you will flail around, like you're doing the upright backstroke, wondering why you're so useless.

Just take your coat from them and say, 'I'll do it myself.'

There we are, I hope this hard-won experience is in some way helpful. May I just state again that I love my hairdresser, so obviously not all of them are horrible.

mariankeyes.com, January 2013.

Personal Shoppers

Personal shoppers. Yes. As Mam would say, it was far from personal shoppers I was reared. All the same, I managed the superhuman feat of shutting down the voice in my head which tells me, *You deserve nothing*, long enough to make an appointment with a personal shopper – we'll call her Alex – in a Large Department Store in London (hereafter known as LDSIL).

I don't know the kind of people who normally use personal shoppers, but I suspected I wasn't one of them. I thought they might be very busy lady executives, or people who go to a lot of charity balls, people who simply didn't have time for traipsing around the shops.

I actually *like* traipsing around the shops. But I was interested in forging a long-term relationship with a personal shopper for one specific reason: shoes. Yes, shoes. Other things, also, hopefully, but specifically shoes.

Because I have very small feet ... sorry ... hold on! Right now, can I stop people who want to tell me how lucky I am that I can buy all my shoes in the cheapo children's department. I am a short-arse and I need heels, I need height. Children's shoes are a) horrible, b) made of plastic, c) too low, and d) have pictures of the Wiggles. I am not lucky at all.

Every spring and autumn, when the new shoes arrive in the shops, I launch myself on the trail for the white truffle of shoes, the holy grail: the size 35. But I don't live in London, and Ireland doesn't stock any shoes smaller than size 37. ('There isn't the demand,' they tell me, while I reply, in despair, 'But *I'm* demanding them.') And the chances of me accidentally being in London the lone day the pitifully few size 35s arrive on the shelves are slim. My cunning plan was that a trusted personal shopper would be my person on the ground to bag the 35s.

However, we were midway between new shoes seasons, so I decided, for a bonding first date, to ask Alex to help me find a dress. A dressy dress, but not too dressy, one that could go from the office to the red carpet, not that I'd be going anywhere near a red carpet, but just in case. A dress like an Issa dress, but not actually Issa, as I already had a shamefully high number.

So we met, and although she was very thin, she didn't call me darling. This pleased me. We went to the store café and she got me an orange juice and quizzed me about what I liked and what my look was and what my size was, and none of this was as easy as it sounds. Then she went away and I stayed sipping orange juice and trying to do a sudoku and in fifteen minutes she returned and led me to a large, off-the-beaten-track changing room crammed with dresses.

Thrilling? Yes, at least in theory. But in practice it was not a success. The dresses were all dresses I'd noticed on a fact-finding trawl earlier in the day. Nothing new or spectacular had been released from a secret vault for the special customers. And nothing really worked. The Temperley dresses made me look like Camilla Parker-Bowles – yes, I know everyone loves her and she can do no wrong now, but there's no denying that something about the set of her shins in a flared skirt calls to mind a stag at bay. Or perhaps a sideboard.

The low-waisted Etro dress made me look like Toad of Toad Hall, like I was all stomach. The Missoni dresses were heart-stoppingly expensive. The DVFs were nice but a little safe, and, like I said, I already had far too many Issa dresses.

Sweat broke out on my forehead and I was suddenly filled with panic. I was *trapped*, trapped in this changing room with all these expensive, unsuitable dresses, and I'd accepted a free orange juice. I *had* to buy something. I was morally obliged to. Alex had gone to all this trouble . . . The room seemed to become smaller and lower and the dresses seemed to cackle, as if taunting me.

In the end I bought an Issa dress – I couldn't, just *couldn't* find the nerve to walk away with nothing – and asked if I could make an appointment for the next time I'd be in London. (Shoe-time.) She said she wasn't taking appointments that far in advance and that she'd call. But she didn't, and as the time got closer, I rang and left a message. She didn't get back, so I rang and left another message. I rang again and it was on phone call four that it dawned on me: Alex wouldn't be calling me back. Oh my God . . . I'd been rejected by my personal shopper!

Why? Why? Was I not stylish enough? Thin enough? Had I not spent enough money? Should I have refused the orange juice? No answers were forthcoming and I faced the frustrating, unpalatable truth: a person like me would never have a personal shopper. Once again, Mammy Keyes was right. Feck's sake!

First published in *Marie Claire*, October 2006.

Kettlebells

I did a kettlebells class. Sweet baba Jay! What happened was, one morning Himself – and this is a fairly regular thing – went off to run up the vertical side of Lugnaquilla, the highest mountain in Wicklow (I'm fairly sure it is, although I might have that wrong, but either way, it's very high).

Himself is always at that lark. If he's not running up the sides of mountains, he's going for fifty-kilometre hikes in the hills in the dark (true fact) or doing them AWFUL wretched endurance yokes. In Ireland there's one called Hell and Back but you might be more familiar with Tough Mudder or similar – you know, when they have to run through lakes and get electric shocks and carry concrete bollards over twelve-foot-high walls and crawl on their bellies under a blanket of razor wire and whatnot.

And it dawned on me that the disparity in our fitness levels was becoming a bit of an unbridgeable gap and that it was time I took myself in hand. So I did a little bit of research and discovered that a kettlebells class was being held that very morning in the local gym in Bluepool. (In fairness, it mightn't be called that any more, but that's what it was called when I was a teenager and these things tend to stick.)

I gave them a ring to establish more details and the lovely lady on the phone said the class lasted forty minutes and wasn't too hard, so along I went, only to discover that the lightest kettlebell was *eight kilograms* – I mean, that's well over a stone!

Which was bad, but there was worse to come because the instructor – a very nice young man with tattoos and fancy facial hair – said we'd be doing the class outside. Outdoors! At the best of times I'm no fan of any space without a roof and walls and windows (preferably closed). But this decision meant that my gasping, wheezing shame would be visible to all the people sitting on the top deck of the number 4 bus. I should mention that the number 4 bus's terminus directly overlooks the all-weather pitch where we'd be doing our class. So the top-deck passengers wouldn't catch a quick glimpse of me as they whizzed by. Oh no. They could have a good fifteen to twenty minutes, planked in a stationary position, able to study me and my cherry-red face in great detail. Perhaps even, to bond with their fellow commuters as they studied my 'form':

'She'll never last the class.'

'Mark my words, that one's going to take a tumble.'

'Hold on! I'd say she's going to puke!'

'You're right, you're right, only a matter of time! I'm giving her four minutes.'

'Put me down for three minutes fifty.'

'Two minutes thirty-five for me.'

Yes, they'd watch me as if they were watching a very-interesting-in-an-atrocious-way sporting event and emerge as firm friends.

Before the class started I realized that everyone else – seven or eight women – knew each other and were regulars, and from ear-wigging their conversations I gathered that their children all seemed to be in school with each other. So I hovered on the edge of their bonded circle, smiling like the anxious, unfit gom I am.

Then off we went! Instructor Boy said we'd start with a warm-up, and my experience of exercise-class warm-ups is of doing grapevines and other sappy easy things, but there was none of that lark. Instead we were made to do sideways-running along the four sides of the pitch. You know when you see football teams training on the telly and they're doing the sideways-running and then they do that strange sprinting where they bring their knees up to their chests and then they bring their heels up to their bums? Yes? Well, that's what we had to do.

It was AWFUL and I thought I was going to die from unfitness, but I couldn't lose face, not with the people on the number 4 bus watching me avidly. (I was too mortified to look directly at them, but I was always aware of a sea of faces clustered the length of the bus, locked in rapt watchfulness.)

Then! We had to start flinging the kettlebells around and I could hardly lift my eight-kilogram one, never mind swing it, and once I got it up I couldn't control it, and it was a mercy that I didn't clatter myself in the head and knock myself out, although I DID actually consider doing that, just to get out of doing the rest of the class, in the same way that First World War soldiers would shoot themselves in the foot and say that the gun had accidentally fired while they were cleaning it, so that they wouldn't be sent back to the front.

But I kept going, even though the class went on for AN HOUR AND TWENTY MINUTES, and despite everything there was a great sense of camaraderie and I liked the teacher and the other people and it was only six yoyos and there was a kind of honesty about the whole thing I liked.

I've fashioned great plans to return but I haven't as yet, because with one thing and another . . . But I will! Yes! Almost certainly! Perhaps . . .

mariankeyes.com, May 2014.

Shite for Goms

It seems like a thousand years ago now, but in August last summer I was on holiday in Italy with my entire family. We were staying in a deeply charming villa near a beautiful hilltop town called Cortona, and you know yourself – Italy, sunshine, tomatoes, the funny pointy trees, saying '*Mi scusi*' – it was *fabulous*.

Everyone had a little wish list: Seán wanted to make pizzas from scratch; Oscar planned to learn to swim; I set myself the challenge of trying every one of the forty-nine flavours of gelato in the Snoopy Gelateria; and Caitríona, who lives in New York, was desperate to visit a designer outlet, an hour's drive from the villa.

All well and good, except she wanted me to accompany her and the thing is, I can't ABIDE designer outlets.

Yes, yes, I know most people love them and they embark with an empty suitcase and return with a lovely new winter coat, three pairs of boots, eight DVF dresses, a leather skirt, a Prada handbag and Tom Ford's phone number, all for a fiver. But there's something wrong with me – I am Bargain Repellent. I never find anything decent in the sales and more than once I've purchased something at full price, only to observe helplessly, five short minutes later, the price being slashed in half. (A subsection of being Bargain Repellent is that I'm the worst haggler on this earth and often end up paying more than the opening figure from the vendor. I don't know what happens – figures bamboozle me and I've obviously got an eejity sort of a face . . .)

Nevertheless, it doesn't mean that I *haven't* bought stuff at designer outlets. I've always felt that I sort of *had* to, that even if I didn't like the stuff, because it was a third of the original price it was my duty to make a purchase and on my return to gather my loved ones around and display the spoils of my trip and instigate a game where I'd tell them the original price of the items, as opposed to the vastly reduced ones I actually paid, and we'd add up all the money I'd 'saved'.

However, although I've put in time in the likes of Bicester Village, Cheshire Oaks and Kildare Village, I can honestly say – even though I'm given to exaggeration – I can *honestly say* that I have never worn any of the garments I bought on those trips.

The way I see it, there's a *reason* they never sold in the first place – basically because they're horrible or they've got three arms or no neck-hole or they're a strange mustardy-khaki-ey colour that you wouldn't dress your worst enemy in. Quite literally, the only bargain that I've ever got in a designer outlet was two turquoise Le Creuset saucepans in Kildare Village that were 40 per cent less than the price in Brown Thomas. But that, my amigos, is it.

So I wasn't enthused about going to the designer outlet with Caitríona. To make matters worse, I had actually visited the self-same Italian designer outlet three years earlier and found it to be so dispiriting that I renamed it 'Boulevard of Broken Dreams'.

But she's my sister and I love her and Himself was commandeered to do the driving so I thought, 'Ah shur, I'll go along for the drive and I can sit in the car and read my book while she's looking at all the rubbish.' But I had to make my position clear and I said to her, 'You do know that "Designer Outlet" is an anagram of "Shite for Goms"?'

So off we went, Himself driving, and it transpired that Caitríona wasn't just looking for a day out, but that she was on a mission – to buy a pair of Hogan sneakers. (Hogan, for those of you who mightn't know, is a US company, the 'little sister' of Tod's, and it does shoes and bags and that sort of thing.) Yes, Caitríona was obsessing about Hogan sneakers. They were all the go in New York, so she told me, but they were very pricey and she was certain that she'd get them for half nothing at the Hogan shop in the outlet.

And you know, I must admit that my interest was piqued. If these yokes were 'all the go' in New York, surely I should be paying attention? So when we arrived at the Boulevard of Broken Dreams, instead of sitting in the car like I'd said I was going to do, I decided to go along for a gawk.

Caitríona had hopped out before Himself had even finished parking the car and she was walking very fast and she had to pause to consult the map of the place but her leg was jigging and she was clearly coming up on an adrenalin surge and she was muttering, 'It's this way, it's somewhere over here,' and then she shouted, 'There it is!' and broke into a run.

Sure enough, there was the Hogan shop and myself and Himself hurried in Caitríona's wake and by the time we caught up with her she was already down the back of the shop where there were MILLIONS of sneakers. Millions and millions and millions of them in all kinds of colours – pink patent and cobalt suede and inky-navy leather – but they were horrible. They had a profoundly strange rectangle-shaped toe and they looked like the lace-up shoes that misfortunate, arthritic old ladies wear.

I was seized with cold fear. This was my sister, my beloved sister – we agreed on *everything*, we liked and disliked *exactly the same things*. But clearly she'd been living in New York for too long. Unbidden, the memory swam into my head of how she hadn't liked *In Bruges*, of how she just hadn't 'got' it, when it was clearly such a magnificent film. 'I'm losing her,' I thought, 'I'm losing her and it's awful.'

Caitríona was prowling up and down, still muttering to herself, and Himself gestured at the horrible sneakers and said, 'As we're here, do you want to try a pair?'

As I've mentioned previously my feet are size 35 – whenever I say this, people seem to think I'm boasting, as if I'm saying something like, 'Christ, I have the metabolism of a greyhound! No matter what I eat, I just can't seem to put on weight!' But it is a bloody scourge having size 35 feet. Because a shoe in size 35 is rarer than a unicorn sighting.

Here in this Hogan place, though, there were walls and walls of boxes of sneakers and more size 35s than you could count. However, because all of them were horrible, I declined Himself's offer and we both got out our phones and went on Twitter, prepared for a lengthy wait.

But within moments, Caitríona was standing, wild-eyed, before us.

'They're dearer than they were in Venice,' she declared. 'They're dearer than they are in New York! It's a fecking swizz!'

With all the compassion I could muster, I said gently, 'Shite for Goms, Caitríona, Shite for Goms.'

I put my arm around her shoulder and led her back to the car, and the mood on the drive home was very subdued.

But anyway, she carried on as best she could and tried her hardest to enjoy the rest of the week, and in all fairness it was very nice: Seán made his pizzas and Oscar learnt to swim and I managed twenty-seven of the forty-nine gelato flavours – and our goodbyes at Rome airport were very emotional.

And then I was home and facing into autumn, and about a

week after we got back I was reading the Sunday paper when something caught my eye: 'Hogan sneakers sell out in minutes.' I seized the page and read with keen interest. Apparently, everyone fabulous in London was lusting after Hogan sneakers and hand-to-hand combat had almost broken out in the shop in Sloane Street. Already they were being sold for vastly inflated prices on eBay.

With trembling fingers I went on the internet and discovered that it was all true, and I thought I was going to vomit. Suddenly I saw how *wrong* I'd been: the funny-shaped rectangular toe wasn't horrible, it was *directional*, it was *fashion-forward*! And to think I could have bought twenty pairs of size 35s in a variety of colours and styles! What a fool I'd been, what a ridiculous, clueless eejit!

I'd let a precious opportunity slip through my fingers and it was unbearable. Worse, there was no one I could talk to because Himself was away for the week (climbing Mont Blanc – can I just digress for a moment and say fair play to him).

Almost in tears, I paced the house, trying to quell the feelings of loss. I should have trusted Caitríona: she lived in New York, for the love of God. *New York!* Of course she had her finger on the pulse!

'This too shall pass,' I repeated over and over to myself, 'this too shall pass.'

But the day went on and the grief – yes, it was actual grief – didn't abate. So I rang the Italian shop! Yes! And the person I spoke to was snotty and pretended he couldn't understand me and hung up on me mid-sentence, and when I rang back, no one answered.

My despair increased – then suddenly I knew what I needed to do. It was all very simple: I'd go back to Italy. Yes. No one need know – I'd fly in and out in the one day. Yes. I'd get a flight into one of them places – Rome, Palermo, whatever (my knowledge of Italy's layout is very sketchy).

And I'd hire a car. Yes. Granted, I've never driven 'out forrin' and the prospect normally terrified me, but not now. No. Like, how hard could it be? Admittedly the Autostrade were scary and the Italian drivers were nutters, but surely to God I too could try to drive like a nutter?

Directions, now they were another thing that could be tricky. I can barely tell my right from left, but where there's a will there's a way, right? Maybe the hire car would have a sat-nav, even if I've never managed to program one and even if I did it would be in Italian and beyond *Mi scusi* I don't understand a word of the language.

But I was going, of that I was certain. Central to my plan was that no one must know: I was too embarrassed by my lunacy. Thursday would be the best day – it was when Himself was doing the final ascent of the mountain, so he'd be out of radio contact. I'd tell everyone else that I was 'working hard' and couldn't be disturbed, it'd all be grand. Grand.

So I started googling flights and I was a little aghast at the cost – but, I rationalized, if I bought enough pairs of the sneakers, I'd end up actually *making* money, because even though they were dearer than New York prices, they were a lot cheaper than the London ones.

Also, the logistics of the whole business were far, *far* more challenging than I'd expected: no airline flew in and out of the same place on the same day. I tried airport after airport – Pisa, Bologna, Rome, Florence – and in the end I had it narrowed down to two options: fly to Pisa, hire the car, drive to the place, drive to Rome, ditch the car, fly home; *or* fly to Florence, hire a car, drive to the place, drive back to Florence, stay the night, fly home on Friday.

At this stage, it was four in the morning and I'd been on the internet for ten hours, so I decided I'd go to bed and when I woke up I'd toss a coin between Pisa or Florence.

So off I went to sleep, and when I woke up I was no longer insane.

EPILOGUE: I managed to buy a pair from an Italian website. I'm still not sure about the toe . . .

First published in *RTÉ Guide*, November 2014.

Bono Boots

I have to tell you about my Bono boots and this is a *complete* stream-of-consciousness, so please bear with me.

Well! I needed new boots. I had a grand pair of boots from Ecco and they had served me well all winter long and worked their humble little socks off, but suddenly they went quare on me and please know I am not blaming them at all, they really gave everything they had, but out of nowhere they went badly stretchy and wrinkled, and started looking like mini-elephants on my feet and that wouldn't do.

So I went out to look for a new pair of boots and every shoe shop I walked into I was assaulted by flimsy yellow flowery sandals and I said, 'No, I need boots!' And the shop people said, 'There ARE no boots, not any more, it's spring now, buy these lovely yellow sandals,' and I said, 'But FTLOG (for the love of God) it's ruddy well SNOWING out there!' And they said, 'Buy sandals, buy sandals, buy sandals!' And I said, 'No, I am going home and I will buy boots on the interwebs! And you are wondering why nobody buys anything from real shops any more!'

So I went home and I tried to buy boots on the interwebs and the thing is, I have very specific things I require from a boot. They need to be quick-in-and-out, therefore no lacers. They need to have 'spring', a certain amount of bounce-back action from the sole. BUT!!! Mark me carefully here! They need to have a heel. Yes, a bit of a heel, for I am 'straordinarily short, a mere five foot, which I'm not sure of the exact amounts in metrics, but only thirty-seven centimetres or maybe thirty-eight. Or possibly forty-one, but not many at all.

So I need a heel. But the heel cannot be too high. I do a lot of 'short-walking'. That is to say, quick jaunts to the optician and chemist and the sobriety emporia and what-not, therefore I need city boots. However, I realize that saying 'city boots' sounds sophisticated and shiny and high and that is not what I need. I suppose I need suburbia boots. A little part of me has just died saying that, but let's move on.

So I went on the interwebs and looked up the Ecco boot but there wasn't a single one left on the planet. Also, as you know, the boots must be size 35, which is a right pain in the hole, if you'll pardon the vulgarity. Because (and you must be sick of me telling you) the size 35 is a rare and elusive beast and I have spent my life having to buy size 36s and eight pairs of insoles and grimly super-glueing the insoles into the new shoes and then superglueing my actual feet into the shoes so they will not lift out.

So there I was looking for a size 35 boot, in March, in a heel that is a little bit high but not too high. Oh yes, also it needs to be an ankle boot because my calves are so stout that a zip won't close higher than my Achilles tendon.

For old times' sake I went on the Camper site, because Camper used to be my friend. Every winter I purchased the perfect pair of suburban boots from Camper, which had the perfect amount of spring in their step and looked well and had the right heel height. And then someone improved their website and now an engagement with it leaves me weeping with frustration and sorrow and without boots.

I tried Clarks, who are SUPER-boasty about their comfort,

but they don't do smaller than a size 36. Then I tried countless US sites who offered 'passable' boots, but then the price quadrupled when they realized they would be posting to Ireland.

And then . . . I went on Net-a-Porter . . . Lovely, lovely Net-a-Porter. Yes, there I was, acting like it was 2007. And I searched for black (another requirement, I forgot to mention) ankle boots, in size 35, and sat back and waited for the site to issue the sound of laughter. But to my great astonishment they produced a pair of black ankle boots with a reasonable heel in size 35. I thought I was hallucinating.

And then I saw they were by Acne – and what do we know about Acne? Yes! They are Swedish. And what do we know about Swedishness? Yes! That it is fabulous. Yes! Acne = Swedish = *Wallander* = Saga from *The Bridge* = Fabulous!

And then I saw the name of the boots – they were the 'Pistol' boots. And I already knew about them, without even knowing that I did. I had heard of them via the *Grazia*s and the *Sunday Times* Style supplement and whispered on the air via the breaths of supermodels. The Acne Pistol Boot IN MY SIZE!!!!!

I saw the price – I was swept along in a tsunami so enormous that I totally disregarded it. I would be cool! I would have *Sunday-Times*-Style-approved boots! That fitted me! I would be practically Swedish. I was so so so so so so excited.

I ordered them! I tracked their little journey to me via Net-a-Porter's DHL magicness. And they arrived this morning! I abandoned work and ordered Himself to accompanize me to the trying-on place (the bedroom). I was nearly sick with anxiety as I wondered if they'd fit. I slid my feet into them. They fitted. 'They fit! They fit! They fit! They fit! They fit! They fit! They fit!' I raced down the stairs and opened my front door and shouted at the passing cars and buses, 'They fit!' The entire top deck of the 46A applauded. People began texting and tweeting wildly, 'They fit! They fit! They fit!'

The day proceeded and at lunchtime I had to go out and some-time while I was out and about I caught sight of Bono. Just from the waist down. But it was definitely Bono. Those tight black jeans, those subtly heeled boots . . . And to my great horror, I realized that the person was not Bono. The person was, in fact, me, reflected in a window.

And the thing is, I have form in looking like Bono (e.g. when I was driving Himself's Maserati – you'll read about it later in this book). Badly shaken, I proceeded with my plans. My next port of call was to my convalescent mammy, who was recovering from pneumonia. She greeted me with warmth and I said, 'Mam, do I look like Bono?'

'You do not,' she said stoutly.

'No, Mam, I think I do,' I said. 'Look at my legs. Look, in par-ticular, at my boots.'

She looked. She looked and she looked. Finally she spoke. 'Have you any sunglasses?'

I replied in the affirmative.

'Put them on,' she says.

I obliged.

'Stamp around a bit there,' she said. 'Would you sing a little bit for me?'

So I stomped around the sitting room and sang a few lines, 'In the name of love. One boot in the name of love. In the NAAAAAME of love . . . lalala in the name of love, how'm I doing?'

'You know,' she said, sort of squinting at me, 'you have the look of him all right.'

A blow, my amigos, a bad blow. Bono is great and Bono's *look* is great. On *Bono*. I am not Bono. I am a lady. I want to look like Alexa Chung.

'What am I to do?' I asked. 'It's these bloody boots, isn't it?'

'I'm no expert,' she replied, 'but it might be. Were they dear?'

'Very dear.'

'How dear?'

'I'm too ashamed to tell you.'

'Dearer than Jimmy Choos?'

'*As* dear,' I admitted.

She whispered something that might have been 'Sweet Mother of the Redeemer'. Then she said, 'And for them to make you look like Bono. That's desperate.'

At this stage, she remembered that she owed me money from when she was sick and I paid her window-cleaner and bought, as she put it, 'sundries', and she began pressing cash upon me.

'No, Mam,' I shouted, 'no!'

'Yes, Marian,' she shouted, 'yes!'

'No, Mam,' I shouted, 'no!'

'Yes, Marian,' she shouted, 'yes!'

I don't know why, it's just the way we carry on. None of us can ever accept money from any of the rest of us. So myself and Mam, we wrestled our way around the room for some minutes, both of us shouting. Then she played her trump card.

'Yes, Marian, yes!!' she shouted. 'I had pneumonia and I had to go to hospital and I nearly DIED. TAKE THE MONEY!!!!'

At that point, I had lost the moral high ground, so I took the money.

'Buy yourself something nice with it,' she said. And, with a flash of her old spirit, she elbowed me and said with a little wink, 'Buy yourself new boots . . .'

marian keyes.com, March 2013.

WHAT WOULD SCROOGE DO?

Driving Home for Christmas

19 December 1986. London to Dublin.

Oh, it was all very different back then – flights costing £1.27 weren't even a twinkle in Michael O'Leary's eye. Aer Lingus and British Airways straddled the Irish Sea like massive costly colossi, rendering air travel far too expensive for the likes of me (twenty-three, a waitress, albeit one who had a law degree, and spending every penny I earnt on drink and clothes). If I wanted to get from London to Dublin, I had to step back into the 1950s and go by train and boat.

On the appointed hour (10 p.m.) I was seen off from Euston station by a small rowdy group of gay friends, one of them my flatmate Conor, who was too skint to even afford the boat-and-train combo so was staying in London for the festive season. The lads fluttered around me, making little adjustments here and there to my clothing, until it was decreed that I was fabulous enough to board the train. And yes, in a floor-length black seal-skin coat, an indecently short black Lycra dress, shiny black tights, red suede gladiator stilettos and a strange little red tricorn hat (made by Conor), I was indeed fabulous. Yes, my dears, in the olden days we dressed *up* to travel. We made an *effort*.

I even had matching luggage: a brown canvas zippy yoke that my parents had got free with petrol vouchers, and an identical brown canvas zippy yoke that Conor's parents had got free with petrol vouchers. The handles were coming loose on one of the bags and the seams were slowly disintegrating on the other. It never even occurred to me to be ashamed.

All around me beaten-looking elderly men carrying cardboard suitcases were boarding the train. I climbed on and bumped my way down the carriage, hoping – like I always did – that when I found my seat the man of my dreams would be sitting opposite me. We'd fall into chat, we'd click instantly, we'd fashion plans to meet up when we returned to London . . .

Alas, no such luck. Across from me was a granite-faced man chomping on home-made corned-beef sandwiches the thickness of a phonebook. Seated next to him was a mild-faced woman with the nail-scissors haircut of the off-duty nun. Mr Corned Beef appeared too ground down by thirty years of manual labour to even look at me, but Off-Duty Nun gave a meek, God-bless-you-my-child-even-if-you-do-have-a-most-peculiar-hat smile which I returned with a cold stare. I had a strict No Conversation policy with any religious types. Or corned-beef men.

As the clock inched towards ten o'clock and the off, the seat next to me remained unoccupied and I began to imagine the unimaginable – an empty seat beside me; I could lie down and sleep! (Those in the know slept with their head on their handbag, to avoid their handbag being stolen. And with their feet towards the window, in case their shoes got stolen. And as shoes went, mine were eminently stealable.)

But seconds before the whistle blew, a young man jumped aboard. Every other seat in the entire train was occupied: this had to be my companion. Initially I was hopeful – he was almost late and I liked late men, the more unreliable the better; in fact, I'd have preferred if he had missed the train entirely. However, he was pleasant and cheery – I preferred tortured and surly – and had the curly-haired, meaty-framed air of a rugby-playing jock. (Strangely, his cheery, friendly demeanour seemed to waver slightly when he focused on my lovely home-made hat.)

With much jerking and slopping of flasks of tea, we were off! Jock-boy transpired to be on his way home from Paris, which elicited oohs of delight from Nun-Woman. They fell into passionate chat about *petty pans o'shockolahhhh*, trying to outdo each other with atrocious French accents.

I decided I hated him.

Despite the cold, the windows steamed up within moments. We rattled through the night, wedged shoulder to shoulder with our fellow passengers, sleeping with our eyes open. There was a distinct smell, a fug of old damp overcoats, of fried breakfasts, of decades of grinding poverty.

I was in the lucky position of having a window seat and occasionally I nodded off and when the train took a corner too sharply I was woken by my skull being cracked smartly against the glass.

Once or twice a trolley came round, trying to tempt us to cough up for tea and sandwiches, but everyone had brought their own. (I hadn't brought sandwiches because for reasons I don't fully understand now, I thought sandwiches were 'silly'. I had a Bounty, a Lion bar and a Twix – that was food enough for me.)

At about 2.30 a.m., amid whistles and hisses of steam, the delights of Holyhead were unleashed upon us. We descended from the train into the perishing night. I hoicked one hefty petrol bag over my shoulder and dragged the other along behind me. The bags felt like they were packed with lead because I'd brought every item of clothing I owned, to dazzle the eyes out of the heads of those back home, but I refused to get a trolley. I had a 'thing' about trollies. In the same way that I had a 'thing' about sandwiches. I thought – I'm afraid this is the best explanation I can come up with – that they were a sign of weakness.

In those days, Holyhead port was grim, grim, grim. A bare, wretched place. No expense had been spent on gussying it up – Irish people weren't too popular in Britain in the 1980s. Handy enough if you wanted a road dug, but you don't want them getting notions. Like cattle at a mart, heads bowed with resignation, armies of smelly-overcoated, bacon-and-cabbage men trudged up the bleak ramps towards the ship.

I trudged along with them, pausing from time to time when I caught the heel of my shoes in the hem of my coat and almost toppled over on to my face. The price, of course, of being fabulous.

Once on the ship, the idea was to find a place as far away as possible from anyone else in order to get a few hours' sleep before the ship docked. There were rows and rows of upright chairs but they were ring-fenced with fruit machines which emitted a constant racket of pings and crunches. I'd go mad. I found a small bare patch of floor and laid down my bags, but a Scouser – the ship was always staffed with Scousers – tried to convey, first with his magical but baffling accent and then by shouting, that I was blocking an emergency exit. Like a refugee, I got to my feet and, dragging all my earthly possessions, moved on to another spot. Also, an emergency exit. In the end I took my rightful place amid the fruit machines.

Rumours reached me of a lounge, an enchanted realm of couches and free coffee. But it cost a fiver – an astronomical sum – to get into. I went to see if it could possibly be real – and sure enough it was. I gazed in through the glass and to my astonishment caught sight of Mr *Petty Pan O'Shockolahhhh*, who was in there with the nun, the pair of them reclining like pashas, guzzling enough free coffee to float a boat. My bitterness overflowed.

Around 6 a.m. we docked in Dublin, the ship stopping itself by – or so it seemed – driving at high speed at the land. Once we'd picked ourselves up from the floor, we streamed out like ghosts into the frozen Irish dawn where, conveniently, public transport didn't start for another two hours. Through the mist the outline of a man waiting at the exit slowly revealed itself to me. It was my dad. He'd come to pick me up. We hadn't seen each other in nine months. He gazed upon me and demanded, 'What in the name of God have you got on your head?' I was home.

First published in *Travel*, December 2007.

Christmas at Marian's

I've always wished I could be one of those women who can cook complicated dinners for twenty people at the drop of a hat, while remaining cheerful, fragrant and unshiny. Those fabulous creatures who can receive flowers, offer drinks, stir an oxtail jus and turn down the oven *all at the same time*.

My lovely mother-in-law, Shirley, is one such woman – she is fabulously capable and makes it look so easy.

I'm convinced this ability is a gift you're either born with or you're not, and sadly I wasn't. I'm not entirely useless – I'm good at crosswords and I'm unusually skilled at untangling delicate gold chains – but I'm afraid I fall down at the hospitality-and-catering interface.

I like having people over and feeding them – I think cooking for someone is a very loving thing to do – but the highest number I'd ever prepared dinner for was . . . four. And the highest number of different foodstuffs I'd managed to have ready to serve at the same time was three (potatoes, chicken, cauliflower, for what it's worth).

Then suddenly, a few years ago – and I'm still at a loss as to how it actually happened – I somehow managed to invite thirteen members of my family, including Shirley, to my house for Christmas Day. Through an appalling mix-up, *I'd mistaken myself for a grown-up*.

I admit I had my own house. I even had my own kitchen, but

my style of cooking was to throw everything in one big casserole and feck it in the oven on a low heat for eight hours. I had quite literally *no idea* where to start cooking a Christmas dinner. I was afraid of turkeys, I didn't like the way they looked so dead, and the thought of having to put my hand into the innards of one of them made me shudder.

It was early summer, probably May or June, when I issued my ill-thought-out invitation, so I dealt with it, like I deal with all challenging situations, by putting it to the back of my mind and telling myself that it hadn't really happened. I couldn't *possibly* have told my siblings and extended family that I'd cook Christmas dinner. And even if I had, they'd forget.

But they didn't forget . . . Oh no, they were excited.

Somewhere around October, I realized it really *was* going to happen and then I was seized by genuine panic. So much so that (I'm ashamed about this, don't think I'm not) I decided I'd have to get an outside caterer in. But not a chance. All the outside caterers were fully booked – had been, in fact, since the previous January.

So there was nothing for it: I told everyone that there would be no turkey or roast parsnips or suchlike this year. We were going to break with tradition and I was going to make my Special Bean Stew.

Well, there was UPROAR. I was quite upset – I'd thought everyone liked my Special Bean Stew, they'd certainly *said* they did at the time. But there was widespread insistence on turkey. Even those who didn't like turkey said we had to have it.

My siblings swore blind that they'd help on the day – but I knew they wouldn't. I know what they're like: too busy lying on the couch, watching *It's a Wonderful Life* and eating cheese straws to come and stir the gravy. (Of course Shirley would have been able to do the whole thing in her sleep, but I wouldn't let myself ask her – after all, she was a guest in my home, I had some pride.)

So this is what I did: I bought everything pre-prepared. I mean *everything*. A pre-prepared turkey, already boned (and stuffed, so no need for me to put my hand into its innards), pre-prepared roast potatoes, stuffing, parsnips, bread sauce, sprouts, trifles . . . *everything*.

But I was still waking in the middle of the night, genuinely overwhelmed. I knew this was too big for me, so – and this is where I stop being able to take any credit – I turned it all over to Himself, who ran the entire operation like a military campaign.

He constructed a detailed schedule: every single thing, right down to the humble chipolata, had a time slot. Because we have only one smallish oven, my dad's beloved hostess trolley was called into action and on Christmas morning Himself closeted himself in the kitchen and began clattering baking trays.

Rita-Anne and Caitríona were commandeered to help, but I was ordered to stay well away, in case my anxiety was infectious. Instead I was placed on cheese-straw detail (i.e. passing them around). Now and again an extra body would be summoned to help in the kitchen and the door would open and steam would billow out ominously and I'd bite my bottom lip and worry . . .

Then, all of a sudden, it was three o'clock – the appointed hour – and bowls of food were being ferried to the table.

Amazingly, everything *was ready at the same time*. Even more amazingly, it tasted lovely and I was so happy and relieved that, as I was looking around the table at thirteen happy faces, I had a wild notion: maybe we should do it all again next year.

First published in *Waitrose Kitchen*, December 2009.

What Would Scrooge Do?

Every year it seems to start earlier and earlier. No sooner is Halloween out of the way than it begins: the bellyaching about Christmas. It's the only topic of conversation and wherever I turn I'm faced with people whingeing that they'd rather gnaw their own ear off than go to their office party. That they wish they could take off to a desert island until the whole wretched thing is over. That there's nothing in the shops but horrible spangly red dresses made-to-order for work parties – i.e. suitable to be torn, puked on, jived in and at the end of the night thrown in a shamefaced ball in the bottom of a wardrobe, never to be worn again.

On and on go the complaints – the expense, the crowds, the family get-togethers, the hangovers . . . It's all such a cliché. However – *and mark me closely here* – just because it's a cliché doesn't mean that it's not true.

For the record, Christmas *is* awful. It's official: more marriages break up around Christmas than at any other time of the year. That and summer holidays, of course. The unbearable workload coupled with unmeetable expectations is what does for most people.

The first sign that the dreadfulness is nigh is when Himself disappears up into the attic and re-emerges with his beloved Rudy. Rudy is a four-foot-high, light-festooned reindeer and for the past five years he has spent the month of December positioned over our front pouch, for all and sundry to see.

It's as if some esteemed visitor has come to stay. Himself watches the weather forecast with edge-of-his-seat anxiety and the words 'high winds' fill him with dread. If we go out for the evening he can't relax, and if it starts raining he insists on an early departure, so he can check that Rudy is all right.

Rudy was a big enough responsibility, but two years ago a life-size Santa was added to the menagerie, then last December I spent one miserable afternoon holding on to Himself's legs as he leant out of a bedroom window, stringing red 'berry' lights from a tree.

It's mortifying. Our house is lurid enough at the best of times due to a misunderstanding with our paint – the patch test looked like a soft, pretty lilac but writ large the colour has somehow mutated into a gaudy, dayglo mauve, which means our home functions as a local navigational landmark ('Turn right at the horrible purple house . . .).

The funny thing is that normally Himself has a great terror of tackiness, but I suspect that if he had his way we'd be adorned and bedecked with Christmas lights and climbing Santas all year round. We'd be like one of those houses that gets on local telly, which people actually make pilgrimages to.

Left to my own devices I'd be quite happy not to put up even a sprig of tinsel – at least then the carol singers might leave me alone. But at the moment, as soon as they clock Rudy on his lofty perch, they mistakenly assume that our household is awash with seasonal cheer. 'This lot will give us a couple of bob,' they think. 'This lot won't turn the lights off and creep around on all fours, pretending they're not in.'

And it's not that I begrudge them the money, it's the standing at the front door in the perishing cold as they sing three verses of 'Away in a Manger' that I can't take. The problem is that I have no idea how to behave – should I tap my foot and move my head jauntily, like I'm humming along? Or should I stare wistfully over their head as if their lyrics have stirred deep thoughts in me?

Instead I'm frozen in a rictus of embarrassment, desperate not to make eye-contact, repeating over and over in my head, *Don't sing another verse, please stop now, oh please God, don't let them sing another verse . . .*

The only way I can cope with Christmas is to ask myself, *WWSD* – What Would Scrooge Do? He wouldn't go to his office party, that's for sure, and at least now that I'm self-employed it's one thing I don't have to endure. God, it used to be awful – the drunken declarations of dislike, the tears, the lost shoes. I was a disgrace.

Nor would Scrooge send Christmas cards. So neither do I. The first year I thought the guilt would kill me, but it's got easier. Maybe it's like committing murder: the first one is the hardest.

Call me mean-spirited. I don't care. I just can't bear seeing people whose lives are already stretched to overload having to take on a ton more stuff.

Come, follow me! Lay down your wrapping paper and embrace your inner Scrooge! You have nothing to lose but a nervous breakdown!

First published in *Marie Claire*, December 2005.

What's Right with Christmas

Every year, around 2 January, I say, 'Right, that's it! Next Christmas I'm going far, far away, to some country where Christmas is actually illegal.' Iran, perhaps. Or Saudi Arabia maybe. A place where there's no turkey, no *Raiders of the Lost Ark*, where hopefully I'd get into big trouble for humming 'Away in a Manger' on the bus.

I always emerge from the festive period exhausted, tubby, smothered with a head-cold, sporting a chinful of stress-induced cold sores and in the grip of a powerful desire to live alone on top of a mountain for the next six months. The worst thing of all is that I feel like a failure, like a curmudgeonly oddball: everyone else loves Christmas, what's wrong with *me*?

But then I made the delightful discovery that I'm not the only one who feels this way. Oh no. Lots of people dread Christmas. And once I knew I was not alone, my attitude changed and I realized that actually there's an awful lot that's good about Christmas.

For some people it's about the birth of Jesus Christ, and if that's your thing, good luck to you, no judgements here, but for me, Christmas is essentially about *food*. Oh, to have the freedom to eat whatever I want!

Here's how it is. For most of the year I feel ashamed of every bite of food that goes into my mouth. My internal monitor, that horrible calorie abacus, keeps track of everything and replays any gluttony in order to shame and reshame me.

What's Right with Christmas

No matter how little I eat in any one day, there's always the feeling that I could have managed on less. My appetite is like an out-of-control Rottweiler straining on a chain, and even as I take the first mouthful of anything I'm already worried about the last and how I'll cope when it's all gone.

Refined sugar is my greatest love and my greatest heartbreak, and trying to stay away from it is like getting up every day and going to war – there's danger at every turn. And then December rolls around . . .

I, along with my four siblings and assorted spouses and children, usually spend Christmas Day at my parents' house, which is transformed into a refined sugar wonderland for the duration of the festivities. It feels like every room I enter, I stumble over boxes of biscuits stacked knee-high. Hidden behind the curtains in the dining room are three incongruous boxes of Black Magic. I open the fridge for some swotty blueberries and there, twinkling at me, is the perfect Central Casting trifle. Dad even gets me my own personal selection box as he has done every year since time immemorial, even though every year I beg him not to.

I haven't a hope, resistance is futile, this is far too big for me. And suddenly it's like a great weight has been taken off me and I grant myself the freedom to eat whatever I want. For a limited period only – like a half-price sale – and I feel skippy and carefree and bingey.

Last Christmas, I began the day, as I have begun every Christmas Day in living memory, by eschewing my usual moral-high-ground breakfast of organic steel-cut oatmeal and instead going back to bed with a tin of Roses, giving myself permission to eat steadily through it until I can see the metal at the bottom. I felt sick long before I reached that happy point, but knowing that there were no limits was what made it so pleasurable. (In fact, this ritual has become so ingrained that, after bitter complaints from my siblings, Mam and Dad are now obliged to buy a second box of Roses for general usage.)

And I felt no guilt. None at all. And frankly the subconscious knowledge that I can go wild at Christmas is probably what makes the denial of the rest of the year possible.

And *that* is what Christmas is for.

People complain bitterly about the *Groundhog Day* misery of being trapped, once again, at close quarters with their family, of time wasted watching shite telly, just like they do every year. But they're missing the point. Christmas is a holiday from guilt, from restraint and from responsibility – and oh, the *relief.* I may not be sunning myself in the Maldives but I'm taking a mini-break from my own rules.

Yes, I know that as I play the Selection Box Challenge with my sisters (basically you eat as much of your selection box as you can in a minute – Dad times us) I'll pay the price in fatso shame in January, but for the moment it's like a ceasefire. I can stop fighting.

It's the same with alcohol – I no longer drink, but those that do are made to feel perpetually guilty. You think you're simply having a couple of glasses of wine with your dinner after a bad day at work, but then you discover that actually, no, you're a binge drinker.

However, at Christmas time, you're *obliged* to drink – the office party, the team lunch, the catch-up with old school friends, the mulled wine at your neighbours . . . the drinking opportunities are endless and, well, you don't want people thinking you're a killjoy, now, do you?

The month of December is the only time of the year when you can get scuttered eleven nights in a row and put it down to sociability, and frankly it's what makes the forbearance of the rest of the year endurable.

Another thing that's lovely about Christmas is the comfort of our own unique rituals – and this is a Keyes one: when we were younger, money was in short supply and because Dad was afraid we'd have all the Christmas goodies eaten before the day itself, we were forbidden to eat any until he blew the whistle on Christmas morning. But Caitríona and I couldn't bear the waiting so, before the appointed time, we used to sneak into the darkened dining room – repository of the selection boxes – and sneakily slit one open, slide out a Curly Wurly and a Crunchie, reseal the box with a handy piece of Sellotape, and tiptoe from the room, like cat thieves. And we *still* do it every Christmas Eve. We leave the dining room and find Dad and sit and ostentatiously eat our contraband, then Dad stares at us hard and forgets that we are now in our forties and suddenly yells, 'Where did you get that Curly Wurly?' Then Caitríona and I laugh ourselves sick.

The thing that people seem to resent most about Christmas is the wasted time. At any other time in the year, if they had ten days off, they'd go skiing instead of watching crap telly in their pyjamas. But the thing is that doing something pointless in a life full of purpose is a precious joy. Under normal circumstances I have a bottomless list of jobs. Always. I should be answering emails or changing the bulb on my bedside lamp or removing my chipped nail varnish, or taking cod out of the freezer or doing sit-ups or charging my phone or buying a birthday present for my god-daughter or looking for lost things or making a new list because I've run out of room on my current one. As a woman, I'm expected to be many different people, all of them fabulous.

But the *pleasure* of Christmas, of watching strange old films which are already half over before the remote lands on them. Bad films. Terrible films. Films of no worth whatsoever. Films that live on in the collective memory and unite the small band of people

who saw them. Every Christmas we STILL ask each other in-
credulously, 'Do you remember that weird film about the man
who lost his memory and married his own wife? Did that really
happen?'

But the very best thing about Christmas – and sadly this con-
fuses and upsets people – is the rows.

Of every lovely thing that Christmas has to offer, this is the one
that is most misunderstood. See, we've bought into that goodwill-
to-all-men business and we expect that it'll be easier to love
others at Christmas time.

But why would it? There's more pressure on us than at any
other time of year: the card-writing, the hangovers, the lists, the
present-buying, the crowds, the brutally relentless socializing,
the cooking, the travelling, the lurking outside Argos at daybreak,
ready to do battle to get your hands on the last delivery of Ninky
Nonks (or Elsas or whatever it is this year) in the universe before
25 December – it all takes its toll. And the next thing, we find
ourselves mired in a sudden shocking shouting match with our
nearest and dearest – and we have the temerity to be surprised?
Ashamed, even.

But there's no need, *no need at all*! We have to stop thinking of
this as a bad thing. No, it's very, very good. See, most of the year we
are small, powerless creatures in a malign world and when bad
things happen we have to swallow back our rage. Our hairdresser
gives us bouffy when we specifically said, 'No bouff!' We get a park-
ing ticket two minutes, *two short minutes* – a mere 120 seconds –
after the meter expires. At work, a toady younger man who is gifted
at golf gets the promotion that should have been ours.

And what can we do? Nothing! We are small, powerless crea-
tures and we have to force a wobbly smile and – yes! – tip the
hairdresser, because if we don't she'll only blow-dry our fringe

funny to punish us the next time. Instead of vaulting across the
bonnet of our car and biting the cruel ticket man, we have to pay
the parking fine. And we have to start reporting to the smarmy
younger bloke at work.

And it builds up, all of that frustration and impotence. Our
shoulders are permanently up around our ears, a bit falls off one
of our molars because we've been grinding our teeth to dust in
our sleep, and we jolt awake at 4 a.m. every day to worry about
the future.

. . . and then suddenly we find ourselves trapped in an over-
warm, over-full house with our family. Tellies are blaring from
every room, there's no privacy and no peace, the kitchen is full of
steam and Brussels sprouts and it's only a matter of time before
all hell breaks loose.

Hard to predict exactly how it'll go – that's the beauty of it really.
But suddenly you'll find yourself shrieking at a loved one about
bread sauce, or lemons being cut into wedges instead of slices, or
overuse of the Sellotape. And of course the rage isn't really about
bread sauce or lemons or Sellotape; it's about all the other stuff, the
not-being-allowed-to-bite-the-traffic-warden stuff.

And my advice is, don't be ashamed of your outburst – *embrace*
it. Have a good old rant. Release all that rage: it'll save you a for-
tune in therapist's fees and dentist's bills and it'll stop you getting
addicted to sleeping tablets further down the line.

Because the important thing is that the boundaries of family
are far more elastic and accommodating than those of any other
social grouping. Families argue. We've been doing it all our lives
and we always bounce back to maintenance-level dysfunctional
(what counts as normal round my way). It's all okay.

And never forget, it will soon be January, sackcloth-and-ashes
month, so enjoy the gluttony, the sloth, the inebriation and the

arguments of Christmas. These are simple, low-cost pleasures – and yet they are priceless.

My five favourite things about Christmas

1) Curling up with a dusty Agatha Christie and realizing seven pages from the end that I've read it already
2) Eating trifle straight from the bowl for my bedtime snack
3) The gym being shut
4) Watching *Moonstruck* for the millionth time with my sisters and saying all the words
5) Sitting around the table, with all the family there, in the aftermath of a giant shouty row, smiling and thinking fondly, 'These are my people, this is my tribe'

First published in the *Sunday Times Style*, December 2008.

ON MY TRAVELS

Maison des Rêves

First let me tell you who Bryan Dobson is: he reads the news on Irish telly every evening at six o'clock (well, a minute past six, but let's not quibble), and there's something about Bryan that I find immensely reassuring. Now, can I tell you about the role he played in a holiday I had in Morocco? Thank you. Well, I visited with Himself, who had climbed Mount Toubkal on one of his mountain-scaling adventures and every day after his return tormented me with, 'Oh, Morocco this, Morocco that. The time I had the delicious tagine in the blah-de-blah.' So eventually I agreed to go.

And Marrakech, a place that Himself had particularly loved, transpired to be not so wonderful for me because – in one of those unfortunate oversights – I didn't have a penis. They're not so keen on women in Marrakech. To put it mildly. But that's a different story.

This is about what happened *after* we left the gropey, hissy insults of Marrakech. We were driven for several dusty hours through barren desert and crucifying sunlight, heading for a palmeraie in a place called Ouarzazate (a palmeraie is something akin to an oasis, a sudden burst of green – yes! – palms in the endless shifting landscape of the desert). Suddenly, out of the emptiness, a sand-coloured fortress appeared, with turrets and narrow slits of windows and a huge wooden door. Do you watch *Game of Thrones*? Do you remember when Khaleesi showed up at Qarth, 'the greatest city that ever was or will be'? Well, it looked a bit like that.

The driver ushered us into the fortress, where the light was so dim that I struggled to see. Behind us the huge wooden door slammed shut and uneasiness started to hum inside me, then an elegant blonde woman stepped forward and said, in a French accent, 'Welcome to Maison des Rêves. This way, please.'

She led Himself and myself down a windowless corridor, off which led numerous rooms and alcoves, but we were moving at speed so there was no time to stop and have a gawk. Eventually we fetched up in a sitting room with big leather couches and a drinks table containing every kind of alcohol ever invented.

'This is a hotel like no other,' she said. 'There is no restaurant, there are no mealtimes, everything is at your pleasure.' She smiled – sort of – and I tried to smile too, but I wasn't keen on the sound of things. I like rules. 'There are no charges. If you desire a drink' – she gestured at the table, which was buckling under the weight of bottles – 'please help yourself. Whenever you need anything, simply come to this room.'

Then we were taken to our first-floor bedroom, which was beautiful – exquisite even – in a simple, deeply tasteful way. The bed was low, the linen smooth and cool; a seating area had a strange-shaped fireplace that looked like the cone of a tagine, and the bathroom was big and modern and stone-coloured. But there was no telly. Or mini-bar. Or phone. Or little book saying stuff about plug adaptors and babysitters. Most crucially of all, there were no windows. Well, I exaggerate – there was one, hiding behind shutters, but when I opened them the window looked on to a small, square, access-free space. We could see nothing of the outside world and, with panic flickering in the pit of my stomach, I knew I needed to ground myself by – please don't laugh – going on Twitter. But – horrors! – there was no Wi-Fi. I *needed* the Wi-Fi. I *needed* Twitter. I felt a thousand million miles away from home and I needed a reminder that it still existed.

So I went downstairs, looking for the special room with the couches and drinks table, but I must have taken a wrong turning because I discovered myself in a tiny dining room. I set off in another direction and arrived at an empty, turquoise-curtained hammam. Back I went, walking faster now, taking left turns, right turns, recognizing nothing, and I stepped into the bright light of an unexpected courtyard – the walls were mosaicked in a million shades of blue and a perfect little fountain bubbled in the middle. Exits led away from all four sides and suddenly I couldn't remember which one I'd come in via.

Panic started to rise in me; I was lost, I'd *never* find my way back. And just as I was about to start shouting for help, a man, dressed in baggy trousers and a long tunic, appeared and, smiling but silent, led me to the sitting room with the couches and the drinks.

French lady showed up and explained that sometimes there was Wi-Fi but it was unpredictable and sporadic. 'Because we are so alone here, so far from civilization.' She gave a helpless little shrug and I wanted to shout, 'I *know* we're very far from civilization, stop reminding me about it!'

When we came down for dinner that evening, candles burnt in wall-sconces and we couldn't find the couch-and-drinks-table room. That scared me because I freely admit I can barely tell left from right, but Himself has an uncanny sense of direction. Eventually someone materialized – smiling but silent, just like the last time – and led us to a tiny, perfect dining room, set for two, with candlelight glinting off golden-coloured goblets and polished silverware. There was no menu and no explanation of what we were getting, which is so different from Ireland these days, where you're practically invited to meet a cow and its entire extended family before you have a cut of beef.

Also, it was so dark, we might as well have been eating blind-fold, and afterwards we were accompanied to the foot of the stairs which led to our room, because if we hadn't been we'd probably still be traipsing around to this very day.

The next morning before breakfast we spent a good ten minutes lost and wandering, until yet another silent-but-smiling man in trousers and tunic led us outside to the garden, to a stunningly beautiful area which featured large wire sculptures of butterflies and flowers, with massive swathes of brightly coloured silk strung between them, creating an outdoor room. We were seated upon cushions shaped like low chairs and we were brought delicious food.

And so it went on for a couple of days. Every time we came downstairs, it was as if, since our previous visit, a few hours earlier, the layout of the corridors had been rearranged. Always, just as we were at the point of panic, someone appeared. It was as if they were spying on us, watching us on CCTV, doubled over laughing in the viewing room, as we took wrong turn after wrong turn, before someone came to rescue us.

At mealtimes, we never knew what we'd be getting or how much – sometimes we got course after course, and other times the parade of strange, delicious dishes would end abruptly.

The staff did a lot of enigmatic smiling, but never spoke, and I began to wonder if they were actually mute. In a dark, fearful moment, I had a flash that they'd offended someone powerful and had had their tongues cut out, and quickly I had to make myself stop thinking that way.

On the second afternoon I made Himself accompany me on 'a turn around the grounds', and although I pretended to admire the olive plants and palm trees I was in actual fact trying to find the wall that marked the boundary of the property. Beaten back again and again by undergrowth that became too thick to get through, I realized I was looking for a way out.

Because what was really, really bothering me was that, no matter how many corridors I went down, no matter how many left and right turns I took, the one thing I never found was the big wooden front door where I'd entered that first day. I had another flash of terrible fear as my mind presented a picture of the doorway having been bricked up.

I 'got' the philosophy of the Maison des Rêves – it was for jaded control freaks, who travelled widely, from Ulan Bator to Tierra del Fuego, and could have club sandwiches and Sky News no matter where they were. The set-up here was to provide something fresh and wonderful and it was to encourage guests to surrender control. Most people would adore it.

Now and again we could hear snatches of distant voices from a room above us – I listened hard, it sounded like two women and they seemed to be speaking French, but I couldn't be sure. And once, I saw two people – a man and a woman – disappearing around a corner. I hurried to catch up with them, but by the time I got there the corridor vibrated with their absence.

Eventually I confessed my anxiety to Himself. 'I feel like I'm being kept prisoner by a benign warlord.' I could actually visualize my jailor – an extremely fat man, wearing rose-coloured silken harem pants, a roomy tunic embroidered in gold thread, curly-toed Aladdin slippers, an orange turban and an elaborately waxed moustache. Despite the bright colours, he exuded a dreadful air of menace.

I named him Pascha Fayaaz and I described my entire, elaborately imagined fears to Himself.

I could see myself being ushered into Pascha Fayaaz's presence, as he lounged on a lapis lazuli daybed. 'Maaaaaarian,' he crooned, in a quare-accented, silky voice, 'I hear you wish to leave us.'

Then he snapped his fingers, rattling his many golden bangles, and a flunky leapt forward and offered him a platter of Quality Street. Pascha Fayaaz's fat, elegantly manicured hand hovered over the sweets and eventually he selected the purple one. With unexpected delicacy, taking care not to rip the tinfoil, he unwrapped the sweet and handed the paper to a meek-looking man. 'For my collection,' he said, and the meek-looking man hurried away, bearing the tinfoil on a silken cushion. Then Pascha Fayaaz popped the chocolate into his mouth and took a moment to savour it, before his attention snapped, once more, to me. 'So, Maaaaaarian, you are not happy here. And this, it makes me so very saaaaad. What are we doing that is so wrong?'

'Nothing,' I stammered. 'Nothing.'

'The food, is it not to your liking? Your accommodation? The people who serve you?'

'Everything is wonderful,' I said, 'beautiful. Especially the . . . er . . . "people who serve me".' It was important to say that, I felt. I didn't want any of them to come to any grief. 'But I miss home.'

'Home?' He sounded surprised. 'What about your so-called home do you miss?'

'Well . . .' My mind seized on one thing. 'I miss Bryan Dobson. I miss the six o'clock thing. Every day after the Angelus – no, I won't get into explaining that, it's not important – but every day after the Angelus, Bryan comes on the telly and it makes me feel . . .' Carefully I sought the correct word. '*Safe*. I've survived the day and I'm relieved. Yes, safe, that's how Bryan Dobson makes me feel. Safe.'

'Safe,' Pascha Fayaaz said thoughtfully. 'Huh. Who knew?' Then he clicked his beringed fingers and I was led back to my room.

About three and a half hours later, there was a knock on my door. It was one of Pascha Fayaaz's flunkies. He said, 'You must come.'

'Why?' I was seized with anxiety. But already he was walking away so I hurried after him. He led me into Pascha Fayaaz's sumptuous quarters, where he was, as usual, stretched the length of his chaise longue, eating things. There was an air of something exciting and terrible in the room.

'So, Maaaarian,' Pascha Fayaaz said. 'You know that I wish for you to be perfectly happy here. So!' He clapped his hands together and called, 'It is time!'

Outside a door that led off to an anteroom I could hear lots of noise – bumps and muffled shouts, as if some sort of fight was going on. Horrified, I watched as several staff wrestled a creature into our presence. It seemed to be a man, a tall one, dressed in a Western-style suit, but he had a hemp sack on his head. The sack was whipped off the man's head and his hair was all tossed and he had a bruise on his cheekbone and a cut on his forehead. 'What the hell is going on?' he shouted. 'Who are you people?'

'Now, Maaaarian,' Pascha Fayaaz crowed with delight. 'Here it is! Here is your Bryan Dobson! All the way from your Ireland! Now, Maaaaarian, *now* you will be perfectly happy here for ever!'

PS: None of this business with Bryan Dobson actually happened, you understand. I mean, I *do* like him and I *do* feel safe when he comes on at six o'clock, but no one actually kidnapped him for me, and after four days at Maison des Rêves they unbricked the front door and we were allowed to leave.

Previously unpublished.

Norway

One summer I went to Norway on a cruise of the fjords with Himself and Himself's parents. I am very fond of Himself's parents (John and Shirley). I am also doing a load of sucking up to them because my sister-in-law, Caron, has recently given birth to delicious Jude, so she is currently enjoying the position of Most Favoured Daughter-in-Law.

So we set sail from Newcastle, and one of the things I fear most in life is being hungry, and I was terrified I wouldn't get fed enough on the boat and what would I be able to do about it, seeing as I was a long way from any shops?

But I couldn't have been more wrong: there was TONS of food – breakfast, morning coffee and bikkies, lunch, afternoon tea, a five-course dinner and, if you were still hungry after all that, there were midnight snacks. It was FABULOUS!

Every day at noon you'd hear this distant rumble, like the ship had come aground on an iceberg, but it was simply the stampede of everyone storming the dining-room doors as soon as they opened for lunch.

Normally I'd be in the thick of that sort of brouhaha, but they were a determined-looking bunch (despite being generally very aged) and I didn't fancy my chances, so Himself and myself usually waited until a bit later, when all the pushing and scratching had calmed down. My mammy had been on this self-same cruise two years ago and when I told her about all the pandemonium, she said, not a bit surprised, 'Oh yes, any time there was food, they were like pigs at a trough.'

Right then! Norway! A stunningly beautiful country – clean and pure and uncrowded and unpolluted and any of the people I met were very nice. We saw glaciers and fjords and the midnight sun and my personal highlight was the Marimekko shop in Trondheim where I went pure BERSERK. I bought two night-dresses (one stripy, one spotty), one light-blue raincoat, one matching umbrella, one pair of pink felt slippers, three tea towels and an adorable little pink dress and matching tights for my god-daughter Kitten. I bought so much they gave me 10 per cent off and two free packets of patternedy paper napkins (one blue, one green). Another highlight was the Noa Noa shop in Bergen, but I managed to be more restrained and no one gave me any paper napkins there (but I am not complaining).

Other Norwegian highlights included four nights of shipboard bingo. John and Shirley had never played before, and when Shirley won forty-eight quid on the last night she was full of talk of taking it up regularly on her return home. I fear I may have corrupted her . . .

mariankeyes.com, June 2005.

Walking in France

Je suis back from France and I had *un temps* lovely. Yes, lovely, despite everyone ROARING laughing when they heard I was going on a walking holiday. 'You in flat shoes,' they said. 'I've seen it all now!'

I don't know why or when the idea of a walking holiday started appealing to me, but it just goes to show how human beings can change. There was a time when I would have thought it was utter hell, but now . . .

Entre nous, mes amies, the thing I was dreading most was the ferry journey from Rosslare to Cherbourg. I once went on a school tour on said same ferry when I was fifteen and I remember it as being full of drunken louts (mostly me and my classmates) and I was convinced it would be a nightmare, but this time it was actually remarkably pleasant.

Himself and myself had a nice tea in a sitty-down restaurant where we were served by a very nice Polish man. After he took our order I said to Himself, 'Russians are taking over the world,' and Himself said, 'He's not Russian, he's Polish.' And then I was a bit mortified as I had thanked the girl at the Information Desk in Russian (because she sounded Russian and her name badge said Svetlana Russiancitizenski or some such), but in retrospect I realized she could just as easily have been Polish and mortally offended by being addressed in Russian when I was only trying to be nice.

This sort of faux pas normally keeps me awake for hours and could culminate in me going back to the Information Desk to apologize for thinking she was Russian (not that there's anything wrong with being Russian) and, if she had knocked off for the evening, insisting on finding her cabin and getting her out of bed in her nightie and face cream in order to be apologized at, but mercifully it didn't happen.

In fact, I had a lovely night's sleep. We had a dinky little cabin with bunk beds (I was on the bottom as I have to get up a lot at night to make wees – too much information? I apologize. It's just that I find a lot of women have this problem and we are all mortified to talk about it) and the motion of the boat was like being rocked, and all in all it was lovely and when we woke up we were in France!

We were headed for Dijon and it took us about seven hours and even that bit was a pleasure because the French roads are very good and when we stopped a couple of times for refreshments and yes, wees, because I am nearly as bad in the daytime, the people in the shops were LOVELY, all *bonjour* and *merci* and *au revoir*.

I know everyone says the French are as rude as anything, but maybe that's only in Paris, and in fairness no one has ever been rude to me in Paris either.

Actually, now that I remember, that's not true. I had one of the worst nights *of my life* in the Georges restaurant on the top of the Pompidou Centre. I'll tell you the story. Himself and myself were booked for dinner and we were 0.4 of a microsecond late and when I attempted to apologize in my admittedly shite French to the exquisitely beautiful greeting girl she stared and stared at me with such complete and utter contempt that eventually my speech of apology meandered to a halt. She picked up two menus, strode across the room, flung them on a table and stalked away without a backward glance.

This was around the time I turned forty and was picking fights with people left, right and centre, and I was so voraciously angry but also burning with shame at the way I'd let her make me feel that I decided I wasn't leaving without doing something. (Every time she passed our crappy table, showing new people to their place, I called out, 'You're a bitch!' But, sadly, the music was too loud and she couldn't hear me. Himself agreed with me that she'd been horrible, and offered to 'say something', but I insisted that I wanted to do it.)

So at the door, as we were leaving (we'd only had one course and I hadn't been able to eat mine because my stomach was all full up with rage and shame), I established that your woman could speak English – she could, perfectly – and I told her that she'd been unpleasant and rude when we'd arrived, that it was unnecessary, that we'd had a horrible evening and that we'd never be back.

In fairness, she was quite surprised, but sadly she didn't break down in floods of tears like what would happen in a crappy American film and apologize for being a bully but say that she'd been bullied as a child and this was the only way she knew how to cope and that even though everyone kept telling her she was beautiful, she felt ugly, ugly, yes, UGLY on the inside . . . Anyway, yes, she was a little taken aback and even though I didn't stop shaking for about three days from summoning up my nerve, I was glad I said something.

ANYWAY, apart from the bitch at the Pompidou Centre, every French person I've ever met has been charm itself.

We arrived in Dijon around six in the evening and went look-ing for a chemist and walked around the beautiful town (city?

Christ, people can be so touchy about the place they live that it's important to get it right), and then we saw the green cross of health, the international sign for a chemist, and we went inside and transacted our business.

As I've mentioned before, I adore chemists. They are such useful places, with so many wondrous, diverse wares. Often Mam and I lie on her bed and list the many, many things you can get. We always start with her shouting, 'Hairbands!' This is a declaration that the game is ON. So I say, 'Cotton buds!' Then she says, 'Strepsils.' Then I say, 'Solpadeine!' Then she says, 'Bonjela!' And so on for many, many happy hours.

The first time we did it, poor Susan (Tadhg's then girlfriend), who was living with Mam and Dad for a while (also with Tadhg, I'd better add) until they got their own flat, had to come in and ask us to keep the noise down as she was trying to sleep, she had work in the morning, and although we tried to get her to join in, she couldn't be persuaded.

Sometimes, out of the blue, in the middle of a conversation about something completely different, even when loads of other people are there, Mam will look at me and shout, 'Hairbands!' And then we're off.

Sadly, the chemist in Dijon was quite small and didn't have the full list of things that Mam and I cover in a session, but Himself and myself had an amazing dinner in Dijon – the first of many – and the following day, the walking began! The weather was magnificent – a bit *too* magnificent, ontra noo, *mes amies*, the kind of weather where you're better off lying beside a cooling swimming pool with a man handy to bring you cooling cocktails. Instead we were marching through vineyards and along trails and I'm not good in the heat at the best of times – being Irish, I'm just not equipped for it – but it's a small complaint and we walked through picture-perfect villages (or should that be *villages*?) with family-business wineries and beautiful chateaux and little boulangeries where we bought Gruyère buns for our lunch and everything was so charmingly French and our hotel was nice and our dinner was fabulous and I was so afraid that I wouldn't be able to get out of bed the next morning (we'd walked about nine miles) but it was no bother to me and all was well with the world.

We did five days of walking and sometimes stayed in sort of bed-and-breakfast places and other times it was more fancy, but the dinners were always magnificent – except that they're not exactly vegetarian-friendly. Not that I'm vegetarian, but I'm a bit squeamish, even about stuff like liver, and Himself is the total opposite: if he sees some piece of innard on the menu, it's almost like a challenge to him, which can sometimes be difficult to stomach, even when it's not me that's eating it.

The worst was when we were in Beaune – the most incredible place (see how I craftily avoided the town/city conundrum there?). I wished I'd had much, much longer there. I bought mirabelle plums at the market and my winter coat in a boutique and they had architecture and oh, all *kinds* of stuff. On the menu was – those of a delicate disposition might like to look away now – a stew made of coxcombs, you know, the frilly things on the top of cockerels' heads.

The minute I saw it I *knew* he was going to order it and gleefully he did, but the waitress looked aghast. She hurried away anxiously and returned with her boss, an enormously fat woman (which gives the lie to the theory that French women don't get fat) with bright purple eyeshadow and black kohl-lines flicking up to her hairline, à la Siouxie Sioux (or however she's spelt) circa 1977.

Boss woman interrogated Himself about his choice – did he

know what he was getting himself into? Had he ever had it before? Did he like tripe? Because it was like tripe, only worse. Then a man in a dinner suit joined in (he might have been the maître d') and a worried-sounding conversation in French ensued. Then they shrugged (for they are French) and decided that if le Rosbif (apparently that's what they call Englishmen, isn't it fantastic?) wanted the joke dinner, they might as well let him have it.

Anyway, when it arrived it was FAR WORSE that I had imagined. When they'd said stew, I thought the coxcombs would be all cut up into little bits and unrecognizable, but it was just a plate with three ENORMOUS coxcombs on it, looking all rubbery and revolting, and when Himself started into it, the entire staff, right down to kitchen porters, deserted their posts and stood staring, marvelling at the sight of le Rosbif eating it. Meanwhile, I was nibbling little pieces of bread, trying to keep from gagging. Christ above.

Other than that, our French adventure was FANTASTIC.

marlankeyes.com, September 2005.

Ulster Says NO!!!

KYLIE!!!! Coming to Ireland! The only fly in the ointment was that she was playing in Belfast, not Dublin, but this is how it all worked out: there were twelve of us, and some were coming from London, but for us Dublin people we hired a minibus and a great day was had by all, except when Ulster said NO!

We'd arranged in advance with the Odyssey Arena people that we could park our minibus, but when we went into the car park we were told by a youth in an orange fluorescent jacket and a walkie-talkie, 'NO! YOU CAN'T PARK HERE! You're too big.' He said there was a separate car park for minibuses, but when we tried to leave for it we were told, 'NO! YOU CAN'T LEAVE TILL YOU PAY FOR YOUR TICKET!' We explained we'd only been in for six seconds, but we were told that rules were rules, then eventually we were allowed to leave and we made our way to the coach car park, only to be told – yes! – 'NO! YOU CAN'T PARK HERE! Normally you could but the council has just said, "NO! NO PARKING HERE TONIGHT."'

We were directed to an official – this time in a YELLOW fluorescent jacket – who sent us back to the first car park, saying there was NO size, weight or height restriction on the vehicles that could park there, where – oh, *mes amies*, it was HILARIOUS – where the original orange-jacketed jobsworth youth came running the entire length of the car park in order to yell, 'NO, NO, NO, NO, NO, NO, NO, NO, NO, NO, NO!' at us.

You should have seen him, he was so THRILLED to have the opportunity to be unhelpful! We made his day, possibly his year.

'NO NONONONONO! Get out, you're too big.'

'But the man in the yellow jacket said –'

'NONONONONONO!!!!!! I have an ORANGE jacket. OR-ANGE trumps YELLOW.'

Before he kicked us out again and sent us back to the coach car-park bloke (who unsurprisingly hadn't changed his mind), he kindly directed us to 'a patch of waste ground around the corner about three minutes' walk from here'.

I wasn't sure which part of that sentence alarmed me most. The 'waste ground'? The 'around the corner' directions in a strange city? The promise of a three-minute walk? Irish people are notorious liars about time and distance, everything is 'just coming now' and 'three minutes' walk away'.

Meanwhile, Himself was ringing the woman who had promised parking in the first place but – guess what? – that's right – NO REPLY.

Then when we tried to go into the Odyssey Arena, the man took one look at our tickets and said, 'NO.' He had already turned away to shout NO at someone else, but when we asked him why we couldn't go in he said, 'You need a letter.' We produced the letter and he was bitterly disappointed, but in the end he had no choice but to let us in. At this stage we were in convulsions.

Then Eileen tried to go outside for a cigarette before the start of the show but she was told, 'NO. NO. NO. NO. Go out if you must but NO WAY will you be coming back in.'

But the best bit, the very best bit of all, was when Suzanne and I went to the loo during the concert. When we came back into the arena, we stood for a second on the top of the steps just to get our bearings and the next thing some official girl yelled in our face, 'NO! NO STANDING! YOU CAN'T STAND THERE!'

We were crying with laughter.

But after all that it was an amazing show: breathtaking sets and costumes and dancers and SHOES. Kylie is a little angel and charm itself.

mariankeyes.com, July 2008.

Cyprus

Cyprus! We were going because Ireland was playing Cyprus in the football, and mercifully we were flying from London and not Dublin as I'd gone to the Israel match in March direct from Dublin and Christ, what a NIGHTMARE! For starters the flight had left at 4.30 a.m. and everyone on the plane apart from me, Himself, Tadhg and Susan were out of their minds drunk and wearing green curly wigs and singing 'The Fields of Athenry' (why? *Why?* Of *all* the songs?). It was like being on a night bus but for six hours, one that they sold drink on and that you couldn't get off.

People (well, men, actually) kept tumbling on top of me and telling me I looked like Eleanor McEvoy (I don't, I've nothing against her, she's lovely, but I just don't) and asking me to sing a song and telling me to lighten up and offering me a drink and the whole thing was badly hideous and I hated myself for not loving it, but then again I AM an alcoholic, one who doesn't drink, so it was bound to be hard . . .

This time, flying from London, there were a few high-spirited green-jerseyed lads in the queue, and Himself did a headcount and said, 'That's good. Just enough to get a sing-song going,' and I said, 'I'll give you sing-song where you'll feel it.'

When the green-jerseyed lads got on the plane, they insisted on proving how good-natured and lovable Irish football fans are by stopping to help the air hostess fit a case into a tight space in the overhead luggage thing. 'Here, let me do that,' one charmer said. Then, from another lovable rogue, 'Ah no, Joxer, you're doing it all wrong, give me a go.' 'No, that's not that way,' said a twinkly ne'er-do-well. Despite the poor woman insisting she was well able, the lads continued to pull and shove at the piece of luggage and only stopped when they damaged its handle. Then they all piled down the back, roaring for drink.

Other than that, it was a grand flight and when we arrived in Cyprus it was 82 degrees! All the others were there, including poor Eileen who'd had to do the night-bus Dublin flight, which was so bad that she couldn't bear to talk about it.

We had a beautiful time, all nine of us, sunbathing on our own little grassy knoll and having lovely dinners, where I had fried halloumi cheese for starters and Cyprus salad (like Greek salad but with halloumi instead of feta) for my mainer.

The match, however, was a tragedy. Although we won, we played atrociously. When we got back to the hotel I repaired to bed, as is my way, but the rest of them piled across the road to a bar, where they spent many happy hours drowning their sorrows.

A lone man in a suit was at the next table, but no one paid him any heed until he stood up to leave and Tadhg suddenly went peculiar. Himself thought that the man in the suit had pinched Tadhg's arse, so thunderstruck was Tadhg's face, but then Tadhg pointed a trembling finger at the back of the man as he crossed the road, and said, hoarsely, 'That's Ray Houghton.'

Now, Ray Houghton, for those who may not know, is a hero, oft celebrated in song and story and comedy routine, because in 1988, in Stuttgart, Ray scored the winning goal in a match against England. It's not that we hold the 800 years of colonization against England or anything, and sure 'tis only an oul' game, but all the same, to beat England!!!

Anyway, Tadhg yelled, 'RAY!' and Ray turned around, lifted

one hand in a gracious salute – and disappeared into our hotel. Immediately Tadhg tried to dash out into the traffic after him and had to be restrained, then he began rounding up whatever the pleasant equivalent of a lynch mob is, in order to find Ray.

But it was late and no one would join his quest except poor innocent Seán (Caitríona's fella). Everyone else sloped off to bed, but Tadhg and Seán apparently spent half the night banging on hotel doors and shouting, 'Ray! RAY! Are you IN there, Ray? Ray? Are you ASLEEP? Can I buy you a DRINK? I love you, Ray!'

Then there was talk that Seán was instructed to cause some diversion by the reception desk so that Tadhg could go through the computer system, in order to discover which room Ray was in.

Some of this is actually a lie, sadly, especially the bit about the diversion and the computer system. All that happened really was that Tadhg and Seán spent several hours in the hotel bar in the hope that Ray might appear in his pyjamas, looking for a nightcap, but we enjoyed ourselves so much the following day with the 'Ray! RAY! Are you IN there, Ray?' stories that I thought I'd write them down anyway.

mariankeyes.com, October 2005.

Brazil

Well, off we went on Valentine's Day to Brazil and, oh my God, Rio, it's EXACTLY like it looks in the pictures. Copacabana was a MASSIVE expanse of beach, jam-packed with millions of people all almost in their pelt, playing music and drinking out of coconuts with the top lopped off and beautiful children running everywhere and women not at all bothered if they didn't have perfect bodies (fair play!) and boys playing volleyball and football and the sun beating down and men selling ice cream and all that.

Round the next headland was Ipanema beach and that was exactly the same. Granted, it was carnival (or *carnaval*, actually) and it mightn't be like that the whole time but I'd like to think it is.

Being Irish, repressed, full of loathing for my body and having received the message from the moment I was born that my naked self was a disgusting, shameful thing and the best garment I could wear would be an all-over body-coverer knitted in itchy wool, Rio came as a bit of a challenge to me. (Actually, now that I think about it, it's strange that the burka didn't originate in Ireland. Not only would it fit in with the message given by priests that all women are shameless hussies who are only gagging for an opportunity to lure good men from the path of righteousness by flashing a square inch of shin or elbow joint, but it would come in very handy with our wet weather. I love a hood. I practically *insist* upon it when I buy a jacket.)

We arrived at the bright, shiny hotel and even in the hotel lobby, people were wearing almost nothing. Lounging by the concierge desk was a standard-issue Eurotrash international play-boy with shoulder-length hair, bright orange Speedo togs (the really, really small, tight, clingy ones – budgie-smugglers, I believe they're called), a matching (yes, *matching*) orange T-shirt and – of course, you could have guessed this – a man-bag (sadly not orange) tucked under his oxter. Himself and myself nudged each other and attempted a snigger, but it was a little half-hearted because even then we intuited we were in over our heads.

After we washed away the grime of our journey, timidly, tenta-tively, Himself and myself, in our roomy T-shirts and lightweight but nevertheless ankle-length trousers, left our hotel, stepped outside into the Copacabana mayhem and were instantly flat-tened against the pavement by the heat.

But I was reminded of what my friend Nadine had told me about Miami. She said when she first arrived there she was intimi-dated to pieces by all the tanned gorgeous bodies in dayglo-pink batty riders, driving around in convertibles and playing Shakira, but a couple of days in, she had successfully infiltrated and was managing to pass herself off as a native. And so it proved with me, my amigos! (Well, almost!)

As the days went on, I wore less and less until the Damascene moment when I bared – totally! – my upper arms. In fact, I actu-ally had a bubble of time when I was able to say, God, I'm really happy. It was when I was on my way back from an AA meeting (it was *unbelievable*, there was an English-speaking meeting just four minutes' walk from my hotel) and the sun was setting and everyone was leaving the beach in droves and heading for the Metrô and here I was, walking along, with the lumpy shame of my upper arms on view for all the world to see, and I was feeling great. Alone but not lonely. A person among people. Lumpy arms or no, just the same as everyone else.

I find it difficult to ever be truly at peace, there's always something that feels like a shark relentlessly on the prowl, somewhere deep in my psyche. Even though I am the luckiest person on earth and have been given an amazing life, it's difficult to get the shark to stop moving, but it stopped while I was in Rio.

Now, I'm not suggesting that a permanent cure for the shark would be to move to Rio, as shark-subduing is a lifelong journey of trying to do the right thing, but it was so nice to get temporary relief, you know?

Our friends Eileen and her sister Deirdre were with us in Rio and we did all the touristy yokes (Cripes the Redeemer and the Sugarloaf and all that), but the best by a million miles was the night at the Sambadrome. I haven't got the words to do it justice. I found it very emotional. I actually cried (not something I do often, except in the presence of Russian orphans) because I was so moved by all the work each school had put into their parade.

The thought of people in the favelas, where I'm sure life is not easy (I don't intend to be patronizing, I really mean it), working so hard and doing it with such pride and producing such a jaw-dropping spectacle (6,000 people dancing along in amazing costumes and on massive floats as big as a four-storey house) overwhelmed me. Human beings are incredible, they really are.

Another thing about Rio, I hadn't expected the people to be so warm. I don't know why. Maybe it was because we'd been warned the place was so dangerous. (We were warned many times to be on the lookout for 'mugglers'. It's my new favourite word.) Or maybe it's because the natives are so good-looking. But they were astonishingly kind and likeable. Even the journalists!

After six nights in Rio we said goodbye to Deirdre, then Himself, Eileen and myself headed for Manaus, gateway to the Amazon. (That's not their slogan, that's just mine.) Manaus used to be a thriving rubber port (not actually *made* of rubber), with its own *opera house* (I know!), but it all went to hell when the arse fell out of the rubber market around 1910. It was an atmospheric place, reeking of decayed grandeur. Himself said he felt like he was in a Gabriel García Márquez novel.

After one night there, we went up the Amazon. Ontra noo, Eileen and I were dreading the whole Amazon thing. We were staying 'upriver' in a lodge with no electricity or hot water, where we expected to be overrun with mosquitoes, anacondas and tarantulas and – worst of all – where meals were communal. God, there's nothing worse, is there? Having to make small talk with strangers over breakfast. Having to ask where they're from and what they do and where they've been and where they're going next (then – aaarrrgggghhh – discovering that you're going to the exact same spot, that you're not in fact an intrepid traveller at all, merely the pawn of a travel agent).

Things got off to a bad start when, just before we got on the boat, I discovered that I'd lost my sunglasses, so I had to very quickly buy a pair in Manaus, and on account of having an abnormally small head my choice was limited. On the boat, watching the banks of the river whizzing past, despair began to creep over me. I was quite surprised as – after a lifetime of depression – I've perked up a bit recently. Yes, everything began to appear malign and tinted with desperation, then I took off my sunglasses – and everything cheered up! Put the sunglasses back on – and I spiralled back down into gloom. Took the glasses off again – and once more all became cheery!

Then I realized that the problem wasn't me at all, it was the fecking sunglasses! There was a yellowish tinge to the glass. Not on the actual *outside* of the glass – I wouldn't run the risk of wearing the same kind of sunglasses as Bono, as the chances of me being mistaken for him are already quite high: we are both short, stout, stocky-thighed, have dark hair, an Irish accent and always wear high heels. Also, I am quite a good singer. (This is a lie.) Also, I have met the Pope and called him 'dude'. (This is another lie.) Also, I have met George Bush and said to him, 'Hey, man, why can't we all jus' get along?' (This is yet another lie, but I am on a roll now and appear to be unable to stop.) Also, we both drive Maseratis. (Would you believe it? This is actually true. There are – apparently – only six Maseratis in the ROI (Republic of Ireland) and Bono owns one, and I (well, Himself really) own another, and often, yes, often when I am out 'motoring', you see people nudging each other, going, 'Doesn't Bono drive one of them yokes? It couldn't be Bono, could it?' And then when I get closer and they see me behind the wheel, short, stout, stocky-thighed, dark-haired, Irish-accented and singing, 'In the NAAAAAAAAAAAAMMMMMEHHHH of LOVVVVVVE! WAAAHHHLURGHHHH ijeh name of LOVVVVVVE,' they go, 'Christ! It is! It is Bono!!!

Yes, so, anyway, the sunglasses. From the inside, looking out, the sunglasses made everything look sort of jaundiced and appalling. How does Bono do it? No wonder he goes around doing good works and badgering the oppressed and the needy if he is looking at the world through jaundice-tinted spectacles. You'd *have* to try to improve things, or else commit suicide.

So once that little problem was sorted out, all was top notch and my time in the Amazon proved to be the greatest surprise of my life.

From the moment we arrived, we went all floppy-limbed and soft-shouldered with humidity and relaxation and spent many hours thrun in a hammock, reading. From time to time we roused ourselves to go alligator spotting or get up close and personal with anacondas, sloths, toucans, piranhas and tarantulas the size of dinner plates.

The best bit of all was going in a canoe into a tributary of the Amazon, then a smaller tributary, then a smaller one, then a tiny one where the boat moved almost silently through a drowned forest where the branches of the trees met overhead and turned the light green and thin lines of blinding sunlight would appear through the cover of branches and I felt like I was in a place where no other human being had ever been before. Eileen said it was like being in *Apocalypse Now*. Even the shared meals weren't a problem. It was wonderful, really wonderful, and even if you're afraid of everything, as I am, I would urge you to go if you ever get the chance.

After four days we left for Patagonia. The thing is, when we'd been planning the trip I hadn't appreciated that Brazil is the fifth biggest country in the world and Argentina is the eighth. I had just thought, 'Well, they're next door to each other, and if we're going to Brazil we might as well pop into Argentina while we're there.'

Big mistake, mucho grande mistake. It took two full days to get from the Amazon to El Calafate in Patagonia (including an over-nighter in Buenos Aires. We arrived at 2 a.m. and left again at the break of day). Also, we crossed back and forth so many fecking time zones in those two days that we didn't know our arse from our elbow.

By the time we arrived in Eolo (twenty kilometres outside El Calafate) on a Sunday evening, we were all in FOULERS. Knack-ered, tired and starving hungry and sorry we had ever left the comfort of our own homes and embarked on so foolhardy an adventure. We made a pact in the car from the airport that as soon as we got to the hotel we were going to demand our dinner. 'We're not even going to check in,' I instructed Himself and Eileen. 'Do you hear me?'

So I had to apologize to all the lovely staff at Eolo who obliged us when I insisted that NO, we did NOT want to see our rooms, and NO, we did NOT want a pre-dinner drink, and YES, we WERE going to go into the kitchen and COOK our dinner OUR-SELVES if they refused to feed us IMMEDIATELY. Yes, I was very sorry indeed. The three of us were very tired and hungry, but I have to admit that I was the ringleader. It was my fault. I led the other two astray. I egged them on. (Hunger-based pun there.)

In the fifteen minutes before the food was put in front of me I stared sightlessly out the window at the frankly astonishing view and bemoaned the fact that we had ever come away and how I wished I was back home in lovely Ireland. I almost sang a sad song about it, as is the way of Irish people when they are twenty minutes outside of Ireland, except that I was too hungry to sing. (Which just shows how difficult it must be to sing for your supper.)

In fairness to me, I did get my period the next day, so not all of my bad behaviour can be blamed on my personality but on that wretched pest progesterone (or is it oestrogen?).

Very, very early the following morning – 6.30 or something ungodly – the other two left to go trekking on a glacier. Himself tried to get me out of bed but, still in the fiendish grip of excessive progesterone, I shrieked that I was 'going fucking nowhere' and eventually, after I bit him for the second time, he said, 'Well, fuck you then,' and stomped out in his crampons.

I slept until eleven, then emerged to roam the halls, demand-ing (yet more) food, and as I shovelled complex carbohydrates into me in front of a floor-to-ceiling window, I was restored to calm. This place was INCREDIBLE. Over our days there we decided it would be a great place to come if you'd had a nervous breakdown.

Have you been to Patagonia? If you haven't I'll try to describe it. It's all wild and windy and beautiful in a barren, bleak, empty way, and if you stand in Eolo's hallway and look one way you see the milky turquoise of a glacier lake, and if you look the other you see the limitless expanse of a mustardy-coloured plain, and if you look over your shoulder you'll see mountains, with another row of mountains behind them, and behind them the snow-capped beginnings of the Andes.

The staff in Eolo were incredibly kind and obliging, and if you go on a walk they might give you a small bag of almonds and raisins, and the place itself is full of cosy gorgeous couches and corners in which to read your book and recover from your nervous breakdown. (Also, there were four puppies, which I think any 'sanctuary' should have.)

After a couple of days I emerged from my slump and went glacier-visiting and hill-climbing and Eileen went horse-riding and all in all we had an excellent wind-blown, outdoorsy, thousand-mile-stare time. (Also, apropos of nothing, the local men were *excessively* good-looking.)

Then Eileen left for Buenos Aires and Himself and I went to Bariloche, still in Patagonia but a two-hour flight away – the *size* of Argentina! – in the Lake District, and it was hilarious. It was like being in Switzerland! Log cabins a gogo. Triangular-shaped houses! Everything made of wood! Jagged snow-capped peaks! Chocolate! (Yes, sadly another lapse from my sugar-free state.) Pine forests! Deep, dark-blue lakes! Stunning, so it was, utterly stunning.

Myself and Himself were staying in this hotel in Bariloche called Llao Llao (pronounced sort of like 'Yow Yow', I believe, or maybe the person who told me was just taking the piss and hoping to make a gom of me).

Apparently it's a famous hotel and it's been there a long time and frankly, *mes amies*, I found it slightly odd. It sort of had a Swiss/Wild West peculiar identity. Lots of wood and stag antlers and wooden banisters and wooden floors and dead animals looming out of walls and cowhide on floors and . . . you know. But nice enough.

In fairness we were in a tiny horrible room with twin beds, although we had asked for a doubler, and if there's one thing that makes Himself cry and put his back out it's twin beds (he puts his back out when he shoves the twin beds together, and he insists on doing it even when they're glued to the floor).

Basically we got off to a bad start. But then things picked up and we went out in a canoe in the lake beside the hotel and all in all a lovely time was had, but from the lake we noticed that there were massive building works going on which we hadn't noticed up to that point. (Bear with me, this becomes important.)

Anyway, two days later, we are in this massive concourse downstairs having our breakfast (I will also explain that) when who do we see wandering in desultory fashion around the breakfast buffet, plate of scrambled eggs in hand? Only John Rocha!

For those of you who don't know who John Rocha is, let me explain. He's an Irish designer and he designs clothing and glasswear and hotels. He 'did' the Morrison Hotel. Also, he is a fairly distinctive-looking character, with waist-length, black-but-greying straight hair, and he was dressed in designer black and he looked – the truth hurts but I am obliged to say it – out of place among the Argentine holidaymakers, who were dressed in jolly holiday shades and fleeces and other relaxed clothing.

Himself and I were TREMENDOUSLY excited to see a famous Irish person and in such an unusual location, and it couldn't have happened at a better time because we were beginning to get homesick. Anyway, Himself decided to climb to his feet and cup his hands together to form a loudhailer and shout at the top of his voice in his best Colin Farrell accent over the heads of the stylish Argentines eating their dolce con leche (they're mad for it, I was fairly mad for it myself, it's like caramel and they have it on their bread, very sweet, gorgeous), 'John, JOHN!!! JOHN, ya mad bollix, what the FOOOK are YOU doing here?' (I should at this point tell you that John Rocha doesn't know me and Himself from a hole in the ground.) Anyway, Himself didn't actually do it, he just pretended to do it, and we got great enjoyment out of it and we concluded that John must be 'doing' the new wing of Yow Yow and that hopefully he'd steer clear of antlers and suchlike. (Was that a pun? 'Steer' clear? Could have been.)

Oh yes. I have to explain what we were doing at the breakfast buffet, because although I love buffets, I hate being in the presence of strangers eating their breakfasts. I'm bad in the mornings, jumpy and nervy, everything seems louder and brighter and – yes, forgive me, *mes amies* – *smellier*. And the smell of eggs – particularly fried eggs, but I will also include poached, boiled and scrambled and any other way you can think of – makes me want to cut my own throat. So I try to avoid communal breakfasts because if I'm feeling in any way at all suicidal, the stench of eggs tends to nudge me that little bit closer to the edge.

However, this was not our first breakfast of the day, but our second. The first we had had several hours earlier, when we had checked out and left for the airport, but en route to the airport we discovered that our flight had been delayed by eleven hours, so we came back to Yow Yow and they let us in and suggested that we kill one of our eleven hours by having a second breakfast. Which we duly did. And to think that if our flight hadn't been delayed we would have missed the sight of John Rocha nosing around the Coco Pops. (I apologize to non-Irish readers. The sight of John Rocha making his own toast may not be as thrilling to you as it was to me.)

After four days, we went to Buenos Aires and we were meant to meet up with Eilers but due to the flight delay by the time we got in it was too late and she left for Ireland early the next morning, so that was that.

Just the two days in BA (as they say). (It would have been three if it hadn't been for the delayed flight.) After extreme forbearance on the shopping front up until this point, I had a mild shoe-and-bag frenzy in some place called Ricky Sarkovy (something like that). I got blue metallic stilettos and a silvery metallic bag and a purple metallic belt.

My friend Conor McCabe had assured me, and I quote, that everything in Buenos Aires was 'dirt cheap'. Sadly, I did not find this to be so. As I may have mentioned, I don't know what it is, but there's something about me that just repels bargains. I think it's because I've an eejity face and when shopkeepers see me approaching, they think, 'This one will buy anything' (which is true). 'I'll just raise my prices by 1500 per cent.'

And now here I am, back home, with the shakes and mild nausea. (Jet lag.) (Also terror at having to resume work.)

mariankeyes.com, February 2007.

The Auvergne

Myself and Himself went to France on a walking holiday. I know it must seem that my life is one big holiday but honestly it isn't, it's just that there was a gap in the schedule: the new book had gone off for the copy-editing and there was nothing for me to do for a little while and soon enough I'd be doing the proofreading, so you've got to take your chances where you can find them, so we went to France.

Also, I feel jackknifed with guilt about going on holiday in these horrible financial times, but this was a very cheap holiday because we were spending our days walking, at no financial cost, and staying in very basic places (lino on the floors, extremely small rooms so that one of us had to stay in bed while the other of us got dressed, that sort of thing. Also, no tellies, not that it would have made any difference, seeing as I can't speak French).

So we had the cost of the ferry and the petrol, which obviously is an expense but it's a bit different from going to Reethi Rah in the Maldives and staying in a villa with its own pool and a butler for two weeks. (I spend a lot of time on the interwebs looking at it and dreaming . . .) So anyway, off we went to France, to the Auvergne.

It's a volcanic region – the place is JAM-PACKED with extinct volcanoes – and the guidebook said it was very remote, and I had visions of inbred peasants throwing stones and shouting, '*Allez chez vous!*' at us as we tramped past in our walking boots and rucksacks, but the book had it ALL WRONG.

It was STUNNINGLY BEAUTIFUL. Lakes and, yes, hills – indeed, you could call them mountains. And – this is the best bit – meadows full of wild flowers, wild daffodils and violets and foxgloves and poppies in the hedgerows, and butterflies and all of that, and it reminded me of the way rural Ireland used to be before they started using pesticides.

There were cows in the fields, and goats and sheep and – unsettlingly – llamas. Yes, llamas. The Peruvian type, not the Tibetan. Twice I saw them. Once I would have put down to a fragile state of mind. But twice made me think that I probably wasn't imagining it. And not once were stones thrown at us. We met hardly anyone, but the few ancient oul' fellas on tractors we encountered were very nice and SALUTED us, like *actually saluted* us, like we were in the army.

It's funny because my mother is a rural type and she uses the word 'salute' when she means 'greet' or 'wave'. But I didn't realize it was something that LITERALLY happens.

We walked miles and miles every day. Thirteen of them. Miles, not days. Six days. Then in the evenings we would arrive at our lino-floored billet and eat enough stodgy food to sink a battleship. Yes, the food was fascinating. Completely not what I expected from French food, which I always associate with complicated reductions and creamy sauces and general gussied-up fanciness.

This was proper rural stodge. Their signature dish is half an acre of potatoes, mashed with a warehouse full of cheese and 112 pints of cream and the side of a pig. The PORTIONS, amigos. MASSIVE. Like rural Ireland, where the woman of the house feels she has failed as a hostess if her dinner guests don't spontaneously develop a hernia in the course of the dinner.

And for breakfast there was no chopped fruit or granola or 'lifestyle' food; what you got was a ginormous croissant and a bucket of coffee, and I was fecking DELIGHTED because I adore croissants but won't let myself eat them because of the continual war that rages between my appetite and the size of my arse. But I had no choice but to eat my ginormous croissant because there was nothing else and I had a hard day's walking ahead of me, so it was great.

Then we'd buy cheese and stuff to bring for our lunch and one day I insisted we purchase ten slices of Parma-style ham, only to discover many hours later when we'd collapsed beside a lake to refuel that it wasn't Parma ham at all, but raw bacon. A low moment, amigos. Yes, some disappointment and – sad to say – a shameful attempt to reapportion the blame, as I sought to absolve myself of responsibility.

But other than that little hiccup, we had *un temps merveilleux*!

mariankeyes.com, May 2009.

Slovakia

While the Praguers were living in Prague, I visited them regularly. And when it transpired that Ireland were playing Slovakia in the European Championship qualifiers, the two things tied in very nicely. So I went to Prague with Himself, Tadhg and Susan, then we drove to Bratislava with Niall to see our glorious boys in green thrash the living daylights out of Slovakia.

Okay, Slovakia. Well, we went there thinking a) the Irish football team would bate the living daylights out of the Slovaks, and b) that the Slovaks were lovely people (Ljiljana had said they were). Neither of these things turned out to be true.

We set off from Prague on the Saturday morning, full of good cheer. We then proceeded to stop at about fifteen different McDonald's on the way, partly because of my bargain-basement bladder and partly because we were all hungry at different times and partly because it was the month for Himself to have his once-a-year McDonald's.

We arrived at the SAS Radisson in the centre of Bratislava to discover that only one of our three rooms was ready (even though it was later than three o'clock). We could hardly hear the conversation with the surly, surly, oh *very surly* desk person because of the singing of 'The Fields of Athenry' from the bars across the street. Undeterred, we went to the one ready room and Tadhg leant out the window, looking at the hordes of Irish fans out there, and said, 'There it is! I've seen my first green inflatable hammer!' And so festivities were declared open!

Out we went. Irish fans everywhere, full of niceness. Slovak police also everywhere, not full of niceness. Making people take down Irish flags. Telling people to shut up the singing. Slovak bar staff. Not full of niceness.

Back to the hotel to see if the rooms were ready. Revelation from (different other) surly desk person: the hotel was over-booked. There was no room for Niall. The whole town was full. But they had secured him some rude lodgings outside the town, halfway to Budapest. All of us very distressed. 'He's our brother!' we exclaimed. 'We don't see him that often! Don't send him half-way to Budapest!'

But nothing doing. Mood low. Arrangements to meet in the lobby at 6.15 for food before the match. However . . . however . . . as luck would have it, weren't we staying in the same hotel as the team! Yes! Before 6.15, Himself and myself were 'grooming' our-selves (i.e. putting on our green gear) when we heard an extra-loud commotion down in the street: a coach had drawn up outside. THE coach. To collect the team and bring them to the grounds.

We were so excited we climbed out the window and on to the roof and then we decided we should rush downstairs to see if we could see them *in the lobby*. And sure enough we did! They all appeared out of the lifts, seconds after myself and Himself arrived, and they disappeared into some back room for a 'chat'. Then they appeared again, a long line of them, being led by Damien Duff. I've always been fond of him because of his alleged predilection for twenty hours' sleep a night.

And – coincidentally, just like me – he too has had his hair recently de-gingered, because he was looking very blond and

Nordic (but small) (but there's nothing wrong with small, nothing at all). As he led the boys out, his eyes connected with my awe-struck ones and he gave me a slow, deliberate wink! (I am afraid this is a complete lie. But I've told it so often that I've started to believe it myself.)

Then we went for something to eat. And my God, the frozen, unsmiling hostility of it all. You'd swear it was illegal to smile in Slovakia. Indeed, maybe it is! Certainly, enough police were around to enforce it. Frankly, we were *astonished* by the unpleas-antness of the staff. I mean, I admit that Irish people can sometimes be a bit wearing, with their constant chat and bon-homie and desperate desire for the craic, but come on!

Then we went to the grounds, where the warm Slovak wel-come continued. There were only two gates for the Irish fans and 279 for the (thirteen) Slovak fans. Tumbleweed was blowing through the Slovak turnstiles but they still wouldn't let us come in. They directed us (curtly, nay *brutally*) to the Irish gates, which looked like Red Cross feeding stations in a famine zone. It was really – genuinely – scary.

Although everyone (by which I mean the Irish people, not the granite-faced Slovaks) was really good-humoured, we were so crushed that my feet were lifting off the ground. By the time we got in the national anthems were playing, and there were still loads of Irish people stuck outside in the throng, so they would have missed the start of the game.

However, the less said about the game the better. All that you need to know is that it looked like we were going to win, then we let in a Slovak goal in injury time. Déjà fecken vu! It was Tel Aviv all over again! We were gutted, gutted, gutted! And to enhance our happiness, the Slovaks sent in a load of riot police, who were so obviously *itching* for a fight.

I've never been so insulted in my life! I've been to Irish games in lots of countries and never, ever, ever have we been treated like this. Irish fans are nice! Everyone knows that! (Like I say, yes, we can at times be wearing with the anecdotes and the good humour, but coshing people over the head with batons just to shut them up surely isn't the way to go.)

Then – the final salt in the wound – the Irish fans were locked in – yes, *locked in* – for fifteen minutes at the end of the match, to let the six Slovak fans home safely (yes, I had originally thought there were thirteen Slovak fans, but seven of them were Irish who had had to buy Slovak tickets because all the Irish ones were sold).

It was a bad business. Doubtless there are many nice Slovakians who spend their days from dawn till dusk laughing their heads off. I am not judging the entire Slovakian nation, only the 417 Slovaks I met. Maybe they were having a bad day. All of them.

In fairness, no wonder it was such a peaceful business when they decided to break away from the Czechs and make their own country. The Czechs must have been delighted! 'Work away, lads, good luck with it all. No, no – no need to feel guilty, we'll be grand. We'll miss you, of course, your little smiling Slovak faces, but we respect that you must do what you must do.'

And of course, out of suffering, great art sometimes comes. So much so that I've been inspired to write a pome about my time there. It goes as follows:

> Slovakia. Oh Slovakia!
> I won't be going back to ya.

Final little piece on the match and then I'll shut up about it. Susan and I were both woken in the middle of the night by a very over-refreshed and heartbroken Irish fan shrieking in the street outside our hotel, 'Staunton. *Stauuuuuuuuuuuuuntonnnnn!'* (Staunton is the Irish manager.) 'We know you're in there! Get down here, you . . .' (pause for breath) *'useless . . .'* (another pause for breath) *'GOBSHITE.'* After a short pregnant pause, sounds of ragged sobbing reached me and Susan.

(Himself and Tadhg did not have their slumber disturbed as they were sleeping the sleep of the very drunk. And Niall, of course, did not have his slumber disturbed either, as he was half-way to Budapest on account of the SAS Radisson Bratislava having given his room away to someone else. I'm not bitter. No. I'm only saying.)

Note: I subsequently heard that the reason there were no Slovak-ian supporters at the match was because they were boycotting it because the ticket prices were so high. Also, that the SAS Radis-son Bratislava is not owned by Slovakians, the implication being that if it had been, they wouldn't have given Niall's room away.

mariankeyes.com, September 2007.

Donegal

It has been the wettest bloody July I can ever remember, and in the middle of it Himself and myself decided to go to Donegal for a few days, in a strange 'if you can't beat them, join them' mentality. Apparently it always rains in Donegal, so if it was going to be wet anywhere, we might as well be there.

Now, I'd never been to Donegal before (neither had Himself, but you'd expect that, what with him being English) and I'd always thought of it as this mad, wild, mystical place, sort of lawless and like a separate country.

When I told people I was going I got two very different reactions. 1) People warned us that it was the worst county in Ireland for 'bungalow-itis' and that as soon as you cross the border into Donegal there are loudspeakers placed every four yards, blaring out Daniel O'Donnell songs, twenty-four hours a day, like the way they do with the teachings of your man Kim Il Kim in North Korea. Or 2) people said it was really, really beautiful.

Well, I can report that although there is a good bit of bungalow-itis in some areas, in other areas (the national park) it is utterly stunning and wild and uninhabited and amazing, but sadly not once, no, not *once*, did I hear the bould Daniel.

The people are extremely friendly and kind, and that beautiful soft, melodic accent! Aye! We got a puncture outside Letterkenny and loads of people came to help and we met some very kindly people in Ulster Tyres who toned down their accent so we could have half a clue what they were saying.

It was so funny, we were on our way to Sliabh Liag (the highest marine cliffs in Europe) and (as always with me) nature called, so we stopped at a tea-house/craft shop called Ti Linn in the middle of nowhere, where it transpired they had beautiful crafts and yokes and I got the itch that I always get on holidays to buy things I'd never buy at home, like cushions and tablecloths.

And while I was browsing, I noticed the place was VERY FULL for a place in the middle of nowhere. Also, at the far end of the room was a table buckling under the weight of finger-food. Because there were many men in suits eating the cocktail sausages, Himself concluded it was the 'afters' of a funeral, whereas I thought it was a corporate bonding yoke – that they were about to have their sangers, before climbing Sliabh Liag.

Well, it transpired to be neither! Instead we had gatecrashed the official opening of Ti Linn (even though it has in fact been open for four years – I mean that, I'm not exaggerating) and we fell into a chat with a beautiful woman called Laoise Kelly – who only happens to be one of the best harpists in Ireland – and Steve Cooney, also a well-known musician. Himself was all star-struck because he is a big fan of traditional music. I explained to them that I hadn't a rasher's who they were because I only ever listen to George Michael, and they weren't remotely offended by this and introduced us to Siobhán, the owner of Ti Linn, and before we knew it we were right *in the thick of things*, eating cocktail sausages for all we were worth and generally having a top-notch time.

mariankeyes.com, July 2008.

Finland/Lapland

One of the jammiest things that ever happened to me was the *Guardian* sending myself and Himself on a romantic mini-break to Finland/Lapland. Well, it was DELIGHTFUL. The fabulous thing was that we arrived in Helsinki at 6 p.m. on the Friday evening and I assumed all the shops would be closed. However! I was entirely wrong. There were about forty-eight – OPEN! – Marimekko shops, all within touching distance of the hotel, and they were ENORMOUS. The biggest collection of Marimekko merchandise I've ever seen. The greatest density of Marimekko merchandise in the smallest radius – it could be in the *Guinness Book of Records*.

I was suitably restrained, as per my New Year's resolution, and eventually purchased only two nightdresses and not an entire crate of towels, bedlinen and clothing. Just the two nighties, one a teal and dark-blue stripy item and the other a charcoal-grey with a fruit-bowl pattern. These are what I wear when I work, they are in essence my uniform, so I didn't feel guilty about buying them.

Then on to Ivalo, the most northern airport in Finland, and there was so much that was beautiful and unusual that I probably won't be able to do it justice. Basically, it felt like we'd come to colonize a new planet. Because the sun never actually rises during January, the sky was strange and beautiful; it was light, but it was a funny colour, sort of lilac, and there was snow everywhere, which reflected the lilac light, and the clouds looked like huge purple satellites, just hanging above us, and everywhere were endless forests of fir trees.

We stayed in a place called Kakslauttanen and there were log cabins and glass igloos and ice bedrooms scattered throughout a snowy landscape, and while we were there they were building an ice church and an ice restaurant.

Now, I must stress one thing: it was very, very, very cold. It was minus 15 every day, and we had to wear several layers of technical long johns before we could leave our little log cabin. Which was the cutest thing ever. I'd expected it to be – yes, loggy – but also quite grim and functional, but it was soft and comfortable and full of delicious little touches, like a carved heart-shaped table, which was nothing like as kitsch as it sounds, but sort of reminded me of Minnie Mouse's house in Disneyland (a very, very good thing).

Also, there was a four-poster bed and other furniture which was carved in a way that reminded me of *Who Framed Roger Rabbit*. Yes, delightful!

We did loads of great stuff. We went on a sleigh ride, pulled by reindeers, through a stunningly beautiful snowy forest. (And could have done a similar thing with huskies if I wasn't so afeerd of dogs.)

We did this mad ice-driving and rally-driving. (Himself LOVED that. In fact he said that although we were having 'a lovely romantic time' that this would be a great place for a stag weekend. Yes . . .) And the best bit of all: a night-time snowmobile trip to see the Northern Lights.

Everyone was at pains to warn us that we probably wouldn't see them, because they're not like trained seals, who entertain on demand. But would you credit it, we saw them! It began by looking like pale-green dust swirling above us. But soon it began to form into shapes – one that looked like a flying saucer and another that looked like a bridge and another that looked like a HUGE cathedral hanging in the sky and many more that looked like massive mountain ranges. The more time that passed, the more they appeared – I've never in my life seen such awe-inspiring, magical sights.

We also met a delightful Japanese girl called Tamoko Ono, who was there with her husband, who seemed like a Japanese Himself (quiet, supportive). You know when you meet someone and you feel like you've met a soulmate, well, that was Tamoko Ono. (We share a love for Marimekko and Hello Kitty, and we are both burdened by being born under the Virgo star sign.) She – being Japanese – had these fantastic disposable heat pads that you put in your gloves or boots or stick to your body and they heat up and keep you from dying of cold. When she and her Japanese Himself left, she bequeathed me her remaining ones. The kindness of strangers . . .

On our last night we stayed in a glass igloo, the purpose of which is to lie in bed and gaze through your see-through roof at the Northern Lights, but sadly there were no NLs on that night. But it was still fun, sort of like glass camping.

First published in the *Guardian*, January 2009.

New York

As luck would have it, Himself and I were turfed out of our house in Dublin due to it being riddled with damp and overrun with builders and this coincided with Caitríona's 'special birthday', so we went to New York and rented an apartment for a month because we are lucky, lucky yokes.

The cast of characters was as follows: Mam, Dad, Tadhg, me, Himself, Suzanne from London, Eileen (Eilers) and Siobhán . . . actually, now that I look at the list it seems very short. It certainly felt like there were lots more of us when we were all together. (I should state that not everyone was staying for the full month – that was only Himself and myself. Everyone else stayed for five days.)

Rita-Anne couldn't come because of being up the duff, and Tadhg's fiancée Susan couldn't come either, and both of these losses came as terrible blows because they are the only sensible ones in the family.

Now, about Siobhán. Siobhán and I have been friends since we were fourteen (her brother was my first boyfriend, and although he dumped me for a posh girl with big knockers, Siobhán and I remained friends). It's one of those lovely friendships where we have absolutely NOTHING IN COMMON but we still love each other.

She has three really lovely girls and a perfect home and perfect blonde hair and wears pastels without mysterious brown stains appearing on them four seconds after she's put them on. Nothing at all like me. And yet we are great pals, and Himself and I are godparents to daughter number 3, Emily.

So we all had great fun for five days, then the others went home and Himself and I stayed, and our rented apartment is lovely, especially because unlike most Manhattan apartments *it has* –yes! – *a window*, although we had to pay extra for that, and the only fly in the entire ointment is that on our first night here I was woken from my jet-lagged slumber by very, very loud music coming from the apartment next to the one next door.

Then on the second night I was woken from my jet-lagged slumber by very, very loud music coming from the apartment next to the one next door.

Then on the third night I was woken from my sleep-deprived, half-mad slumber by very, very loud music coming from the apartment next to the one next door. The walls were practically pulsing, it was so loud and bassy, but wait till I tell you the most bizarre thing – it was a Cher song! A Cher song remixed so it had a dancey bassline but it still had that stupid, singing-into-a-plastic-pipe wobbly singing bit. Talk about adding insult to injury! If I have to be woken in the middle of the night, I'd at least like it to be by someone good, like George Michael.

There were so many things that were wrong about this Cher song that I hardly knew where to start. I decided that the fact that it was 2.30 in the morning was as good a place as any, so I lurched from my bed, Himself trying to restrain me, out into the corridor – where the music was so loud the ceiling was crumbling – then banged and banged and banged like a maniac on the door of the apartment where Cher was coming from. (Himself, still mostly asleep, was staggering around the bedroom, trying to find a pair of jocks to put on to accompany me.)

Afterwards, when I was telling the story, many people expressed shock and said, 'But this is New York, people have guns, you could have been killed!' But the way I was feeling I'd have been *delighted* to have been shot! I need my sleep. I need an awful lot of it. I can't function without it.

Eventually a young man with curly, neatly cut hair opened the door, and I nearly went blind from the force of the music, but he didn't shoot me and instead he found the whole thing wildly funny, which is probably fair enough, seeing as I was standing there in my nightdress, my hair askew, and sobbing with frustration.

After much negotiation, and pauses for him to writhe with mirth, he agreed to turn the music down. Every night since then, going to bed I've been clenched with fear, afraid to go to sleep because I'm terrified of being woken by Cher or worse.

Although I know next to nothing about the Cher-lover, every time I pass his door I stare hard and 'feel' him, and my imagination has conjured up all kinds of things, mostly based on the fact that he doesn't seem to have a job, because his telly is always on in the daytime and he can dance his little hooves off in the middle of the night without any apparent worries about having to get up for work in the morning.

Also, his apartment has a window, so he's clearly no stranger to the finer things in life, like natural Manhattan daylight. So where is he getting the money from? From his rich daddy, is my (admittedly baseless) conclusion.

Now and again he gets late-night visitors (other nicely turned-out young men) who bang on his door and say, 'Yo! Open up, man!' and I lie in my bed and curl my lip and repeat, 'Yo!' with great scorn, because the young man is very young (about fifteen) and his haircut is most definitely not the haircut of a 'Yo!' kind of person.

Strangest of all, New York is a really noisy city, but I've no problem being woken by police sirens or cars beeping or disembodied voices shrieking, 'You didn't do that, motherfucker, you DID NOT DO THAT!!!!' But still, a teenage youth who likes nothing more harmless than dancing around his apartment to Cher in the middle of the night can reduce me to lunacy.

Now, wedding dresses! Caitríona is getting married in August and a lot of my time in New York has been spent in specialist wedding-dress shops, looking at Caitríona in the most beautiful dresses.

I don't know if any of you have done the accompanying-a-loved-one-as-she-tries-on-wedding-dresses thing, but I think I've found my niche, my hobby, my passion, call it what you will. I LOVE it. I find it endlessly absorbing, soothing, exciting and enjoyable; it completely takes me out of myself. I have a terrifyingly short attention span, but I could look at loved ones trying on wedding dresses for ever.

Sadly (or maybe not, it couldn't have gone on indefinitely) she has actually found a dress, stunning, fabulous and really special. Maeve Binchy once wrote an article called 'The Woman Who Walked into Weddings' about a woman who gatecrashed weddings because they made her feel so good. Maybe I should start hanging around bridal shops and infiltrating dress-viewing parties of women – there are usually so many people present that I should be able to mingle unnoticed.

Finally, I had my legs waxed – by the only blind leg waxer in New York. Even in a city full of gimmicks, this is going too far. I don't think the poor woman knew she was blind but I kept having to point out patches that she'd missed, and now that I've got my legs back to the apartment and am examining them in the light shed by our expensive (but worth it) window, my legs look like a field of crop circles! Nevertheless, if that's all I have to worry about, I'm doing okay. As my mammy would say, at least I *have* legs.

Altogether now, DO YOU BEEEELIEVE IN LIFE AFTER LOVVVVVVE.

mariankeyes.com, February 2008.

Portugal

Portugal! Myself and Himself suddenly found four days when we could go away, and decisions had to be made fast because we had no notice and it's the only chance we'll have this summer, so we needed a direct flight from Dublin (because if you go via Heathrow you lose five hours, also the will to live), and Lisbon was only two hours away, and half an hour's drive from there was Sintra, and it was unexpectedly atmospheric and wonderful!

I was enchanted: all those mountains and huge, prehistoric trees and the switchback roads and the green light and – best of all – those mad Gothic castles and houses, with their underground tunnels and the Initiation Well. It reminded me of Donna Tartt's *The Secret History*, and I swear I could imagine Byron and his ilk (who spent a lot of time there) dancing around in their pelt, smeared with the blood of a sacrificed rabbit, beneath a full moon. Magnificent!

The whole thing was an absolute delight, and not a screed of jet lag because Portugal sticks out so far into the Atlantic that it's on the same time zone as Ireland. This has never happened to me before.

While we were there the European football yoke was on and Portugal were playing, and in honour of the delightful time we were having we decided to support them, but on account of being the kiss of death for any team I support, I should have supported the other team. Because any team I (or Himself) support, they take a sudden and inexplicable nosedive. On the rare occasions I put money on a horse, it breaks its leg and has to be shot at the end of the race.

Portugal lost, of course they lost. All the same, it was a laugh: we were in the bar with lots of other people (an alarming number of Irish people – I always get a fright when I'm on holiday and I hear Irish accents – and apparently Irish people love Portugal. As indeed so do I now. It wasn't just the landscape and the weather: the people were sweet and kind and sort of innocent).

If I had any complaint at all, it would be that the food was beyond bland. One night we went out to a seaside place for our dinner and the waiter tried to tempt me with fish made with 'a traditional Portuguese sauce'. And when I enquired about what went into this traditional Portuguese sauce, he replied, with great pride, 'Boiling water.'

'Just boiling water?' I asked.

'Well, a little bit of bread,' he sez, 'but mostly just boiling water.'

So of course I *had* to have it to see if it was as bad as it sounded. And I'm happy to report that it was – it tasted of absolutely nothing!

And now I know why Irish people love Portugal! Ireland is famed for its crap cuisine; we are known the world over for boiling our vegetables until all flavour has been bet right out of them. It's almost a national slogan – 'Guaranteed! No pesky flavours present in our food.'

But in Portugal, we Irish are able to swank around, behaving as if our native cuisine is as flavoursome and tasty as Korean, or French, or Peruvian.

mariankeyes.com, June 2008.

Chile

Yes, well, lookit, I went to Chile with Himself.

It all began because I have a 'thing' about Easter Island – well, a combination of 'things': the hundreds of massive carved stone heads dotted about the place; it being the most remote inhabited island on the planet; etc., etc.

And because it belongs to Chile you have to fly via Santiago, and Himself said that if we were going to Santiago could we please go to the Atacama Desert. Please. You see, Himself subscribes to a magazine called *Wanderlust* and it's always urging people to go to remote, rough places, and now and then he comes to see me, with his *Wanderlust* in his hand, trying to get me enthused about some faraway undeveloped place, and in the old days I used to say, 'Does it have shops? Does it have a Prada outlet? Well, does it? No? That's right, no. So be off with you and take your ridiculous magazine with you.' And he'd slink away, head bowed, good and chastised.

But I'm different now and I haven't a clue when the change happened, except that it has and I'm now open to 'activity' holidays. Well, in a way. I still don't like getting my hair wet, but I'll walk. Oh yes. Even in hideously unattractive 'technical' clothing. Up hills and things, so long as they're not steep. So I graciously granted him a go in the Atacama Desert and off we went.

First to Easter Island. Which was everything I'd expected and more. The stone heads were EVERYWHERE, there are nearly

900 of them and they're thrun all over the place, and the island is made out of volcanoes and is entirely free from modern-day ugliness. There is only one town and hardly any other buildings, and there are no power lines or rubbish, and even though it's in the middle of the Pacific it reminded me of County Clare. Except it was warm.

The population is 4,500, and they all know each other and each do about thirteen different jobs – we met a fisherman who is also an air host on Lan Chile – and there are 6,000 semi-wild horses, and the people are a mix of God knows how many races because colonizers kept coming along and interfering with them, but there's a very strong Polynesian strain and as a result they are INCREDIBLY good-looking.

The first person we met at the airport was a girl called Tammy and you should have seen her, the almond-shaped eyes and the radiant skin and shiny long hair. But the gas thing is that even better-looking than the girls are the men. Mother of God!

It's hard to describe them without sounding like a lecherous old woman, but I'll give it a go. Right! They're big. Like, tall and very muscular and broad-chested and with beautiful Polynesian-style tattoos, and they'll take their shirt off at the drop of a hat. Tanned and brown-eyed (mostly), but the best bit, *the very best bit of all*, is their hair. Long and lustrous and thick and flowy. I would KILL to have hair like theirs. And they're great men for 'items of flair', like feathery yokes in their hair or shell necklaces or shark's tooth bracelets, you know yourself. But mostly stuff in their hair.

I get the impression that these young men (every one of them looked like they were twenty-two, but surely they can't ALL be) have the time of their lives with the visiting girl tourists. We had one 'guide' who went haring up the side of a volcano, on the trail of two blondey girls, leaving me and Himself for dust. When we finally caught up with him, he waved us vaguely in the direction of the petroglyphs and the other archaeological wonders we were after hiking up the side of a volcano to see and he glommed on to the blonde girlies, and after Himself and myself did our best to figure things out, we went back to your man, who had the nerve, yes the BLOODY NERVE, to ask us for a pen! (To get the blonde girlies' phone numbers, of course.)

Even Himself got annoyed. I'm always getting annoyed, but Himself hardly ever does. So when your man asked us if we had a pen, I stared at him stonily but Himself said, with unconvincing bluster '. . . Er, no. Ah, no! I haven't.' And as we made our way back down the mountain, Himself whispered to me, 'I actually do have a pen.' I whispered back, 'I know you do.' Himself always has a pen. Himself is an organized person. Which is why I married him. One of the reasons, anyway.

But all the other guides were delightful: charming and informative and caring. With lovely hair.

We stayed in a place called Explora and everything about it was perfect. It's hidden in the landscape and made of wood and natural stuff and there's no excess, but it's very comfortable and the views are stunning and the food is fantastic – but again no excess: you get two choices for your dinner and that's plenty.

The staff are charming – very warm, but also efficient. They know everything about your activities, but not in a spooky authoritarian way.

Like when Himself and myself booked to go to a show, the kitchen staff knew about it and fed us earlier than the normal dinner hour so we wouldn't be late for the show. Which actually I didn't want to go to because it was described as 'local dancing' and I thought it would be the usual oul' tourist shite.

And as we sat in a taxi, bumping down an unpaved boreen, and drew up outside a corrugated iron barn, my expectations were in the gutter.

Cripes, was I wrong! It was extraordinarily powerful: the dancers took what they were doing very seriously and not once did I feel that it was a tongue-in-cheek money-making exercise. The dancing felt mystical and ancient and deeply authentic, almost spiritual.

The gas thing was that the first dancer out looked really like Tammy, the stunner who'd met us on our first night at the airport. We spent most of the first half going, Is-she-or-isn't-she? Until Himself positively identified her, based on her tattoos. Normally I would hit Himself a clatter for having paid another woman so much attention, but honestly, she was so beautiful that I didn't blame him.

The thing about Explora is that it's an 'all-included' place, so you can have as much Sprite Zero as you like (it doesn't have to be Sprite Zero though, it can be wine or pisco sour or whatever), and I spent some of the most peaceful times of my life just sitting in their open-to-the-elements bar area, looking out at the sea and the grass and the wild horses and the absence of ugliness. I was very, very happy . . . nearly as happy as the time I overdosed on the Emla cream.

Then we went off to Santiago for a couple of days. We'd been strongly advised that a couple of days in Santiago is a couple of days too long, but bullishly we insisted that we wanted to see the real Chile.

Well, how can I put it? It's no Rio de Janeiro, is probably the best thing to say. You see, what I hadn't appreciated is that Chile is the most successful economy in the region, so they're a right crowd of diligent hard workers. And even though they have the biggest Palestinian population in the world outside of Palestine, and a big Serbian community, there was no evidence of a vibrant, melting-pot culture. And the shops were *crap*. Whatever it is they're making with their successful economy, it isn't shoes.

Next we headed to the Atacama Desert, for trekking and suchlike. This was Himself's side of the trip, so I hadn't paid it much attention. I just thought it would be miles and miles of nothingness, it being the driest place on earth and all that. God, *how wrong I was*.

So yes, the Atacama. Very high up. Very cold at night. Near the Andes. Every day we went a bit higher (we were there for five days, so we had to do it slowly in case we got altitude sickness).

On our second-to-last day we were up to 14,000 feet (4,300m) and we were about to start our walk and the guide says, 'We'll start our trek here.' And I thought, 'TREK? Good God, am I . . . *trekking?*' Then I looked around and couldn't see some of the smaller Andes, and when I asked Himself about where they'd gone, he said we were actually *on* them.

'The Andes?' I said. 'I'm *on* the Andes? And I'm trekking. So does that mean, I'm . . . trekking in the Andes?'

And yes, it turned out that I was. The oddest bloody thing, if you ask me. I don't know when I turned into a trekking-in-the-Andes person, but it appears that I have. Just goes to show.

mariankeyes.com, January 2009.

Bulgaria and Amsterdam

As I've said before, I know my life seems like one long holiday, but I HAD to go to Bulgaria, to do my patriotic duty, because Ireland were playing Bulgaria in the World Cup qualifiers (football, *football*, not rugby).

So off we went, with our green jerseys and our tricolour wigs, to Sofia, with Tadhg and Susie. And I had no idea AT ALL what to expect from Bulgaria.

Apparently it drives them mad, their lack of coherent identity in the world. All I knew was that they had nice yoghurt. However, from the small bit of dealing with them on the phone while I was trying to find out about hotels and that, they seemed warm and pleasant. And so they were!

The Sofia people were astonishingly welcoming. With very good English. Which I didn't expect at all. Also, very cheap shops. VERY cheap.

The result (a draw) was a good one and we were there for three days and it was the best fun. There were five Irish pubs in Sofia, but they obviously weren't *real* Irish pubs because on the first night one of them (McCarthy's, I think) RAN OUT OF DRINK!!!!! For the love of God!

Also, one of the others – the one we went to the most, JJ Murphy's – had bar staff that were in no way equipped for a stampede of Irish fans. It took up to an hour to get a drink, and the staff were so overwhelmed that the fans were telling them how to pull pints, and when one punter ordered ten pints the barman just walked away and was last seen sobbing in a corner.

Then we said goodbye to Tadhg and Susie, and Himself and I went to Amsterdam for the promotion of the Dutch publication of *This Charming Man*.

And such beauty! I'd never been to the Netherlands before and I'm not sure why. Maybe it was that most of the people singing Amsterdam's praises in my past were stoner gobshites who kept going on about blem being legal, and the funny thing is that, even though I'm a TOTAL addict and could get addicted to just about anything, the few times I got stoned in my youth, I hated it.

I hated the way time slowed down and I'd think, 'I have to stand up now. I have to stand up and I'll have to do it soon. Maybe in twelve seconds, maybe in thirty-seven,' and I'd be lying there incapacitated and paralysed and then a sentence would speak in my head and several hours would pass and I'd think, 'Did I say that with my mouth or just in my head?' HORRIBLE, HORRIBLE, HORRIBLE!!!!! So, yes, I think that must be why I never went, because I was afraid I'd have to smoke a load of the quare stuff.

But Amsterdam is NOTHING like that. We arrived on the Sunday evening, and it was raining, which I found astonishing because I've always had this belief that it never rains 'on the continent'.

The light was very North European (sort of thin and clear, which I love), and I knew in theory that there were canals in Amsterdam, but when you see them for real! There are loads!

It's all so pretty and clean and intact. Hundreds and hundreds of narrow merchants' houses from the eighteenth century, and cobbles and bridges and trams, and people on bicycles.

I was working, so I didn't have much time to sightsee, but

when I finished work on the Monday evening I a) bought a choc-
olate bun, and b) went on a boat on the canal, and because I was
wrecked from the interviews it was indescribably pleasurable to
just lie back and watch the beautiful city drift past me.

Apparently there's a handbag museum! Yes! Can you credit it!
But sadly I didn't have time to see it. And there many other mu-
seums in Amsterdam, including the Van Gogh one. I love his
paintings, I find them very heart-wrenching. Before we went,
Himself and I went on Pronunciation Guy to learn how to pro-
nounce 'Vincent Van Gogh', and God, it's hard. You say it like this:
'Finchent Fen' – and this is the really hard bit: you have to cough.
'Finchent Fen COUGH!'

We didn't have time to go to the Finchent Fen COUGH gal-
lery, so that'll have to wait till another time. Also, I have a
confession to make. On our first night, when we were staggering
around, trying to get a feel for the place, I passed a shoe shop!
Yes! What are the chances! And they had the most amazing shoes
in the window, sort of like pieces of architecture. But the shop
(Jan Jensen) was closed. So I took a note of the name and men-
tioned it to some of the journalists who were interviewing me,
and they all said, 'He is the Netherlands' most famous shoe
designer.'

So on the Wednesday, just before I left for the airport, I ran
over there and thought, 'They'll never have anything in my size,'
and sure enough they didn't, but they had one size up (36) and
the girl put new holes in the strap and gave me – free! – gel insole
yokes and, amigos, they fit! They are astonishingly beautiful and
architectural. According to Himself the heel is 'cantilevered'.

Even though they're works of art and indeed architecture, I
felt guilty about buying them (oh, why break the habits of a life-
time?), because I was after getting a pair of FitFlops. Are you

familiar with same? They've a funny-shaped sole so that you exercise your legs and bum while you're walking, and I walked down to the cinema in them the first night I had them, to see the Eric Cantona film (God, I love him), and the next morning I could hardly get out of bed, my leg muscles were so exercised. Could I justify a pair of Jan Jensen sandals as well as my FitFlops? Well . . . I decided that they fulfilled two very different roles in my life.

mariankeyes.com, June 2009.

Laos

I went away with Himself to Laos (although it was reported in the papers as Lagos, with an earnest line, 'Keyes has travelled to Africa in the past for charitable reasons'). But no, it was LAOS I went to. Laos is in Asia; it borders Vietnam, China, Burma and Cambodia and has Thailand on the other side of the Mekong.

Before I went, people kept asking, 'Why *Laos*? For the love of God, what's wrong with the Maldives?' And I had no answer for them. Except the nasty suspicion that if I was confined to a place with nothing to do but sunbathe and get scuttered (neither of which I do), the unbearable feelings that live in my solar plexus might get out of control altogether.

So off to Laos we went, with the roof of our house removed and the whole place covered with scaffolding and walkways, like it was a prison, and every single thing, every SINGLE thing, covered in dust: the knives and forks in our drawers, the cotton buds in their box, the teeth in the very back of my mouth.

I must say though, they are really nice builders – not like the old days of the Celtic Tiger when they didn't give a shite, when they just knocked lumps out of your 100-year-old mouldings with their ladders and chortled and said, 'Sure, it was fecking ancient, wha'?'

RIGHT! So Laos. We'll never get there with all the asides I'm doing. Okay, long journey, via Heathrow, Bangkok and finally Luang Prabang, the old royal capital of Laos. And it was fecking

ROASTING. I'm breaking out in a sweat even thinking about it. Humid like you wouldn't believe. Instantly my fair frizzed up like I was Krusty the Clown.

Luang Prabang (furthermore known as LP) is after winning city of the year two years in a row in Himself's *Wanderlust* magazine. It's on the Mekong and is very pretty and riddled with temples with Buddhas and we were made to tour them. (My personal temple limit is thirty-one; after that, I start becoming short-tempered, even disrespectful.)

There are almost no cars but millions of motorbikes and tuk-tuks and many new fancy French-fusion restaurants. But almost no shops; everything is sold from stalls or huts or at the market. A very innocent sort of place. Even at the crafts market, no one would be shouting, 'Over here, pretty lady! I have good price for you!' You'd look at their stuff and they'd yawn and you'd wander on and it's a wonder anything gets sold at all. No entrepreneurial spirit. Lord Sugar would give them a right scolding.

We were there three nights, and every night the whole city (ah, it's not really a city, it's more like Dún Laoghaire) plunged into darkness as the power failed – we were enchanted by this. Himself got to wear his head torch, which he was THRILLED by.

The next day we went 'up country' with a guide and a driver, and it really did feel like uncharted territory. The alarmingly narrow roads were on top of mountains with sheer drops of hundreds of feet, sometimes on both sides.

We stopped at a hillside H'mong village and the guide was insistent that we call in and visit some poor locals in their humble homes, and I was equally insistent that we were NOT going to call in, because I've done that sort of stuff in the past and I come out hating myself and I'm fairly sure the visited ones hate me back. I feel voyeuristic and exploitative and embarrassed to be invading their privacy, and also I hate making small talk, which is fecking obligatory – you have to ask about their goat and how often they milk it, and you have to pretend to laugh when the rooster makes a huge big screechy noise at the sight of you.

Nor do the villagers have any interest in me. One time in Thailand, I tried starting a conversation with a woman, about how my granny boiled water over an open fire in exactly the same way that she was doing, and she just stared at me with, 'What the fuck do I care?' eyes.

I'm perfectly happy to give the money so that I DON'T have to visit the villagers.

After about eight hours we arrived in a biggish city called Phonsavan – a lively place, full of markets, where business was brisk in galvanized buckets and nylon knickers and live bats (I swear to God, I'm still not right after seeing them).

And then! Something incredible happened! I saw a box of BB cream. *ASIAN* BB cream – i.e. the best, most *authentic* BB cream. Up to now, I've been riding the BB cream bandwagon with my Estée Lauder version, which I find HIGHLY satisfactory and looks lovely on my skin, but on Twitter everyone's been saying, 'The best BB creams are the Asian ones,' and there I was, looking at one!

I flung myself on it, extracting it from between the bats and the buckets, and this shrewd stallholder looked me up and down and eventually decided I could afford £2.50. Clearly she thought she was robbing me blind, whereas I was overjoyed and my guide was beyond baffled. BAFFLED. 'What does it do?' he asked (as everyone does), and I said, 'I don't really know, but you have to have it if you care about beauty products. The BB stands for "blemish balm" and every self-respecting make-up bag has one and . . . look! I don't really know! But it's a good thing and I need it!'

Then it dawned on me that there would be other people who'd be interested in owning an authentic Asian BB cream, so I set myself a little project that every town I visited I would trawl the stalls looking for them. (See, they don't have chemists, like in the 'developed world'. Their stalls are more like jumble sales, where Lux soap is next to a bowl of crickets and beside a huge big pile of Valium, which you can buy like pick'n'mix – much as I wanted to, I desisted. I'm bad enough.)

That night we stayed in a hotel that was jam-packed with all these shouty *Toor of Dooty* men, who looked like they were still fighting the Vietnam War. Buzz cuts and camouflage and other pieces of tomfoolery. Finally it dawned on us that they were land-mine disposal people – Laos is the most bombed country in the world. During the Vietnam War, more bombs were dropped by the US forces on Laos (even though they weren't at war with them) than were dropped on all of Europe during the Second World War. Often the bombs were dropped because the US planes hadn't been able to get to their targets in Hanoi and they didn't feel like flying back to their base in Thailand with all their goodies, so they just fecked them over Laos, like Laos was a big rubbish bin.

To this day, vast parts of arable land in Laos are unusable because they've got bombs buried in it, so these kindly *Toor of Dooty* lads were off to do some bomb clearance. After an extremely strange tay in which nearly everything on the menu wasn't available, we retired to our room, where the electricity promptly failed. Out with Himself's head torch!

The next day we went to the Plain of Jars, which again, like the BB creams, I'm at a loss as how to explain. It's a massive area, covered with . . . well . . . *jars*. Big stone jars. Up to three metres high. Some say they might have been burial urns, others say they were for storing . . . well . . . *jar*. But nobody knows. Nevertheless, it's very atmospheric, especially if you go to Sites 2 and 3, where we saw no one.

That's the thing about Laos, it really does seem to be untouched and uncorrupted and the people seem very innocent.

That night we stayed in a very basic place – no electricity – like, *officially* no electricity, unlike the other places, which had electricity for some of the time. And the rooms were little wooden huts and there were windows but they had no glass in them, and we were right beside the river, which was some tributary of the Mekong. And, in general, I'm not a person who's comfortable with 'basic' – mostly because I'm afeerd of everything, and specifically beasts, to wit, spiders, animals and that sort of thing.

But God only knows what got into me, because I was very happy. We sat outside on wooden benches and drank mango smoothies (well, I did; Himself had Laos beer) and admired the river, and when we went to bed there was a mosquito net over us, which I decided would protect me from all predators. Just before I went to sleep, I put my anti-mad tablets out on the bedside yoke for easy access in the morning.

And when I awoke, after a lovely slumber, weren't they all ett?! Yes! My anti-mad tablets! By insects or small beasts unknown! Who must have been going around in TOP form all day.

So, yes, Laos is a country where the ants will eat your anti-mad tablets, but it's still a lovely, lovely, lovely place.

mariankeyes.com, April 2012.

Antarctica Diary

Hello, and welcome to MAD! (Marian's Antarctica diary!) This is a very long 'piece' and it's written in a diary format. I'm just telling you this so as you can 'pace' yourself.

DAY ONE

Greetings from the Heathrows, where I am a nervous wreck! Yaze! The flight from Dublinland was delayed coming in, and there are only two and a half hours before the flight leaves for Buenos Aires, and I have A VERY REAL fear, founded in FACT and empirical PAST EXPERIENCE, that my suitcases won't make it to Argentina and I will be in the Antarctics without:

1) Thermal warm clothing
2) My anti-mad tablets

I'm so convinced that this is going to happen that I've bought a notebook and a pack of three (3) pens from the WHSmith to draw up a list of all the things I will need when I get to Ushuaia (the world's most southerly city, and not hot like you might think when you hear the word 'southerly', no, not hot at all, but actually very, very cold).

Those of you who know me will know that on planes my bags fail to turn up more often than they arrive. And any transit through Heathrow almost certainly guarantees that I'll get on the flight and my luggage won't, and obviously you'd think I'd have learnt by now and at least brought enough anti-mad tablets in my hand luggage to last a few days, but no, I haven't learnt, and it makes me wonder if fundamentally I am an optimist when I'd thought all along I was a pessimist, and isn't life one long process of learning about oneself?

Himself (for Himself is my travelling companion) asked a British Airways 'man' if he could tell us anything about the whereabouts of the bags, and the 'man' was helpful! He couldn't actually be persuaded to say that the bags would make the flight, but he did admit that they'd left Terminal 1 and arrived in Terminal 5.

(A quick aside on British Airways: I used to call them the World's Most Supercilious Airline because I felt that they were told in staff training to channel Mary Poppins. 'Be brisk, dears! Brisk, patronizing, cold, yes, *withhold*. And DO feel free to pull the passengers up for not having scrubbed their faces properly and polished their shoes. *Scold* them.'

You see, I have my reasons for this assessment . . . *mutters darkly* . . . once upon a time, on a business-class flight on British Airways, I found that I was seated not next to Himself, but to a smelly man (he may not have actually been smelly, I just say these things), and it was an overnight flight and the overnight chairs are in little pods of two, curled around each other, and it would be like the man and I were sleeping with each other, and Himself was way down the back next to a lady, so I tried to flag down a stewardess and said, 'Miss, miss, please can I not sleep next to the smelly man and –' And she planted herself in front of me, tall and bony and with her scarf tied abnormally neatly, and said, 'Do sit down, dear!' Then she breezed away briskly to scold a man for taking his shoes off, leaving me feeling foolish and chastised and worried about sleeping with the smelly man (who probably wasn't smelly at all; like I said, I just say these things).

But that was all a long time ago! Yes! In another lifetime, and I feel British Airways staff have definitely 'warmed up'. And anyway, I am not one to hold a grudge, no, that is not my way, except perhaps it is, and if so I shouldn't be boasting about it.

So I am still here, waiting to board the plane, and I am anxious, so anxious that I bought myself a Moshi Monsters toothbrush and I flirted with an Alexander Wang bag in the Horrods, in the most delightful 'shade' of sort of pale blue-green, and I would have bought it except I knew that I wasn't in my right mind, and I even said it to Himself: 'I'd like to buy it but I'm not in my right mind. I'll give it thirty-six hours and see if I still love it.' (Actually, I've just gone on the Net-a-Porters looking for it, and it's not there, and I'm wondering if I should run back to the Horrods and buy it. But what would be the point, seeing as I've nothing to put in it, seeing as my luggage is 'lost in transit', which is quite an apt description of my state of mind.)

So anyway, Antarctica! It's been very funny, people's reactions, when they've heard that I'm going there. They kind of seize up, then an expression – ConfusionJudgementPity – zips across their face and I can see they're thinking, 'Is she INSANE? Who would go to Antarctica? When you could go to Lanzarote?'

Then, after a second, they gather themselves and say, too cheerily, 'Well! That'll be . . . cold! Yes. But you'll see polar bears?'

And I say, 'No, you only get polar bears in the North Pole.' And they say, 'You're actually going to the actual North Pole?' And I say, 'No, you thick-arse, didn't I just tell you I wasn't?'

. . . Listen, I've got to go, I've to get on the plane. Himself is anxious.

DAY TWO

Buenos Aires!

The flight was fourteen hours long, which I was worried about because I was afeerd I might go a little mad in the confined space, but actually it was GRAND and I slept for most of it and woke up feeling optimistic and that was nice. So we arrived into some sort of strike – after all, this is Argentina and this is their way of show-ing their gratitude for your visit. The airport was CRAMMERS, hordes and hordes of people milling about the place, queuing to be let out. (It was like when the Irish passport people went on a strange strike, a 'go-slow' I suppose you could call it, when they stopped everyone and 'made talk' with them for far too long, to hold everyone up, but I always enjoyed the little chat and I felt sure that visitors to our chatty little country would also like it.)

And so to the luggage belt, where to my EXTREME surprise, *both of our suitcases arrived* and I was so relieved that I might have shed a little tear. Our run of good luck continued when, queuing for passport control, myself and Himself, we got the most Argentinian-looking of all the passport checkers. FERRY handsome, and frankly so Argentinian-looking he looked like he'd come straight from a polo match and that his horse was crouched down next to him in the booth and assisting him, hand-ing him up the date-stamp and all. Indeed, they are a *very* attractive crowd, in general, the Argentinians.

I was in Buenos Aires a long time ago, maybe seven years ago, and these are my memories: hand-made Minstrels and blue metallic shoes. God, it was great!

But today there is no time for buying beautiful blue metallic shoes: we have to transfer to the domestic airport, which is about an hour's drive, and I tell you, you'd think you were in Chicago, or Melbourne, or cities of similar ilk. Prosperous-looking place. Lots of parks and trees and people out jogging, and there was an open-air gym-playground place where a load of buff-looking mens were doing pull-ups with their nippers.

And now we are in the domestic airport, which is BEJAMMED with people. Also, it is roasting hot and we've come from the cold and we're going to the cold tonight and I feel a little quare, but that could be down to several things, including the 'quare air' you breathe on planes and the culture shock and the feeling of being in transit and (temporarily) without a home.

It's funny because even though I'm very grateful to be going on this holiday, or indeed any holiday, I always get overwhelmed with a terrible uneasy melancholia before I go away. I was like this even when I was a nipper, I hated leaving home, and it eased off a bit when I was doing a lot of book tours, because I had to keep moving, but it's back for the last few 'difficult' years, and for most of last week I was hoping something would happen so the trip had to be cancelled, but it didn't and it'll all be grand.

Mind you, you'd think I wouldn't keep going to such quare spots – like Laos or the Atacama Desert or – yes – Antarctica. But I've just realized that extreme places suit me: because I feel edgy or downright scared all of the time, when I find myself in a place that seems other-worldly or freaky, my feelings are appropriate. It's the one time when my state of mind chimes with my surroundings and I am 'right' with the world. 'Feeling quare? Well, you *should* be!'

This is why I want to never go to Italy again. 'Oh, the art, the beauty, the cypress trees, the medieval towns, the men, the girls, the beauty, the blue skies, the Tuscan hills, the beauty, the leather bags, the haircuts, the beauty, how could anyone ever feel unhappy here?' *Coughs apologetically* 'Sorry, I feel like I'm in hell here. You've all been lovely, yes, lovely, but I have to go home now.'

Right, I'll be back to you later on with my 'first impressions' of Ushuaia, the Beagle Channel, the ferocious cold and all that.

7 p.m.

We arrive in Ushuaia!
The other passengers applaud when the plane lands!
This worries me . . .!
Okay, here are my first impressions of Ushuaia. Windswept and rocky and a triumph over nature = Ushuaia. The entire town looks like it's built of corrugated iron and cornflakes boxes. It's quite spectacularly horrible, but at the same time admirable. It's balanced on the end of the earth and it's got massive other-worldly, black-and-white mountains behind it, looming over it, shunting it into the sea. It makes me think of a tiny tenuous outpost on another planet.

The whole place looks like it could be washed away in five minutes, but clearly that doesn't happen because it's still here, despite the high winds and perishing cold. The roads are packed mud and all the cars are filthy and you can tell just by looking at them that their suspension is but a distant memory.

But there are bursts of unexpected beauty: there are loads of flowers – they might be delphiniums? Long skinny yokes like fox-gloves?

Our hotel is on the edge of the town and it's overlooking the Beagle Channel and on the far side are more and more and more of those terrifying mountains. Rows and rows of them keep appearing, popping up into infinity.

The hotel is lovely and glassy and full of views. Loads of people arrive to check in at the same time, so I'm guessing they're probably going to be on the ship too, so myself and Himself are discreetly checking them out, but I told Himself, 'Do not, under any circumstances, make eye-contact with them!' We are shy peaceful types who find small talk difficult.

PS: I've entirely forgotten about the Alexander Wang bag. Things are different now. New perspective. Yaze.

DAY THREE

Downtown Ushuaia!

Christ. What can I say? If I lived here, I'd end up in the nuthouse in double-quick time. It feels so bleak and abandoned and god-forsaken. Although, mind you, there are a fair few churches, which always flourish in places of despair, I find. There are two shoe shops, selling the kinds of platform boots that Ginger Spice used to wear twenty-nine years ago, and there are 400 souvenir shops, selling penguin T-shirts and penguin snow-globes and penguin bookends and penguin carvings and fluffy penguins, and in the windows, instead of human mannequins modelling the clothes, they have penguins (not real but as big as humans and unexpectedly glum-looking).

I would buy any old shite, I'm famed for it, but after a while of this, even I flagged. 'I can't look at another penguin thing,' I said. 'My head will burst.' So we went back to the hotel and watched the first episode of *The Good Wife*, which I liked. Himself said it wasn't bad and I said, 'No, it's better than not-bad.'

DAY FOUR

The ship!

11.30 a.m.

We had to check out of the (lovely!) hotel at 10 a.m. but the bus isn't coming until 3 p.m. so we're all sitting here in the lobby, still studiously not making eye-contact. Everyone has discreet anti-seasickness patches behind their ears (except me, because I'm on too much anti-mad medication and have to make do with Kwells) and they've all gone slightly lurchy and glassy-eyed.

I got a look at the passenger manifest last night at the orientation meeting and I am the only Irish person! At least half, maybe even two-thirds, of the passengers are from the United States and lots also from Canada and some from the UK and Australia. One Pole, two Japanese, two South Africans and one Braziliard. Oh, and two from Taiwan!

1.29 p.m.

I have dulce de leche ice cream and Himself has dulce de leche crème brûlée. They are magnificent.

4 p.m.

We board the boat! I'm so excited. We're on our way to see the penguins! There are about 120 passengers; the demographic seems to be almost entirely baby-boomer people, but there are little pockets of texture – three Asian-looking hipster lads with amazing hair and groovy glasses and bright neoprene T-shirts, for examples.

Also, there are two young Australian backpackery types and their conversation seems to consist of dire stories of how they were 'ripped off' buying four beers in São Paulo, or 'ripped off' when they were changing money in Montevideo, or 'ripped off' when their tent was stolen from above their heads while they were sleeping in a public park in Lima. They seem to have very bad luck, God love the pair of them.

5 p.m.
The orientation meeting in the Oceanic Lounge, where we meet the staff of twelve who do the excursions and talks and whatnot. They're all scientists of some ilk – geologists, marine biologists, game rangers – but they also drive the Zodiacs (the little boats that bring you from the ship to the land) and are cheery and enthusiastic and really lovely.

They are at pains to tell us that the crossing is expected to be as smooth as the Drake Passage ever can be. That at around 11 p.m. the ship will be leaving the protected Beagle Channel and will go into open sea, but really it's going to be freakishly calm.

7 p.m.
Dinner. Delicious. The two young Australian backpackers have just discovered that the cruise is 'all in' and that they can have as much beer as they want without having to pay for it. They can hardly countenance such a notion. They have never been so UN-ripped off, in all their days! Their delight is – well – delightful!

8.45–9.45 p.m.
We watch a show about how cold the Antarctic is.

10 p.m.
We turn in.

10.59 p.m.
The sea is as calm as a millpond.

11 p.m.
The ship turns into a roller coaster! The sea goes wild, the swell is enormous, the ship feels like it's balancing on its side, then it swoops down into a hollow, then swings up on its other side. This continues all night. I swalley Kwells by the fistful.

DAY FIVE

The 'notorious' Drake Passage!
I accidentally have breakfast with a creationist!
First I have to tell you that the sea was so rough and the ship so bouncy that when I was putting my sock on, I took a tumble into the shower. I had to lie on the floor to put my jeans on. And when I lurched down to the breakfast place, the staff told us that this was the calmest crossing they'd had in living memory.

Right. The story about the creationist. See, in the dining room, most of the tables are for six people or eight so you get your grub at the buffet and then you 'join' people already sitting at a table, and you say, 'May we join you?' It's bad form to go off and start a 'new' table until the partly occupied one is full. And obviously you have to make chat with the people you've joined. But last night, due to a stroke of tremendous good fortune, Himself and I got one of the very rare tables for two (I think there might only be three in the whole dining room). So last night we only had to chat to each other as, all around us, everyone else bonded. 'SO WHERE DO YOU GUYS COME FROM?' 'WHAT DO YOU GUYS DO OUT THERE?' 'IS THAT A FRANCHISE?' 'YOU MAKE A LOT OF MONEY DOING THAT?', etc., etc.

I live in dread of being asked what I 'do', because:

a) They ask, 'So have I heard of you?'
b) Or they *have* heard about me but say, 'I don't trouble myself with that kind of trash.'
c) They say, 'YAH, I GOT A GREAT IDEA FOR A BOOK!'
d) They say, 'Where do you get your ideas from?
e) They say, 'Any of your books been made into a movie?'

In order to avoid these eventualities, Himself and I have several cover stories ready. 'Himself here pretended to get injured at work and we scammed a big fat wedge out of his employers and we're living on the settlement money. Jump up there and show the man your limp' is the one we elect the winner.

Anyway, this morning there was a woman sitting on her own, and Himself and I asked if we could join her, and she said, 'Sure. My husband is sitting over there.' And right enough, her husband *was* at another table, and it wasn't full, there was still one empty chair at it, so I thought, 'That's a bit strange, but each to their own.'

Then we were joined by two of the staff, two lovely mens who have PhDs in continent formation and albatross feathers and similar. And we were chatting pleasantly about the Andes and how they were formed 33 million years ago – you know, nice, uncontroversial, breakfast conversation, appropriate to an Antarctic cruise, when suddenly Missis-My-Husband-Is-Sitting-at-a-Different-Table-to-Me pipes up, 'Let's not forget that the planet is only 5,000 years old and that human life originated in the Middle East.'

Well! I admit I thought it was some sort of joke! But then she says, 'All life is thanks to God the creator.'

She was serious! And we were all mortified. And I was thinking, 'What are you doing, coming on a trip like this, you raving lunatic?'

Very quickly we finished up our toast and made our excuses.

My first breakfast on board was not a success.

All day

The weather is extremely bright and there's heat in the sun and the water is very blue. But the sea is as rough as a badger's arse and many of the passengers seem to be seasick.

Outside our window is a massive white bird, staring in at us, giving us the quare eye. It stays with us all day and Himself says it is an albatross.

You see, Himself, though he denies it until he is purple in the face, likes birds. He set up a bird feeder at home and gets annoyed when the pigeons sit on it and scare away the smaller birds, and he's always looking out the window and saying, 'Is that a *dove*? Well, you hear the phrase "dove-grey" and it's definitely grey.' Chatting away to himself, like.

But whenever I say, 'You're fond of birds,' he says he isn't. I tell him there's no shame in it, but he is adamant that he has no interest. I think he thinks it's a boring thing to like. Or maybe an 'old' thing.

DAY SIX

Land ahoy!
Humpback whales ahoy!

10.30 a.m.

We weren't expected to make landfall until tomorrow, but due to the 'freakishly calm weather conditions' we've gone much, much faster than expected, so much so that at 10.30, when Himself came back from the geology lecture, we spotted some things on the horizon that we thought might be clouds. But we stared at them and stared at them until we realized that they actually are land – the South Shetland Islands. And now we've just got an announcement that we'll be getting off the ship and going on an expedition this very afternoon!

I do a hasty dress rehearsal of my expedition clothing: one technical vest, a second technical vest, a technical fleece, a down parka, a special yellow waterproof jacket that 'lock-hard' men and lollipop ladies favour, a pair of technical long johns, a second pair of technical long johns, 'furry'-lined trousers, waterproof over-trousers, two pairs of special thick knee-socks, a blue hat, a pink hat and a white furry hat, a pink ear-protector, a purple neck-gaiter, two pairs of technical gloves and a pair of white mittens which look like boxing gloves. I can hardly stand up for the weight of clothes, but they'll be needed by all accounts.

The land is hurtling towards us. Big, black, looming, sheer cliffs, and pointy, flinty islands and icebergs which look like they're made of frozen marshmallows. It's coming up on us really fast and it's awe-inspiring and a bit scary.

Does anyone feel like writing a dystopian novel set in the near future, where the world powers are jostling to own Antarctica because the rest of the world is used up? I'd be no good at writing that sort of thing, but I'd love to read it.

And here are the whales! Two humpbacks and there's just been an announcement that due to all the stuff to look at, Liliana's lecture on penguins has been cancelled.

Another announcement: the ship's stabilizers are being taken in – be carefuls!

PENGUINS!!!!!! Penguins at one o'clock! Swimming in the open sea. Doing little curvy lepps, like dolphins do. And, oh my

God, an iceberg has just gone flying past with a load of chinstrap penguins standing on it. Really belting along, they are. They look like they're actually driving the iceberg, like they've decided to escape from Antarctica and the iceberg is their get-away car. 'Keep the foot down there, Patsy!' Very good at maintaining their balance. And now they're gone, but there are several more gangs of them swimming all around the ship.

Himself has just taken a tumble – it must be something to do with the stabilizers coming off – but he's up on his feet again and he says he's grand.

Every twenty or thirty seconds another batch of penguins appears out of the black water, like they're putting on a show for us.

Out on deck, the cold is phenomenal but one of the Asian hipsters is wearing a pair of paisley-patterned shorts and khaki-green Crocs. Maybe it's because he's young that he can withstand the cold. No sign of his two comrades. Perhaps they are in the cabin, throwing down some sounds or maybe making a short experimental film or doing their (frankly magnificent) hair.

We're really close to land now and the water isn't exactly black, it's like a gunmetal grey, and the icebergs aren't white but sort of a pale-green colour, not dissimilar to the 'shade' of the Alexander Wang handbag that I've entirely forgotten about.

12.30 p.m.
And here is the bing-bong announcing lunch! Run!

1.45 p.m.
We took lungeon with a lovely lady from South Africa and her niece, who are travelling together. We exchange pleasant small talk and no one asks what anyone 'does'.

2.30 p.m.

We leave the ship and whip across the sea in the little zodiac boat. The sky is blue and sunny and the snow on the mountains glares like silver.

We land on Half Moon Island, which is RIDDLED with chin-strap penguins. Thousands and thousands of them, all along the beach and up on the cliffs. They behave *exactly* like penguins – they waddle, they hop and they slide downhill on their bellies, using their wings like oars. They are delightfully comical!

They have really cute pink feet and they're not a bit afeerd of us humans: they come right up to us and cut across our paths and bustle along, looking like they're in an almighty hurry, like they're late for something or they've just remembered that they forgot to turn their iron off. 'Out of me road, I'm in a ferocious hurry!'

Up on the cliffs, being minded, are the fluffy baby penguins, which look nothing like their parents.

And the racket out of the adults! They shout in unison, like they're doing a football chant. 'Luton are shit! Luton are shit! Luton are shit! Come on, everyone, Luton are shit!'

They stretch their necks long and throw their heads back and open their gullets and howl at the moon like mad yokes.

7.30 p.m.

Dinner. We have got a bit of a handle on the other passengers now. Mostly from the US, like I said. The three Asian hipster young lads, they are FABULOUS! One has hair like Sideshow Bob and looks like he's wearing a black sweatband just on his hairline. The second has an auburn-coloured quiff and matching goatee-facial hair. The third has ginormous Perspex glasses, the type you wear if you are working for Securicor. *At all times*, at least one of them is wearing a lumberjack shirt. Himself says it is only a matter of time before they cycle into dinner on a 'fixie'. We cannot establish what land they're from because they're chatty with each other, but in general very quiet.

There are many solo travellers on board, which I find admirable in the extreme. Many young mens – some Scandinavians, some US citizens and an Asian (am I allowed to say 'Asian' without incurring the wrath of someone?) who might be Japanese or Korean or Taiwanese. And a fair few lone womens also. So far I have identified an Australian and a French lady.

DAY SEVEN

Deception Island!

A misty, colour-free day. We make landfall on an island that is a deserted Norwegian whaling station and, well! The atmospherics! Ghostly and spooky and strange and sad and fascinating and fabulous. It's a (still active) volcano, so the island is surrounded by sulphur pools which are steaming up into the terrifyingly cold air. The smell! Mother of divine! Like there are 40,000 hard-boiled egg sangwidges sitting on the shore.

I love it here. Love, love, *love* it. It should be called Desolation Island. Because of the volcano-ness, the sand is black. Everything is in shades of charcoal – dark grey, light grey, medium grey.

Two wooden fishing boats, bleached to the colour of nothing, lie rotting on the black sand. Whitish whale bones litter the place. A long, low farmhouse – once the home to the poor-bastard Norwegians – still stands but the roof has caved in. A short distance from the house are piles of stones, each topped with a cross and bearing Norwegian-looking names.

There's a collection of massive metal drums that look like that famous museum in Bilbao that was designed by Frank Gehry.

Himself is palpably uneasy: 'It's all a bit post-apocalyptic. It's like one of those dystopian books you love so much.'

Really, I'm *begging* someone out there to make a ten-part series about a post-apocalyptic world, set here. And if it could be in Swedish or Danish or Norwegian, so much the better.

There aren't many penguins on this part of the island. We pass a group of four, deep in earnest conversation. Abruptly, three of them waddle into the boiling sea for a swim, but the fourth stands stubbornly on the beach. One of the penguins gets back out of the water and seems to be reasoning with the one who won't get in. 'Would you not give it a go?' he seems to be saying. 'Ah, go on, you're making the other lads feel bad.'

But the fourth fella says, 'No. Don't be "at" me. I'm just not in the form right now, I'll stay where I am, thanks.'

'Well, feck you anyway,' says the third one, 'you're after ruining it for all of us.' And off the third one goes.

The Asian hipsters are wearing wonderful things. Even their waterproof trousers aren't boring black ones, like everyone else's, but blue, red and green. Also, they are garlanded with many 'items of flair', for example Securicor-glasses has an 'ironic' little black cuddly dog hanging from the zip of his rucksack.

Sideshow Bob is lying on the snow on his belly, taking an up-close photo of something, and I said, 'There he is, instagram-ming the living daylights out of a rock.' And Himself said, 'Instagram? Not at all! He's on some new, fabulous social-media thing that we won't hear about until next July.'

7 p.m.

We try hard, for once, to not be the first people down for dinner. But alas . . . Mind you, we are not alone. It's a stampede.

We notice that the lone Asian young man has been co-opted by the three Asian hipsters! I tell you, it would gladden your heart! There they all are, the three hipsters and the very ordinary-looking other bloke, all chatting and laughing away in their shared quare foreign tongue.

The expression on the ordinary-looking bloke's face is a delight! He is lit up like a Christmas tree, and you can tell that he's thinking to himself, 'I can't *believe* these hipsters have befriended me. I am *so lucky*! I wonder if they'll still be my friends when we get home to Japan/Korea/maybe Taiwan?'

I'm going to give you a quick example of what a day on board looks like. Please bear in mind, the times are all approximate.

7.30: Awoken by the bing-bongs for an excellent buffet breakfast.
9.30: You put on all your weatherproof clothes and go off in the Zodiac to land on an island with penguins or seals or other lovely things.
12.30: Lungeon back on the ship.
14.30: Another expedition off the ship.
16.30: Tea and cake served in the bar.
18.30: A recap of the day and a 'first look' at the plans for tomorrow. Also hot savoury snacks served.
19.00: A magnificent four-course dinner.

After dinner there is sometimes a talk on 'Bayshtes of the Antarctics'. Or similar. Also there is a film on your telly in your cabin.

Just an observation: people are very prompt for mealtimes, and the snacks with the 18.30 debrief prove particularly popular.

DAY EIGHT

Mainland Antarctica!
I 'take agin' Argentina!

7.30 a.m.

It's snowy and blizzardy when we wake up. We've been lucky with the weather until now, but not so much today. I elect to opt out of this morning's excursion because I have to wash my hair and I haven't the energy to do both. You'd think the bracing cold would make you more alert and full of vim, but actually it's the opposite. The extra effort the body has to make to not succumb to hypothermia makes people chronically tired.

Even the protective clothing is exhausting because it's so heavy; the neoprene boots each weigh about a stone, so taking a single step is knackering.

So anyway, under the best of circumstances, washing my hair is a major operation, but harder here because although the shower is sometimes hot or sometimes perishing, whichever flavour you get, you only get a thin trickle. (This is the *only* non-de-luxe bit of the trip, the rest is fantastic and really cushy.) I am too cold to take all my clothes off, so I wash my hair standing in my neoprene wellingtons and my togs.

11.50 a.m.

Himself returns with photographs of baby penguins hatching from their eggs and I am *sickened* with jealousy and regret that I stayed home and washed my hair.

12.30 p.m.

The bing-bong announces lunch and we break into a run, colliding with everyone else in the doorway to the dining room. We take our lungeon with a delightful couple of newly-weds and no one asks what anyone 'does'.

2.20 p.m.

We sail into Paradise Bay and the snow has stopped and the sun has come out. Once again, the landscape and colours are different from anything we've already seen. The sea is like diamonds which have been melted down, all silver-grey and crystalline, almost syrupy, like water that sugar has been dissolved in. There are lots and lots of icebergs; maybe it's the melting snow that's giving the water such gloopiness.

Suddenly a ghostly ship appears out of nowhere; it's entirely dark brown, just like a shadow. It's not like a modern ship, but like one from *Pirates of the Caribbean*, in that it has three rigs for sails, which is mandatory for any ghost ship, no? I have to check with Himself that I'm not hallucinating it.

He confirms that he does *indeed* see it and says that there's an Argentinian military base near here, and we conclude the ghostly ship has something to do with them.

2.30 p.m.

An announcement! The Argentines will not let us land! Feckers! We are standing by, sweltering in our eighteen layers of clothing, awaiting further instructions.

Another announcement! The Argentines *definitely* won't let us land! Plan B: we are to go out in the little Zodiac boats for a mini-cruise.

I shake my fist at the Argentine ghost-ship and shout, 'I have TAKEN AGIN you!'

2.45 p.m.

Himself and I have a conversation where we do the Irish version of whatever the Argentines said when they wouldn't let us land. 'A ship, you say? And you want to land here? Yes, but I don't know if I'd be let. I mean, it's against regulations. I'm sorry now, I am. We're all sorry, but it's more than our job is worth. I'd better go now because myself and the lads have a lie-down every afternoon between 2.30 and 5 p.m. Dead to the world we are. We notice *nothing*. Nothing at all. Well, good luck now and enjoy your trip and you didn't hear any of this from me.'

3.15 p.m.

As we board the little Zodiac for our mini-cruise, a man, a US person, is complaining bitterly about what cheeky bastards the Argentine military are, and I look at him and unwelcome words come into my mouth, looking for escape: 'No, indeed, it is not like *your* military ever behave in a high-handed fashion!' But I suck my tongue and suck my tongue and swallow down the thoughts and eventually the words go away.

3.30 p.m.

The sun has come out and we're on a huge silver lake, in the centre of a circle of radiant white mountains. The water is dazzling and shiny and very still, like a flyblown mirror (but in a nice way). Icebergs, like frozen waves, break the surface. These are some of the shapes I see: a giant crocodile; a helter-skelter; the starship *Enterprise*; a Mr Whippy ice cream; a comb going through curly hair; the royal palace in Lhasa; a jet ski; the back end of a whale; a brain; a giant anvil and a white Crunchie. Some of the icebergs are white, but others are a luminous blue colour, as if they've got LEDs built into them.

At times I feel as if I'm in a huge modern sculpture museum with giant sculptures made of white glass or white marble.

We're on the same level as the water, which makes everything shockingly immediate. I could jump off the boat and sail away on an iceberg if I wanted.

Every now and then there are deep boomy noises like thunder – ice avalanches. Then we actually see one happening – a huge chunk of ice tears away from the rest of the glacier and topples into the water – and we're told to brace ourselves for a massive wave and I am really, really worried that I will get Water in My Bad Ear (I have the 'Keyes Ear', and at all costs must avoid getting Water in My Bad Ear). Mercifully the wave doesn't make it as far as our little boat and my ear is saved.

6.23 p.m.
We leave our cabin for the daily debrief. We are seven minutes early but I'm thinking of the snacks that are served – lovely things like you get in Marks & Spencer at Christmas time, for example cocktail sausages and mini-onion bhajis and spring rolls – and I really want to be at the head of the queue.

6.24 p.m.
There are already sixty people ahead of us. 'Honestly,' I say, in tones most judgemental, 'you'd swear no one ever got fed around here.'

7.03 p.m.
I formally withdraw my grudge agin Argentina. Life is too long.

8.16 p.m.
Himself's face is bright red – he's after getting sunburnt! In Antarctica! I give him a stern talking-to about using sun protection.

Tell me, *what* is the problem with mens and sun factor? They behave as though it is a girly affectation and a sign of weakness.

9 p.m.
Himself leaves for his overnight outdoor camping on the Antarctic ice shelf. I was meant to be going – before I'd left home, I'd signed up for it and already had my boasting prepared. 'Oh yaze, well, I camped outdoors in the Antarctic. Cold? Oh yaze, shockingly! I thought I would die. But I reached deep inside myself and found the inner strength.'

But yesterday the preparatory talk put THE FEAR OF GOD in me!

Dave the guide said several things that made me reconsider:

1) There would be no coming back to the ship, no matter what. If a person changed their mind and found it too cold and windy and life-threatening, that was TOUGH! No one was going home till morning.
2) The temperatures would go down to minus 10, maybe minus 15.
3) It would be better if you had no wees to make, as to do so you would have to get out of your sleeping bag and put on your hefty boots and four layers of trouser and several protective jackets and walk 'some distance' on the ice and through the snow and wind to find a makeshift jacks. Seeing as I generally have to get up about twelve times a night, this is a worry.
4) The important thing was to try to stay warm, but this would be very difficult.

Then Kevin the guide came on to give his advice and he said, 'The important thing is to try to stay warm, but this will be very difficult. Some people dig trenches down into the ice, but if you do that, please fill the hole in when you leave. Try not to drink anything at all tomorrow because it would be better if you did not have to get up in the night to make your wees because you could get cold, and the important thing, the *really important thing*, is to stay warm and this will be very difficult.'

Then Dave the guide came back and said, 'One more thing: the most important thing is to stay warm, but this will be very difficult.'

Then Kevin the guide came back and said, 'One more thing. You could be ett by a tiger seal in the middle of the night. Finally! Stay warm! But it will be very difficult!'

So it is sad, but I will not be able to swagger about in boasty fashion, bragging of my icy endurance.

DAY NINE

6.30 a.m.

Himself is returned to me after his night camping on the ice. He says that the group was composed almost entirely of mens whose wifes had intended also doing the camping but changed their mind after the scary talk from Dave and Kevin. Apparently the wees-makingness was a big deterrent.

So anyway, Himself found a sheltered spot and created a little ice wall up around his sleeping bag. But there is a young man among the passengers, from a snowy Scandinavian country – we will call him 'Rolf from Sweden' to protect his identity – and Himself says that Rolf got a hold of the shovel and, in a blur of activity, dug a hole about six feet into the ground, and people were slagging him for digging his own grave, and Rolf took it well and said he needed to do a bit of exercise. Then Rolf dug a tunnel connecting his little icy home to the centre of the camp (where the makeshift jacks was). *Then* he started digging branch-lines to connect all the other sleeping bags to the centre of the camp. *Then* the shovel had to be taken off him. 'Calm down, Rolf, calm down, or we'll have to send you back to the ship.'

General information that I want to tell you but isn't connected with any particular time of the day
There is tons of food and everyone is sleepy a lot of the time and we're all strangely passive. We get up when we're told and eat when we're told and go to briefings when we're told and it's all really nice. I'm feeling quite well in the head. I'm tired more than usual and finding it easier than usual to sleep, but I don't feel in the horrors, far from it.

We were told at the start of the cruise that every day we'd be dealing with sensory overload, and it's true. It's just too mad to look out of the window and see a three-mile-high snowy Everest-lookalike looming in at you. There's probably a point where my brain thinks, 'Right, that's enough of all this unbelievable stuff, let's go into cocoon-mode and stay safe.'

Another thing that's nice is that the mood on the ship is deeply unglamorous – no one dresses up or even combs their hair. It's days since I've bothered with make-up. It's all about keeping warm.

2.30 p.m.
We're due to make landfall at a little place called Port Lockroy. But the wind, as the ship approaches, is at fifty knots (I don't really know what that means, but the ship is leaning on its side, if that helps). And, oh my God, Port Lockroy hits a new level of bleak! It's a tiny, grey, wind-scalped rock with a black Nissen hut perched on it. Apparently four people live there (doing some sort

of scientific work, I don't mean like *normal* living) but they've no fresh water, so they've no washing facilities, so they have to wait until a friendly ship comes to visit and lets them on board.

This is where we were due to post our postcards and get our passports stamped, but we've just been told that the winds are too high for us to make anchor. However, the scout Zodiac has whipped over to the island and brought one of the people back to talk to us.

Also, we've been told that we'll wait it out for a while and see if conditions change for the better. I'm going to try to put into words how absolutely incredible the guides on this ship are. They're very safety conscious, which is a comfort, but they're unbelievably innovative and resourceful and manage to adapt to extreme and constantly changing weather conditions and do their utmost to make sure we get the best possible experiences. Also, they're constantly cheery, upbeat, informative and funny.

4.03 p.m.
The wind has dropped enough for us to be let over to Port Lockroy, and over we go in the nippy little Zodiac!

On the island, there are gentoo penguins *everywhere*, in every crag and on every rock, and there are many newly hatched chicks, being fed by their mammies. I *die*! ATYPS (as the young people say).

Also, there is a gift shop! And post office! And museum!

And the best bit about the museum is that it isn't like a museum (i.e. dull but worthy) but like an Antarctic house from the 'olden days', maybe sixty years ago. There's a kitchen with – what's that word for little red-and-white squares? Gingham! Yes, gingham. Yes, gingham curtains.

And cupboards full of tinned food, for examples sardines and

Spam and other foulery. Also powdered stuff, for examples custard and blancmange! (Blancmange! Let's start a campaign for its return.) There's a range, and airing above it are long johns knitted in really, really thick, very itchy-looking wool. There's a (perishing cold) sitting room, a radio room, a washroom and a bedroom with very narrow bunks and – yes! – with pictures painted on the walls of ladies with extremely large knockers!

In the post office, we post our post cards and purchase souvenirs.

6.19 p.m.
Back at the ship. Himself has just looked over my shoulder to see what I'm doing and said in a portentous voice, 'Day 9, and the penguins were getting restless . . .'

7.36 p.m.
At dinner, Himself is staring at another table for ages. Then he says, 'Has your man done something to his hair . . .?'

'Who?'

'The ordinary-looking Asian lad. The one with the hipsters.'

I take a look. He is right. The ordinary-looking lad's hair has a definite 'coiffed' air to it.

Also . . . we say it together, 'He's wearing a lumberjack shirt!'

8.04 p.m.
Himself says he has a confession to make. 'I've never done it before,' he said. 'I don't know what came over me and I'm certain it was just a one-off, but . . .'

'Yes?'

'. . . but . . .'

'TELL ME, FOR THE LOVE OF GOD!'

'Today . . . I . . . looked in a bird book . . .'

'Christ alive!'

'Yes, I saw a bird out of the window and I was wondering what make it was and the next thing I know I was looking it up in a reference book.'

'Shite,' I say. 'This is worse than we thought . . .'

10.45 p.m.

Just before we go to sleep, Himself says to me, 'Do you pronounce it "glassy-er" or "glay-shur"?'

'"Glassy-er",' of course,' says I. 'Like Fox's Glassy-er Mints. Or Fox's Glassy-er Fruits.'

After a pause he says, 'Trust you to bring everything back to sweets.'

He is a fine one to talk, him and his birds.

DAY TEN

Inspiration strikes!

Listens, lads, there's no need for you to write the dystopian telly series set in the near future in Antarctica, because I think I can do it myself! Yes!

Here's my pitch . . . The year is 2036 and the planet has almost run out of fuel and the race is on between several nations to bag Antarctica. The United Nations has managed to prevent an all-out war, but hostilities are bubbling away.

Himself and I are brainstorming about names. I want to call it *The Dead Land* and he says it needs 'Ice' in the title. But now he has suggested *The South*, and I agree that it is memorable.

Okay!

Opening scene

Fabulous woman alone in a black Zodiac in a calm sea full of icy-bergs and surrounded by icy-mountains. She is wearing a red waterproof parka and big sunglasses and what looks like no make-up, because she is one of those derring-do women who wouldn't be bothered with that sort of thing, but all the same she has lovely skin and you can tell she wears her sunblock.

Her hair is long and dark and thick and curly and she has no trouble with frizz. She is steering her little boat and she sees a couple of penguins 'dolphining' around and a couple of lazy-arse seals stretched out on ice floes. She is smiling, even though she is by herself, and you can tell she is 'in her element'.

Suddenly there is a REALLY LOUD boomy noise and she looks concerned. She consults a couple of instruments and she looks even more concerned, but she doesn't start talking to herself like Sandra Bullock did in *Gravity*, which was annoying and dis-believable. Then she gets on her walkie-talkie and says, 'Camp South? Camp South? Do you read me?'

But there is only crackling noise.

Then she looks behind her and a MAHOSSIVE wave is coming from about a mile away across the mirrory sea, and she looks really shocked and says, 'Oh shit!'

Scene ends

New scene

An aerial shot, moving fast, following a little propeller plane as it swoops over huge ice shelves and snowy mountains and a rocky colony of rowdy penguins and over silvery water with whales and seals breaking the surface. The plane lands on an icy runway and an INCREDIBLY HANDSOME man gets off, swinging his bag over his shoulder in a manly fashion. I am debating who should play this incredibly handsome man. I am thinking maybe Pasha or Benedict Cumberbatch or Tom Dunne.

But no, I might need Pasha for the Russian part of the plot, which will come in a couple of episodes, because there is a Russian base down here, also a Chinese one, also a Scandinavian one.

All right, so Tom Dunne, playing the part of 'Tom Dunne', swings down the aeroplane steps, in his outdoorsy gear and wraparound sunglasses, and swaggers into the base, where he is greeted by Sawyer from *Lost*, Sayid from *Lost* and Freckles from *Lost*. (I never really got over *Lost* finishing.)

Tom Dunne: 'Hey! Looks like the gang's all back together.'

Sawyer (*surprised/alarmed*): 'I thought you'd done your last winter out here!'

Tom Dunne: 'Changed my mind. Where's my bunk?'

He walks down a short, curved-roof corridor with no windows.

Sayid: 'You're back? I thought . . . ?'

Tom Dunne (*gives a short mirthless laugh*): 'They let me out.'

Tom Dunne finds a narrow bunk built into the wall. He starts emptying his bag into a metal locker and puts a quare, futuristic, holographic photo on his bedside yoke. Out in the corridor, Sawyer and Sayid are talking.

Sawyer: 'Looks like you're rooming with Psycho. Good luck with that.'

Sayid: 'Just so long as he stays away from the spoons.'

Scene cuts to a control room, where a woman is sitting, watching gauges and screens and that sort of thing. I've decided that this woman is played by me. On the CCTV she sees Tom Dunne at his bunk, unpacking his stuff.

Me: 'Oh my God. He came back . . .'

Scene cuts to a group shot, where maybe thirty people of obviously different nationalities are gathered together for a welcome/ motivational speech from the base commander, who is played by Krister Henriksson, who is (as always) charismatic, avuncular, kindly, wise and Swedish.

The camera scans over the faces, which look earnest, keen, enthusiastic and a little apprehensive. Some of the faces are: Zayn from One Direction,* Mary Berry, Paul Hollywood, Claudia Winkleman, Leonard Cohen, Sarah Lund, José Mourinho, Michael Bublé, Dermot O'Leary, Cher, Graham Norton, Beth, two very short red-haired Irish brothers (the Redzers), Kerry Washington, George Michael, Gianfranco Zola, my mammy, Cathy Kelly, Fran from *Love/Hate*, Tommy from *Love/Hate*, Judy McLoughlin, Fergal McLoughlin, Sali Hughes, Margaret Mountford, Posh Kate, Nile Rodgers, Angélique Kidjo, Louise Moore, JohnEamonChippyBill, India Knight, Mary Kennedy, Djocko Djokovic, Michelle Obama, Jean Byrne the weather girl, Jonathan Lloyd, the entire cast of *1864*, Jojo Moyes, Zoë Ball. And other people I like but can't think of right now.

Krister Henriksson: 'Welcome back for another polar winter! People don't know how or why we put ourselves through this, but this year, more than ever, our presence is vital down here. Blahdeeblah . . .'

Back to the control room. I have made contact with the Scandinavian base. Lars Mikkelsen's face appears on my screen. We smile warmly at each other. We are friends 'of old'.

* I have since taken agin Zayn and no longer want him in my show.

Me: 'Here we are back again for another winter, Lars.'

Lars: 'Krister already said that. There's no need for you to say it too. Keep things moving.'

Me: 'Very well. Have you made contact with the Chinese base?'

Lars: 'Negative.'

Me: 'Me either. A bit worrying, isn't it, Lars?'

Lars: 'It *is* worrying, Emkay, but it's early days. This is only the first episode.'

Me: 'You're right, Lars, it's early days indeed. Okay, over and out.'

Lars: 'Over and out. And Phillip Christensen says hello.'

Me: '. . . hello back to Phillip.'

I take a look at some gauges and seem startled. René, the French bloke, is beside me. (He is played by Jérôme out of The Returned.*)*

Me: 'René, my readings are compromised.' (*Or some such technical guff.*)

René: 'Let me check. Hey, that's funny. The numbers are falling. Hey, HK, take a look at this.'

The base's second in command, HK – a tall, handsome, kindly man, played by Himself Keyes – comes and looks over René's shoulder. HK watches the figures and seems terribly alarmed.

HK: 'Take cover, take cover! This is not a drill!'

There is a big bang and the walls and everything shakes and all the people in the meet-and-greet topple over and fall on the floor and the lights flicker and go out and the whole place is in darkness.

A voice: 'Is that your hand, Mary Berry? Well, you dirty article!'

Outdoor shot of the igloo-shaped base blazing with light, then going completely dark.

opening credits folley!!!

So what do you think?! Himself and I are going to pitch to Nick Marston on our return from the Frozen South. Hopefully it will be on your telly-boxes for the autumn. It all depends on Tom Dunne's availability.

Palmer Station!
Adélie penguins!

10.30 a.m.
We set off, on a blindingly blue day, in a Zodiac, for Palmer Island, a US research station. The sea is so full of chunks of ice, it's like driving through a white Slush Puppie (vanilla flavoured). However, we are very lucky because until shortly ago the island was iced in and no one could get to it *at all*. And the people living there had no way of getting out. Imagine!

Yes, so Palmer Station is a US research station, with forty-four staff on it, doing research into krill and things, and hardly any ships are allowed to visit, only ten a season, and we are among the lucky ones.

The buildings are metallic and basic and have *many signs* sellotaped to the wall, a bit like a hostel would. For examples: 'Turn off the light' or 'Do not sleep upside down' or 'Do not torment the krill.' And that sort of thing.

I read a book called *Antarctica* before I came here, and it suggested that from time to time people go a bit bananas here and suddenly try to stick a spoon into their colleague's ear. (You will note my reference to that in my dystopian telly-box show.) But then the madness passes and they are all pals again. Until the next time . . . They call it being 'toasty' or 'going toast'.

I walk around and stick my head down corridors and open

doors that maybe I shouldn't and in general take many, many mental notes for *The South*.

There is a gym and chocolate brownies and lots of krill in a white bucket, which everyone takes photos of. (I cannot see the thrill myself.) Apparently they used to have pet dogs out here but now they're not allowed.

We asked the 'man' what he missed and he said 'Fresh vegetables.' So there you are. I would miss the Twitters. Also the telly.

2.45 p.m.
After lunch we set sail for an island which is an Adélie penguin colony, and do you know Adélie penguins? They're a bit different from gentoo penguins (which are your 'classic' penguins) because they have a FABLISS hairdo. Sort of like they've shaved their hairline and then backcombed the rest so it is sticky-uppy. Hippest of all the penguins.

As we came in to land, I saw a couple of them tap-dancing in the distance, but the minute I tried to show Himself, they stopped and put their flippers in their pockets and started whistling instead.

There were lots of chicks, and most of them were as big as their mothers but looked like a totally different species: they were round and goofy and looked like they were trying to wear grey fake-fur coats. They were adorably ungainly, trying to stand up and then falling flat on their faces. One of them had just discovered his flippers and was waving them around, delighted with himself.

The parents and nippers were clustered in groups of about thirty, but now and again two or three of the parents would break away from the group and hurry off at top speed, looking from the back like they were old women in black headscarves and long black topcoats, who were late for Mass.

Also, from time to time a pair of them would take a notion and stretch their bodies really tall and long and wrap their necks around each other's and make trumpeting noises at the sky, like totally mad madzers. Perhaps a mating ritual? Or maybe just letting off steam?

4.49 p.m.
I have changed the name of my dystopian telly series to *The Frozen*. Or maybe *People of the Ice* (Himself came up with that one).

5.42 p.m.
Sweet baba Jay, there's been an announcement over the bing-bong – an invitation to the Polar Plunge, where they take passengers out in their togs in a Zodiac and then they jump off the little boat into the icy sea, and I am *not* going to do it! I don't care. I do not need to experience everything once. I find life challenging enough without jumping into an icy sea. Himself is doing it though. And I cannot bear to even go and watch him. It feels cruel and dreadful and terrible and I just want it all to be over.

5.50 p.m.
Himself says, 'You don't have to be involved in any way.'
    I say, 'I'm not going to be.'
    He says, 'You don't have to be involved in any way.'
    I say, 'I'm not going to be.'
    He says, 'Do I have slippers?'
    I say, 'Go in your runners.'
    'With my togs?'
    'Yes, with your togs.'
    'It'd be better if I went in my slippers.'
    'You haven't got any slippers.'

'But they said on the bing-bong I was to come in my slippers.'

'But you haven't *got* any slippers.'

'Help me look for the slippers.'

'There are no slippers! There are no slippers! THERE ARE NO SLIPPERS!'

6.01 p.m.

He's gone. To calm myself, I will count my Solpadeines.

6.13 p.m.

He's back! He admits that it was 'shockingly cold'. He said he just 'jumped in and jumped out' but that the Dutchman swam out to an iceberg and preened a little. I said, 'What Dutchman?' He said, 'Have you not met the Dutchman?'

In other news, his lad is 'much shrunken', but should return to normal, given time.

In other other news, he reports that the M&S-style snacks are 'out but covered in cling film'.

6.16 p.m.

He says no one came down in their slippers. He says, 'I don't think there *were* any slippers.'

8.45 p.m.

After dinner, there was a chocolate buffet. With chocolate penguins! And other chocolate beasts! And then! We were looking out to sea, at the quare, beautiful light on the ice mountains, and we saw eight penguins swimming towards us, looking like the arrival of the cavalry. And then!!! Yes! Three whales. Humpbacks. A mother and a father and a baby, and they swam right up beside the ship and swam alongside us for a good while, doing their blowhole stuff, until one by one they curved up and showed the fin on their back and then, like they were saying goodbye, showed us their tail-fins and then disappeared, down into the deep, leaving behind three circles of water.

I haven't got words to even start to describe how rewarding and enriching this journey has been. It's like I'm drunk on beauty. Everywhere I look, I see astonishing natural magnificence. Just now I'm looking out the window and there's a mountain that looks like K2. And beside that there's another one and another one, and there's nothing, not a single sign, that human beings have ever existed. Everything is still and poised; not even the clouds are moving. It's so surreally perfect that it almost looks like a painted backdrop.

Also, my mental state while I've been here is different. I feel slowed down, like my brain has been wrapped in a duvet. I have literally forgotten what day it is. I feel like I've been on this ship for ever and that I'll be here for ever and all there is is right now, but in a fluffy, giggly, carefree sort of way, rather than in that grim, clenched-jaw, I'm-in-the-moment mindset that seems to riddle so much positive thinking.

It's not like I've surrendered control, but that it slipped away from me while I was staring, slack-jawed, at yet another too-astonishing landscape.

At home I find the days far too long. A half-hour can take a shocking amount of time to pass. But time is nothing here. I'd brought lots of box sets to watch, but haven't got further than Episode 1 of *The Good Wife*. And I've barely read anything, and yet I never feel bored and I rarely get the fear where I'm desperate for something to calm me.

Also, I've gone almost feral in my appearance. It's goodbye to make-up, it's goodbye to combing my hair, my Gelish nail varnish has peeled off several of my nails and it seems utterly unimportant to do anything with them.

There is nowhere else like this on earth. Nothing even close.

Another thing that adds to my cocoon-brain feeling is the loveliness of every single one of the staff. Everyone, from Iris the receptionist to Joseph who always remembers my Sprite Zero, to Marvin the plumber who had to come and fix our jacks, they are all warm and treat me with a generosity of spirit that seems genuine.

I spend a lot of my life agonizing about economic inequality and worry that people who have to work as hard as these people do must really resent the spoilt, rich Westerners they take care of. But I don't feel like that here. I feel everyone takes great pride in doing their job excellently and they sincerely want us to have a great time. I feel everyone who works in the dining room is (justifiably) proud of the delicious food and thoughtful service they provide.

As for the twelve guides, I am *humbled* by how they have gone out of their way to make sure everyone had a wonderful trip. Also, everything is extremely tightly organized, but there's never any sense that any of the guides are stressed or tired. They all seem to genuinely love the Antarctic and are passionate about getting the best out of the trip for every single person. Really, I cannot praise them enough.

7.44 p.m.

Sideshow Bob hasn't come down for dinner! Himself says he must have done the Polar Plunge and 'collapsed' his hair. Himself says he might have had to take his hair to the medical bay.

7.59 p.m.

Sideshow Bob appears in the dining room and his hair looks freshly 'done'. It is unusually pineappley and sticky-uppy and sway-ey. Himself says that he has obviously been to the medical bay and 'had a shot'.

DAY ELEVEN

Whales everywhere!
I have made friends!

6 a.m.

The bing-bong awakens us with news that there is a pod of TWENTY (20) humpback whales just off the ship. We pull on our thermal long johns and puffy jackets and other warming devices and run for a look. We are just in time to see them before they turn tail.

2 p.m.

I watch four orcas for an hour. They are so curvy and graceful and sleek in the vast expanse of navy ocean and I feel very peaceful.

I should mention that apart from one snowy morning the weather has been magnificent every day I've been here. Sunny, and the skies have been gloriously blue. I've barely been cold. Admittedly I've worn an awful lot of technical clothes, but still.

5 p.m.

We take a Zodiac cruise beside cliffs and under flint archways and through staggeringly quare landscapes. There is a fair bit of bouncing and getting splashed and Himself says, 'This will play merry hell with Sideshow's hair.'

I agree but I am also focused on how FABLISS this will be for my telly series – Zodiac chases through the narrow canyons of rock and beneath flinty arches barely big enough to fit a boat and into ice caves and down blue icy tunnels. I tell you! It will be *Lost* meets James Bond meets a cold place!

Another thing about 'my' show: all of the main characters will have thrilling and interesting back stories. Including – yes! – possibly having died.

Other news

Himself and I have made friends with some of the other passengers – an Englishman, a Swiss woman, an Australian man and an Australian woman. Yes! I didn't want to tell you about it until I was sure it was for real, but it is! We have got into the very happy habit of 'taking' our meals with them, and they are great fun and excellent company and very nice.

7.30 p.m.

Sideshow Bob appears for dinner and his hair looks much subdued.

I ask Himself if *The Frozen* will include people coming back from the dead like they did in *Lost*. He says no. But secretly I plan to overrule him, and when we are sitting in Harvey Weinstein's office doing our pitch in LA I will throw in the part about the dead people reappearing and there will be nothing Himself can do about it! Hahahahaha!

DAY TWELVE

We head for home!

Yes, that is the end of our excursions. Now we have two days at sea, until we get back to Ushuaia. I'm a little bit sad, but it has been an incredible trip.

9.30 p.m.
. . . d'you know what? I feel a bit sick . . .

10.01 p.m.
Yes, I definitely feel sick.

10.11 p.m.
. . . Christ, I'm dying . . .

DAY THIRTEEN

In the 'jaws' of the Drake Passage!

The sea is wild rough and the whole ship seems to have the gawks. I spend the day in bed, even forsaking my lungeon. Himself goes downstairs for one of the lectures and he says there were only fifteen people there and they all had their faces in gawk-bags.

6.03 p.m.
The ship has reached calmer waters and I am well enough to 'rise' for our final dinner, which we are 'taking' with our new friends.

7.11 p.m.
At dinner I take a last look round at my fellow passengers . . .

. . . and then there were four. Hipsters, that is. The ordinary-looking lad's metamorphosis is complete. His hairs, his clothing, his spectacles, his everything. He leaves the ship a fully-fledged hipster!

THIRD-LAST DAY

7 a.m.

We come into port in Ushuaia and get off the ship and I have a little cry because it was all so wonderful. But still, I feel incredibly lucky – this has been the trip of a lifetime!

Our flight isn't until one o'clock, so we go – with our four new friends – to Los Cauquenes, which is the beautiful hotel we stayed in for our first two nights. We have coffee and lovely conversation and at 11.30 Himself and I leave for the airport to go to Buenos Aires, where we will be staying overnight because we're not in time for today's flight to Heathrow.

Our flight is delayed but that is grand. When we were in Argentina seven years ago, we were delayed eight hours at El Calafate airport, so it is all par for the course. The plane eventually comes and we take off and make a 'short' stop in a place called Trelew and most of the plane troops off and then comes stomping back on five minutes later, complaining that this is NOT Buenos Aires!

7.30 p.m.

I will not bore you with the airport/lost baggage details. You've heard it from me too often, too many times before. Then we go to the Park Hyatt, where we discover that we have been upgraded to the Presidential Suite! Oh my God, I cannot tell you! It is beautiful and lavish and HUGE! We have a sitting room and a dining room and a kitchen and TWO (2!) bathrooms.

We've no idea why we've been upgraded (I'm not being coy, it is all booked in Himself's name. Perhaps Himself is famous here . . .).

SECOND-TO-LAST DAY

As we drive to the airport I remark on what wide streets Buenos Aires has and say that some of the streets are almost as wide as O'Connell Street, to which Himself says that some of them are *wider* than O'Connell Street.

. . . but this cannot be true. O'Connell Street is the widest street in the world, no? (This reminds me of when I was visiting this part of the world seven years ago and Eileen and I were in Brazil on a scenic flight across the Amazon and the pilot told us that the Amazon was the longest river in the world and I said, 'Indeed it is, except for the Shannon.' And the pilot was a right cranky-arse and said, 'What are you talking about?' And I said, 'The Amazon is *indeed* the longest river in the world. Except for the Shannon. Which is the *true* longest. So the Amazon is the second-longest river in the world. Apart from the Dodder. And perhaps the Dargle.' And he was really, really annoyed and did not 'get' me at all.)

11.10 a.m.
They are playing tango music at the passport control.
And I am *not* lying about that.

LAST DAY

Heathrow!
Then Dublin!
Boo, we are home! And here ends Marian's Antarctica diary.

mariankeyes.com, January 2014.

MARIAN MEETS . . .

Tom Dunne

Right, I'll tell you the whole Tom Dunne thing. He's really famous, especially in Ireland, because he was (is? As far as I know they've never broken up) the lead singer in a band called Something Happens, which was GINORME in the early 1990s but I was living in London then so I missed it all.

Then he got a job as a radio presenter on *Newstalk* and I STILL didn't know about him because I never listened to the radio except when I was in the car and I was never in the car because I was meant to be at my computer working.

But then I was at the dentist, I was lying in the chair, having stuff done to my teeth, and Seán Moncrieff was on the radio and he was so funny and dry and witty and clever that it took the sting out of the dentistry somewhat.

So I changed the setting in my car to *Newstalk* and I said to Susie, 'Isn't *Newstalk* great?' And she said, 'Yes! Isn't Tom Dunne fantastic?' And I'd been all set to launch into praise of Seán Moncrieff and I said, 'Who's Tom Dunne?' And she said, 'You don't know who Tom Dunne is?????'

Then she turned to everyone else and said, 'Marian doesn't know who Tom Dunne is!' Then the entire room erupted with laughter and total strangers were wiping away tears of mirth.

So, yes, Tom Dunne. I started listening to him and very quickly I fell in love with him and veered dangerously close to becoming a Tom Dunne window-licker and that was okay because Himself loved him too. In fact, everyone I've ever met loved him and we were all manufacturing excuses to drive places in the morning at the time that Tom was on.

He has a beautiful voice and I've laughed out loud SEVERAL times while listening to him, and he talked about himself and his family and home life and weekends with such warmth and humanity that he is a FORCE FOR GOOD in this sometimes-frightening world.

Then! One Wednesday he said, 'Bin night tonight,' and Wednesday was OUR bin night too, so Himself and myself realized that we must live quite near to him and we obviously had the same bin collectors!

In my next monthly newsletter I wrote about this 'connection' I have with Tom and he must have found out about it because – yes! – he played a SPECIAL SONG for me on his show about Wednesday nights being our 'special' night.

It caused a sensation among my friends and family! A veritable SENSATION, I tell you. It began with Posh Malcolm ringing me and saying, 'I don't know what's going on, but Tom Dunne is sending you coded messages on his show!'

And it continued from there. A torrent of jealousy from other Tom Dunne window-lickers (formerly my friends) was directed my way, but I didn't care.

However, I'd never met him and was quite certain that if I did, I would DIE!

Of course there was a small chance that I might bump into him, seeing as we live near-ish to each other (seeing as we shared the same bin night, like). And even though I'd no idea where exactly he lived, it didn't stop me having a mental image of it.

However, Suzanne, who also has a fondness for Tom, she *also* has a mental image of where Tom lives, which differs from *my* mental image, and the last time I met her, we drew out a sort of map on the table, using napkins and salt and pepper yokes as landmarks, and we nearly fell out over it. ('No,' she insisted. 'When you get to the traffic lights, you go up the road.' 'You don't,' I replied. 'You go straight on and he's in there on the right.' 'No, no, no!' she said. 'You go UP the road. Up!' And so on. And relations between us have been slightly frosty since.)

Anyway, one cold, sleety, miserable day a few weeks ago, I was 'down the town' and I was looking particularly unattractive. I'd overdone the mythic oil in my hair, so my fringe was looking all bitty and greasy (like Tommy's in *Love/Hate* actually, *just* like Tommy's) and my hair was up in a ponytail. BUT! I'd put a hat on *over* the ponytail and it was a particularly unattractive hat but good at keeping me warm but all the same I looked like I had a particularly strange-shaped gargantuan head. I was wearing my North Face duvet-coat and was laden down with bags filled with turnips (or something equally grim) and I was feeling knackered and bet-down and I'd just come out of Ecco shoes (I know!) where I'd been looking for insoles and who did I see, when I emerged, only Tom Dunne!!!!!!

Horror zipped through me. Horror! Our eyes met and he looked sort of horrified himself. 'Tom,' I said haltingly. 'Hello. I'm sorry. About the hat. It's only because it's so cold. Tom, I've fantasized about meeting you and my hair would be just blow-dried and I'd be looking fantastic and moving in slow motion and, oh Christ, I can't believe this is happening.'

With extreme kindness Tom said, 'You look great, Marian, we both look great.'

'Do we?' sez I. 'Okay.'

I gestured at the sleet, at my appalling hat, at my bagful of turnips, and said, 'Living the dream, Tom, living the dream.'

An awkward little pause followed, then I exclaimed, 'Will I give you a hug, Tom?!'

So he let me hug him and then I let the poor man go on his way and on trembling legs I made my way home. I couldn't get my key in the lock and Himself had to open the front door and I said, 'You won't BELIEVE what's after happening!!!'

Himself looked concerned and I wailed, 'I met Tom Dunne down the town!' And Himself looked aghast and said, 'In *that* hat? Oh God!'

mariankeyes.com, August 2013.

Robert Plant

Right! Himself! Well, for years and years and years and years, since he was aged about twelve, he has been in wild bromantic love with Robert Plant. He adored him in Led Zeppelin and in more recent decades has been a fan of Mr Plant's other groups and collaborations.

I, too, have been a big fan of Mr Plant's. When I was fifteen, I had a boyfriend with excellent taste in music. Actually, it was his older brother who had the excellent taste in music and even though the older brother hated me (it's grand, all grand, I hated him too, it was fine) he let us listen to his records. (Yes, actual vinyl records.)

And many of those excellent records were by Led Zeppelin, so I was well versed in their 'oeuvre' by the time I met Himself and it was one of the reasons that convinced him that I was the perfect woman. (At this point I must add a caveat and say that George Michael is my *actual* all-time favourite music-type person.)

Over the years, I've been to Robert Plant gigs. There was one night, many years ago, when Robert (you'll have noticed I'm now referring to him as 'Robert' as if we are friends . . .? Yes, well, pay heed) . . . yes, there was one night when Robert was coming to Dublin to do a gig and I couldn't go because I was down the town learning how to make beef casserole. And when Himself came home (it was late), I woke up to ask him how it had gone and he said, all dreamy and star-struck, 'He was a golden rock god . . .'

And I couldn't get a word of sense out of him for several subsequent days.

When Led Zeppelin reformed for that one gig in 2007, we paid a large sum of money to a charity for tickets. And in more recent years we've seen Robert with Alison Krauss (twice) and with the Band of Joy. So we are TRUE BELIEVERS.

Right. Having established these facts, can I fill you in on some more stuff, basically about my day-to-day life. See, you might think that I live a high-octane life of extreme glamour, but I really don't. I eke out a small, local existence in a suburb that is partly pleasant and partly *un*pleasant. (It is on the sea (pleasant) and they welcome you to the neighbourhood by burgling your house (*un*pleasant). Do you see? Pleasant and *un*pleasant. Yin and yang.)

And the people I cross paths with are not fabby famous types but the likes of my mammy, the Redzers, Posh Kate and Posh Malcolm, Steve from DHL, Mary and Owen from round the corner, Fuzzy Mahon, Lovely Judy, Nawel from the second-hand furniture shop, and occasionally Tom Dunne, but only when I'm down the town and looking spectacularly dreadful.

I'm very happy with my set-up. But the odd time, I leave my pleasant/*un*pleasant suburb and am thrust into a situation that is extremely glamorous and sometimes during these glamorous events I meet people who are very nice; and that happened to me recently. I was at a thing and got talking to a wonderful, wonderful woman who is a great raconteur and as an adjunct to an anecdote she mentioned that Robert Plant was her neighbour and I immediately began to choke but The Lovely Woman (henceforth known as TLW) was already several sentences ahead of me.

I flailed and coughed and waved my hand and eventually managed to croak out, 'Stop! STOP! For the LOVE OF GOD, you can't just say that Robert Plant is your neighbour, like that's something unremarkable. This is the most REMARKABLE thing I've ever heard in my life.'

So TLW came to a halt and she thought about it and agreed that yes, perhaps, Robert Plant *was* a bit of a legend. And a very nice man. 'You'll meet him next month,' she said. 'When you come to me for tea and then I take you to visit a local knob-shop.' (To buy knobs for my furniture-banjoing, not the other kind of knob-shop . . .)

Well! There was so much in that sentence that was abundantly wonderful – I was being invited to TLW's for tea! And we'd go to a knob-shop! And I'd meet Robert Plant! Then she said, 'Unless he'll be away on tour.' And the thing was, she was right – I knew she was because Himself and I had tickets to see Robert Plant and the Sensational Shapeshifters in Dublin on 24 November.

So I told TLW that and she said, 'Okay, leave it with me. I'll sort something out, get you backstage passes or something.' And she said it with such confidence that I sort of believed her. But at the same time, it seemed so incredibly impossible that I was already throwing buckets of cold water over the flames of my appalling, painful hope.

A few weeks passed and we moved on into November and Himself's lovely mother, Shirley, went into hospital to have open-heart surgery and it was all a bit tricky: the first attempt to operate on her had to be abandoned and although the second attempt had gone okay, she was still in intensive care.

I was at home one day when Himself rang from the car and he was on speaker and he sounded a bit odd, so I asked, 'Are you okay?' And he said, 'No, not really.' And I thought, 'Oh Christ! His lovely poor mother's after pegging it.'

So I said, very gently, 'What is it, sweetie?' And he blurted out, sort of half-crying, 'Robert Plant's just rung me on my mobile. I might never be right again.' And then we were both shrieking and shouting and I was jumping around the room but quickly I realized I had to be sensible. 'Pull in,' I said. 'Pull in. You're not safe to drive.' However, it transpired he'd already had the cop-on to pull in and he promised to stay parked until the shaking had stopped.

Eventually he came home and I sat him down and made him tell me the whole story. 'I was driving along,' he said, 'and I saw an English mobile come up on the phone and I thought it might be work-related so I answered it and a man said, "Can I speak to Tony?" And I said, "Speaking." And he said, "It's Robert here. Robert Plant."'

'Jesus Christ!' I said. 'Just like that? And did you nearly crash the car?'

'Of *course* I nearly crashed the car!'

'And then what happened?'

'He said he'd leave tickets for the after-show party at the box office for us to collect on Monday night.'

'For real?! We're actually going to meet him?! And then what happened?'

'We talked a bit about football. I said about how his team [Wolves – even I knew that] hadn't done so well at the weekend.'

'But how did you hold it together?' I asked, and in bewilderment Himself said, 'I don't know, I really don't know.' And we stared at each other for a startled second, then we started shrieking again and yelling our heads off and jumping around the place and I had to hop on to the couch because I wasn't getting enough spring from the floor to express the extent of my glee. It was FECKEN FANTASTIC!!!

The night of the gig came around and we kept saying to each

other, 'Do you really think this will work? Do you think it'll really happen?' So we promised each other that we wouldn't get too hopeful just in case it all went sideways. But, sure enough, at the box office there were two passes to the after-show party.

And the gig itself was AMAZING! All the musicians were wildly talented but it was Robert, as always, who stole the show. His voice! Still as good as it was forty years ago. And his presence, his . . . yes . . . his *extreme sexiness* . . . Witnessing him singing 'Whole Lotta Love' . . . Sacred *Heart*!

Eventually, after several encores, the gig ended and people started to drift off home, except myself and Himself, who went to Maureen's Bar (as instructed) and presented our passes and I was still waiting for something to go wrong.

But we were on the list and we had to wear the pass and in we went and the man himself wasn't there yet, but other people were and my eyes were flicking back and forth, like knives, as I assessed the situation. See, I'd never before been to an after-show party and I'd no idea of the protocol. Would millions show up? Would we queue to meet Robert or would it be every man for himself?

More people arrived. Not lots. But some. Including some famous faces. Well, one that I recognized – Joe Elliott off of Def Leppard. And Joe Elliott off of Def Leppard was quite alpha – he sported an air of great confidence, an air that he very much *belonged* at an after-show party. I quickly identified him as 'competition'.

Every time the door opened, Himself and I would jump, hoping that it would be Robert Plant himself, but it never was. And then it WAS! In he came, simply *radiating* charisma. But not being grandiose either. Just being HIM.

As I'd feared, Joe Elliott off of Def Leppard was in like Flynn! Yep – up-close and chatting away immediately and surrounded by other members of his party. Perched anxiously on my seat, I trained my eyes on him, thinking, 'Please make him stop soon.'

Himself was scoping out the situation just as much as I was and it was dawning on him that we were going to have to actually make this thing happen.

Now, Himself is the most self-effacing man on the planet. He's extremely shy and unpushy, to the point where people often forget his name and call him Tom or James or John. But he'd suddenly developed an uncharacteristic glint in his eye. 'Come on,' he said to me. 'Up you get.'

So we got up and we went and stood beside the circle and we 'hovered with intent'. We almost 'hovered with menaces'. We kept our eyes fixed on Robert in a way that demonstrated that we meant business. Joe Elliott off of Def Leppard was still chatting away with great animation – then something happened: a split second where Joe Elliott off of Def Leppard blinked and broke his connection with Robert and next thing, Himself is IN!

Yes, in that tiny sliver of time he'd shouldered his way between Robert Plant and Joe Elliott off of Def Leppard and before my startled eyes he was introducing himself to Robert Plant!

And OH. MY. GOD!!!! Robert Plant was so, so, so, so, so, so, so, SOOOOO lovely. He instantly and immediately knew who we were and welcomed us warmly and then he hugged me! Yes! I HAVE BEEN HUGGED BY ROBERT PLANT! And it was a lovely hug – full, expansive, generous, humane, everything a hug should be. And yes, it was incredibly strange to be standing right next to a living legend, to a man who's been part of my life for almost forty years, to be looking into his face and thinking, 'You're Robert Plant. YOU'RE ROBERT PLANT!'

But even though he was definitely Robert Plant, we managed to talk about things – music, obviously, where Himself got a chance to tell Robert how he has always loved him.

Then, mano-a-mano, Robert and Himself talked about climbing mountains because Robert is fond of the mountains in Wales, and Himself is fond of mountains in general, and we told Robert about all the lovely walks in Wicklow and he said he'd have to come back and do some and the chances are that he probably won't but it doesn't matter!

Honest to God, it couldn't have gone better. The funny thing is that Himself is a quiet man, I'm the chatty one, but suddenly he'd become as voluble as bejaney, and in the end I had to give him a little 'Settle the head there' look because we were hogging Robert and there were other people 'hovering with intent', hoping to talk to him.

So, before the 'hovering with intent's turned into 'hovering with menace's, I prised Himself away and Robert hugged me again and it was just as nice as the first one and he shook hands with Himself and clapped him on the shoulder with his other hand. And off we went and as soon as we left I whispered, 'He hugged me,' and Himself said, 'And did you see the way he clapped me on the shoulder?'

Then Himself stopped me and acted it out – the handshake and the shoulder-clap – and repeated, 'He didn't just shake my hand, he *clapped me on the shoulder.*'

It was wonderful beyond description and the warm glow generated by meeting him is still there. As for those people who say you should never meet your heroes? Well, FECK them! If you get the chance, *meet* your heroes, meet them, meet them, meet them!

Previously unpublished.

Aung San Suu Kyi

I want to tell you about my Aung San Suu Kyi experience! (From now on I'll refer to her as ASSK.)

It began with a phone call. I'm always terrified when the phone rings, and I poke at it with a stick and shout, 'Shut up, shut up! Stop ringing. Be peaceful! Please, I implore you.' But for once the phone wasn't bringing scary news, it was bringing thrilling news. It was Himself who actually answered the call and he came back into the room, where I was huddled fearfully, and I said, 'Who was it? What did they want?' And he says, 'Would you like to meet Aung San Suu Kyi?'

I took a good long look at him and thought, 'Well, that's lovely, that is, now the both of us are mad and he'd always seemed so sane, but there we go.' Slowly and loudly I said, 'You can have some of my anti-mad tablets. At least for tonight. But we'll have to get you to a quack in the morning.'

However, it turned out he WASN'T mad and WASN'T having audio hallucinations. I will explain . . .

I'm sure you know who ASSK is, but in case you don't, I'll tell you. She was under house arrest in Burma for fifteen years between 1989 and 2010 – imprisoned by the military junta for having the audacity to be the democratically elected leader of the country. Several times the junta told her she could leave the country, but she knew she'd never be able to get back in, so she stayed, even when her husband – who was living in the UK at the time, because the Burmese wouldn't give him a visa – was diagnosed with terminal cancer and then died. She was also separated from her children.

Throughout her years of imprisonment I thought about her so much, about all the sacrifices she was making on behalf of her country, and I was in total awe. Whenever I was asked by magazines who my favourite dinner guest would be, I always said ASSK because if she was able to have dinner with me it would mean that things had improved enough in Burma for her to be able to leave and that her sacrifices had meant something.

I admired her strength, her dignity, her serene intractability, her intelligence and, most of all, her powers of endurance. I mean, it must have been horrific. How did she survive, second by second? At what stage did she realize she was Burma's 'chosen one' and all the personal sacrifices which that entailed? When did she realize that her personal attachments and love for her family and her husband had to be put to one side? How did it dawn on her that this wasn't going to be over in six months or two years or five years, that she was in it for the long haul?

It made me think of that quote (and I know I'm not saying it right) that people aren't born great, they have greatness thrust upon them. And how awful that must be. ASSK was just an ordinary person – admittedly her father negotiated Burma's independence from Britain, but she wasn't looking for the role as Burma's saviour.

So, as I said, I'd cared about her and worried about her for a long time. I knew that Amnesty International were doing their best for her (sorry, veering off a bit here. I was just thinking that even when I was living in London in my twenties and drinking my head off and spending the electricity money on shoes and was totally skint, I coughed up enough lolly to be a member of Amnesty International).

Anyway, in November 2010 she was finally freed from house arrest and felt that the ruling junta had made enough concessions to enable her to leave the country.

Now, I don't know exactly what happened, but between Amnesty International and Seamus Heaney and Mary Robinson and Bono and maybe other people, and forgive me if I haven't listed them, she was persuaded to visit Dublin and accept the Amnesty Ambassador of Conscience award. She was coming to Dublin *for literally six hours*, between accepting the Nobel Peace Prize in Oslo (twenty-two years after she was awarded it) and going to Britain. And it was decided to hold a concert in her honour in Dublin.

The tickets sold out in a nanosecond and I was very disappointed not to get one, but that was that . . .

And then came the phone call from a mystery benefactor offering me two tickets. (The mystery benefactor was not actually a mystery to me, but they've asked for anonymity in case all their friends and family round on them and screech, 'Why didn't you invite ME, you selfish article!!!!' Indeed, what IS a mystery to me is why I was the person chosen to be invited, but I am not going to analyse the situation, I'm just really, really, really, really, really, really grateful.)

There was just one fly in the ointment . . . I was going to be in Poland for the football. 'Football!!!!' I scorned. 'Football!!! You think I'd miss the ASSK concert just because of some oul' football!'

Himself and I had a chat about things and he was very conflicted about it all, because he has also been a supporter of ASSK (even before he met me), but in the end it was decided that I

would go to the ASSK concert and he'd go to Poland. As it tran-
spired, I was able to go to Gdansk for the massacre by Spain and
I flew back to Dublin on Sunday.

Now, I'm skipping out *so much* – the fun in Gdansk when we
weren't being massacred by the Spanish, my happy hour in Oslo
changing planes, my lost suitcase, my lost car, my shame at the
car-park exit, the fact that I hadn't a single thing to wear to the
ASSK concert because the one good dress that still fits me was in
the AWOL suitcase, along with all my make-up – but we'll
fast-forward to Monday, when I picked up my mammy at three
o'clock to go to the event.

When we arrived at the theatre, it was mobbed with media! Tel-
evision stations from around the world, photographers, journalists,
satellite dishes, a big stage set up in the outdoors. The excitement
was indescribable. The mammy and I were brought to a reception
room and ALL KINDS of hobnobs were hobnobbing, then I got
up to get my mammy a cup of tay and brushed shoulders with –
as in LITERALLY my shoulder brushed against hers – Vanessa
Redgrave! *That's* the calibre of hobnobs we're talking!

Myself and the mammy were paralysed with nerves. Canapés
and stuff were put out on tables but our joint self-esteem was too
low to allow us to eat. But after a long time had passed and none
of the hobnobs had spoken to us, she gave me a nudge and in a
low voice said, 'Hop up there and get us a couple of bikkies.'
There was an impressively WIDE selection of biscuits, but I
cleared the platter of all the Bourbons and brought them back to
her and we ate them and after a while I got up and went to
another platter and took all the Bourbons off that and we ate
them too – it looked like none of the hobnobs were eating any-
thing – and after a while we'd eaten every single Bourbon biscuit
in the place.

Then! Finally we were told to go 'below' to take our seats. But we had to go to the loo! And we went the wrong way looking for it. So then we had to go back through the biscuit room and out the other side, and the staff were clearing things away and looked startled and alarmed at our reappearance, and I was beginning to panic. 'Quick, Mam!' I was yelping. 'Quick!'

'I'm going as quick as I can,' she said. 'I've arthritis!'

'I KNOW,' I said, dragging her towards the Ladies. 'But you'll just have to put it to one side for today. Pretend you're young! We can't be late. It's Aung San Suu Kyi!'

We found the Ladies and then we made our way back through the biscuit room, where the staff had nearly finished clearing up and were looking really, really worried about us, so much so that I thought one of the lovely waiters was going to throw Mam over his shoulder just to get her to her seat in time.

'Wouldja come ON,' I said to her, heedless of who heard me. I can't handle being late at the best of times, but ASSK is my hero of heroes. 'I'm COMING,' she said. And then we were in the lift and then we were in the lobby and then we got to the auditorium – just in time for the announcement that we ASSK's plane had been delayed and the concert wouldn't be starting for another half-hour. All credit to Mam, she said nothing, she didn't even pinch me and she'd have been *well entitled*.

We took our seat and, amigos, we were *surrounded* by hob-nobs – the mayor of Dublin was in the row behind us, the fiddler Martin Hayes was two rows in front of us. People whose names we didn't know but who certainly LOOKED like hobnobs were on both sides of us . . . and then a ripple started. Like a breeze blowing over a field of corn. Electricity starting moving through the crowd and murmurs of, 'She's here, she's here, she is, she's here.' And then! There she was! Aung San Suu Kyi! Free! And on the small little rock that is Ireland! Climbing down the steps of the Grand Canal Theatre. I thought I was going to pass out. To be so close to this woman whom I'd admired and cared about for the last twenty-two years. For all that she'd done and all that she symbolized. To be in her presence was one of the most moving experiences of my life.

Everyone was going mad and standing and cheering and clapping and taking photos (even though we'd been told no photos). And eventually she took her seat – *in the row in front of me and the mammy* – accompanied by Bono and Seamus Heaney and other bigwigs. At this stage I'd have been happy to go home, the night just couldn't get any better, but the concert started and it was utterly brilliant.

All kinds of artists – I'll say some of them: Declan O'Rourke, Dónal Lunny, Angélique Kidjo, Damien Rice, Bob Geldof, and Saoirse Ronan, who read one of Seamus Heaney's poems.

But – for me, anyway – the most mesmerizing performance was from Martin Hayes. I'd seen him once before, so I knew how gifted he is, but he just came on, humble as can be, one man and a fiddle and a grand head of hair (his hair alone deserves a credit) and started playing slow. And I don't know how he does it, but he quietens people, he casts a calming spell and then starts to gather people up, like a fisherman tightening the ropes on the net of a big catch. He started playing faster and people were with him, sort of attached to him, in captivity to him. He played faster and faster, and many of the foreign hobnobs, who'd flown in from around the world just to see ASSK, started to consult their programmes, thinking, 'Just who IS this man?' Martin played faster and wilder, and it was hard to believe that the sounds and the emotions were coming from just one man, and when he finished up he brought the house down. He is AMAZING. He made me

so proud to be Irish, and it was a fittingly magnificent perfor-
mance for ASSK.

Then came the moment everyone had been waiting for: Aung
San Suu Kyi took the stage. She's very beautiful and she looks
very young, even though she was sixty-seven on Tuesday and has
endured a lot of physical and emotional deprivation. She wore
simple clothes and a flower in her hair and she spoke with aching
sincerity. One of the things that affected me most was when she
said, 'I had no idea so many people cared.' And I was thinking, 'If
only you *knew*.' If only she'd been able to feel the collective love
and concern and admiration from around the world all these
years.

But maybe she intuited some of it, because how else did she
keep going?

It made me think about all the people, all the individual
human beings, around our globe who campaigned for her, or
who paid a small sum every month to Amnesty, or who refused
to go on their holidays to Burma, even though there are mag-
nificent hotels and resorts there (built by slave labour), simply
because she had asked us not to, and it made me aware of
how powerful any individual is, once they align themselves with
others with the same beliefs.

Then there was more singing and at the end all of the artists
were on the stage and everyone, including the audience, was
singing 'Get Up, Stand Up', and I swear to you it was like a reli-
gious experience, it was utterly transcendent.

ASSK was hurried outside – things were running much later
than had been anticipated – to receive the freedom of the city,
and Mam and I were despatched to a reception room and were
told that after the ceremony outside, ASSK would be 'doing a
quick walk through' the room and that there 'might be an oppor-

tunity to meet her'. And I got the message: there wouldn't be an opportunity to meet her. And that was okay.

It was a long, thin room and it was rammed with hobnobs, far, far more than at the earlier do, and I was starting to think that maybe we should just go home, that we'd had a wonderful time and there was no point waiting, when a good Samaritan – and I've no idea why she chose me to be the recipient of this bountiful news – whispered me a little whisper: that ASSK was not going to come through the door everyone was expecting her to come through, that she was going to come in at the far end of the room.

I didn't know whether or not to believe this person; I didn't think this person was deliberately misleading me, but I thought they might have it wrong.

Nevertheless, I made up my mind to chance it. First I consulted with my mammy, who urged me to go it alone. 'I'm old and decrepit,' she said. 'I'll only slow you down. I'll mind your bag. Off you go and do your best.' So I made my way towards the far end of the room, where the crowds were thinner and thinner and eventually there was no one at all. Wondering if I was being taken for a right eejit, I loitered by the door . . .

And suddenly it was all action! Organizey men appeared beside me and there were walkie-talkies and urgent words and extreme tension. 'Just a quick walk through the room,' they were saying. 'She's exhausted and she's got a plane to catch.'

With a shock of surprise, I realized I was in *exactly* the right place, and apart from the organizey men there was no one else near me, not for yards. Then someone was saying, 'Three seconds, two seconds, she's coming, she's coming . . .'

And the door opened and in she came, tiny, powerful, brave woman that she is, her entourage hurrying in her wake, and I took my chance and jumped into her path, and she looked a little startled to see me but recovered well, and I stuck my hand out and she took it and I said, 'Thank you for enduring,' and she looked me in the eyes and said, 'Thank you for helping me to endure,' and of course, she wasn't talking about me, she was talking about all of us, about you, about every single one of us who has wished her well over all these years, so I just thought I'd tell you.

marian keyes.com, June 2012.

Pasha

Thank the Lord, *Strictly* is back and as soon as I watched the preview show a few weeks ago, I felt a huge uplift in my mood! Genuinely, seriously. More effective than any antidepressants I've ever been on.

I can't pinpoint what it is that I find so joyous about *Strictly*. The glitteryness? The music? Seeing people who don't really look like dancers suddenly start to blossom? Anyway, I immediately applied for tickets for the live shows and – of course – they were all gone, they've been gone for months.

I brooded upon the matter as I sought a solution. I even considered asking *It Takes Two* if they'd have me on the Friday panel, just to get 'close' to the show. (I planned to do the panel, then kiss everyone goodbye – 'Goodbye, goodbye, leaving now, off I go, out of the BBC, very much leaving, practically gone, indeed I *am* gooooone' – but it would be a ruse, see. I'd only be *pretending* to leave the BBC. Instead I'd sneak down to the studio floor and hide under the bandstand for twenty-four hours, with a stash of cereal bars, and I'd watch the Saturday show from there.)

In the end I discussed the matter on Twitter and many of my folleyers asked the BBC if they'd rustle up a couple of tickets for me – and would you believe it?! – they did! I am so grateful to all the people who lobbied for me and to the BBC for the tickets. But do you see how great the Twitters is and how we help each other when we can?

I had two tickets and myself and Himself discussed this long and hard and it was decided that, even though he loves the show nearly as much as I do, he'd fall on his sword and give the spare ticket to Jenny.

Now, let me tell you about Jenny. Jenny has been my friend since 1986 and she's probably the most 'true and good' person I've ever met, and her kindness to me goes way beyond the call of duty. But the thing is she's very hard to thank. She says she has everything she needs and, for example, she thinks flowers are a waste of money (for herself, she'd happily send them to someone else).

However! She's a massive *Strictly* fan, perhaps even more than me, because Jenny does dancing, as in she can do salsa, tango, jive, jitterbugs and all the rest. Jenny Boland could be a *judge* on *Strictly*! She knows all about 'kicks and flicks' and 'finishes' and other judge-speak.

So the long and the short of it was that Jenny and I went to the *Strictly* ACTUAL show! Himself had to disappear to an unknown location because Jenny would have insisted that he go instead of her, but when I told her – honestly – that I hadn't a clue where he was, she eventually gave in.

And oh God! If you're a fan of the show, you'll know how excited we were. The first thing is that you have to get there HOURS before the show starts. People had been queuing from eight that morning, and Jenny and I got there about three. We waited in a BBC canteen till we were called at about 5.30 and when we walked into the studio, I nearly puked with the excitement.

I know people always say this about television sets, but it really was much smaller than it looks on the telly. Everything was so near! There was the judges' table and there was the band

and there was the stairs – all a matter of yards away. We were in the second row from the front and it was then that Jenny and I discovered that we were in with the friends and family of the celebrities!

Denise Van Outen's husband was there, and I was sitting beside someone who was a friend of Johnny Ball's, and next to her was someone who might be JB's wife. Supporting Louis were some very clean-cut-looking young men. Athletes, allegedly. But they looked sort of holy, you never saw such neatly combed hair!

Antony Cotton was in the front row, and other people that I recognized but didn't know from where. Then, at the very last minute, who comes in, only Nadine and Nicola from Girls Aloud, to sit in the front row! Thrilling it was, thrilling I tell you!

I'd show you photos of all of this glittering glamour except that our phones had been taken away from us. So I can't.

Am I conjuring up anything at all like how thrilling it was to be within touching distance of the dancers and to see their nerves before the music started and to watch the reaction of the judges?

I have seventeen favourite couples, which takes some doing as there were only fourteen couples, thirteen now, in fact only twelve now, they're dropping like flies! My favourites are – obviously – Nicky Byrne because I'm Irish, and Lisa Riley because her cha-cha-cha in week one was the most uplifting thing I've ever seen, and Fern Britton because she's dancing with Artem, and Artem is Himself's favourite (of the men dancers; Aliona is his favourite female).

But if I had to have a *favourite* favourite, it's Pasha. And Kimberley, obviously.

So the dancing started and at the end of each dance I was

jumping to my feet and giving rowdy standing ovations. (I was close to being out of control.) But not everyone was as excited as me and Jenny. I'm going to whisper you one tiny little piece of gossip. I shouldn't, and Christ knows, I don't want to blot my copybook with the BBC, but I can't stop myself! During the show, a certain famous 'friend and family' was approached by a poor man from the BBC to tell them that the celebrity they were there to cheer on would be the next to dance and that the cameras would be on this 'friend or family' so would they please smile.

I'm not the only one who commented on this certain person's sour puss throughout the show, so I suppose I'm not giving away too many secrets.

Eventually the Saturday-night show ended, but instead of the professional dancers all rushing away and shouting, 'No, no, no! Leave me be!' they loitered on the dance floor, chatting to members of the audience they knew. At this stage I'd decided that the person I really, really, really, really, really, really wanted to show the love to was Pasha. I don't know why I particularly picked on him, because I love everyone in the show, judges, dancers, celebrities, male and female, young and not-so-young.

And he was tantalizingly close. A matter of yards. He was chatting to Nicola Roberts from Girls Aloud, who is the cutest little thing; she had a lovely pink jumper on. Because I was in the second row, my route to the dance floor was barred (the front-row chairs were sort of glued together, so I couldn't just shove them aside), and I watched Pasha with mounting hysteria.

The clock was ticking, soon he would be gone, and just when I was considering clambering over the back of the chairs, I got a lucky break in the form of Brindan, who came to chat to the Johnny Ball supporters seated next to me. With uncharacteristic rudeness, I interrupted and said, 'Ah hello there, Brindan, we meet again! Yes, we *have* met before!'

Politely he prepared to engage in chat with me, but I said briskly, 'No need, Brindan, no need. But would you do me a favour?' I'm sure he was expecting me to say 'Would you autograph this torn bit of paper for my granny?' or some such. Nevertheless, he gamely agreed. So I said, 'Would you go over there and get Pasha for me.'

Instead of being offended, instead of saying, 'What am I? Your pimp?!' he said, 'Okay.' He went over, had a little whisper in Pasha's ear, Pasha looked up and clearly didn't know me from Adam, but he made his apologies to Nicola Roberts and immediately he came over!

This is what I said: 'Pasha, my name is Marian, you don't know me, I'm nobody, nothing, and you are Pasha and I love you, yes I do, you remind me of my nephew, his name is Luka, he is eleven, and I love you, you are Pasha, I saw you in the live show in Dublin in January or it might be February and I thought you had a very lovely kindliness about you, you are Pasha, you are sweet, I sound mad to you, I know it and I can hear myself and yet I can't stop myself, I love you, but not in a stalkery way, yes, everyone always says that, especially the stalkers –'

At this stage, Jenny, keen to release Pasha from his torment, interjected with some nice words and broke my unstoppable gush. Now, the thing is I've met a few famous people over the years and most of them have been (all, even) pleasant. But with a lot of them, they're so used to hearing star-struck love and praise that even though they try to hide it, something shuts down behind their eyes. I suppose it's very hard to engage when someone is shouting facts about yourself at you that you already know. But not Pasha. I was right up-close and I'm telling you, he is real! He's as sweet as he seems. His eyes did *not* go funny! He was genuinely friendly, not just ticking off the seconds, being polite to a manic fan. Trust me on this! Please!

He hugged me. At least twice. Possibly up to four times. Jenny says it only happened twice. But it FELT like four.

mariankeyes.com, October 2012.

Writers I Love

May I tell you about what turned out to be one of the happiest days of my entire life? I may? Tanken yew! Well! You know Sali Hughes, the brilliant journalist who writes for the *Guardian* on a Saturday and the *Pool* on a Wednesday? And has her own website, salihughesbeauty.com, where she does great videos called 'In the Bathroom', where she visits the bathrooms of famous and/or interesting people and discusses their beauty products and skincare and whatnot? Well, I've been a fan of hers for a long time because while she really loves all things beauty, she's entirely honest and reliable and informative. She knows *everything*.

We first came into contact when I twittered asking people what I should do about the little broken capillaries on my face and everyone told me to email Sali – and she emailed me back immediately, giving me a variety of options and telling me the upsides and downsides of each. And after that we stayed in touch, and even though we hadn't met in real life I loved her already because she has great sweetness and gentleness coupled with razor-sharp intelligence.

Also, she gives airtime to all kinds of brands, they don't have to be big names and expensive, so she's in nobody's pocket, so I know that what she writes in her columns is genuinely impartial. Also, she's wonderful for giving exposure to new and emerging brands, which thrills me because I am a divil for 'New and Exciting'.

And now she's after writing a book, called *Pretty Honest*, and it is the ABSOLUTE BEAUTY BIBLE – it covers everything from the very basics, such as identifying your skin type, to how to manage your beauty when you're going through something awful like cancer, and she demystifies the 'anti-ageing' industry, separating out cod science from things that do actually work. (As well as acknowledging that there's nothing wrong with looking your age – basically she gives you every option.)

Every woman should have this book. Because beauty stuff is a passionate hobby of mine, I thought I knew a bit, but compared to Sali I know nothing and I've already consulted the book many times.

So anyway, there I am, living in Dublin and, you know, living a quiet life, seeing my mammy and the Redzers and the Praguers and going for walks with Himself and Posh Kate and Posh Malcolm – when Sali sends me this invitation to a lunch. A foncy lunch – being thrown for her by Bobbi Brown – yes! The make-up brand Bobbi Brown! And I was invited!

There were only twenty people invited and I was one of them – and when I saw the list of the other invitees, didn't I nearly get sick! They were all writers or journalists that I hold in HUGE regard: India Knight, Jojo Moyes, Sam Baker, Polly Samson, Miranda Sawyer, Hadley Freeman, Lucy Mangan, Maria McErlane, Georgia Garrett, Julia Raeside, Jo Elvin, Camilla Long, Sophie Heawood, Bryony Gordon and Sarah Morgan. Also invited were three amazing women from the Estée Lauder group: Jay Squier, Cheryl Joannides and Anna Bartle.

My immediate impulse was that I couldn't possibly go, that I didn't belong, that I wouldn't fit in, and then I thought, 'Feck it! I want to go. I'm GOING!'

And this was huge for me because I've been mad in the head

(MITH) for so long that I've had to keep my life very small and safe because it was all that I could cope with. But I realized I was ready to go into a daunting, intimidating situation and try to hold my own.

And off I went. And I really hope you don't think I'm being a boasty-boaster, I just wanted to let you know that if you've suffered from the MITH-ness yourself and you think you'll always feel terrible, it may not be the case for ever.

I 'jetted' in from Dublin – normally, when I travel by air, I simply fly, but because this was so glamorous I 'jetted' – and the lunch was upstairs in the private room in Balthazar and I had to scuttle past the welcoming committee to go to the Ladies to do last-minute checks on myself, only to discover that – horrors! – I'd somehow managed to leave Dublin without my comb!

For a brief but very real moment I contemplated scuttling back past the welcoming committee, leaving Balthazar and going back to the airport and flying home – yes, 'flying' home, no 'jetting' this time, it would be an ignominious return – and never contacting any of the people here today ever again. Then I remembered a day long ago when my mammy couldn't find any of her combs, because all of her daughters had stolen them, and she had to go to Mass (not a Sunday but a holy day of obligation) and she ended up having to comb her hair with a fork. Inspired by her ingenuity, I resolved that as soon as was polite, I'd secrete a fork from the table into my handbag and race back to the Ladies and sort my hair out that way.

So in I went to the room and I was appallingly nervous – the first person I saw was Camilla Long – Camilla Long! In real life! And then I met Sali and my hands were shaking so much, my fingers were all fumbly. But she was the kindest, nicest woman you could meet, and exquisite-looking, like a doll.

And as it transpired, everyone was INCREDIBLY nice. The only person I'd properly met before, apart from the amazing Jay Squier, was the wonderful novelist and co-founder of the *Pool* Sam Baker, who is very grounded and calm and kind, and she passed on a little of her calmness to me. And she was with Jojo Moyes – Jojo Moyes! My love, my admiration, my *downright jealousy* of Jojo's talent knows no bounds. But would you believe, Jojo had also forgotten her comb! So I decided that if someone as amazing as Jojo Moyes had forgotten her comb, forgetting one's comb was actually admirable. Perhaps it could become a 'thing'. A bit like the ice-bucket challenge – where you go out for the evening without your comb . . .? No, maybe not. Sorry. Not all my ideas are runners . . .

Then I met Miranda Sawyer, the music journalist, who is so cooooollll! But she was *extremely* welcoming and warm and fun and that did a huge amount to put me at my ease.

So we were standing around having drinks, and I went mad and had a Diet Coke because of the day that was in it, and before I knew it, I was in the thick of things.

Initially I was acting, trying hard to chat and act normal and not keel over with intimidation, but after a while it became real – and then I discovered I was enjoying myself. Like, *really* enjoying myself.

And when we sat down for the lunch I discovered several things:

1) A personalized name tag – while we'd been doing our chatting and mingling an illustrator had sat in the room and sketched each of us. I've never encountered a more charming, delightful gesture ever.
2) I was seated on Sali's right hand, which was a massive honour.

3) On my other side was India Knight, and oh my GOD! She's incredible! Utterly hilarious – I nearly got sick laughing – and entertaining and warm and vital and alive and passionate and smart as a whip.

4) A Bobbi Brown goodie bag next to my side plate. It took EVERYTHING IN MY POWER to stop myself from ripping it open and kissing the things inside.

5) I was seated opposite Hadley Freeman, who is the nicest, nicest person and was so complimentary about Ireland that I totally fell in love with her.

6) Maria McErlane was sort of diagonally across from me and she was another one that had me choking with laughter.

7) Diagonally across from me on the other side was the afore-mentioned lovely Miranda Sawyer.

What was very interesting was the atmosphere in the room – there was nothing but love. I'm very attuned to undercurrents and unspoken tension and there was absolutely none. Everyone was so happy for Sali and everyone seemed genuinely thrilled to be in such a beautiful room, eating such delicious food, and being with such lovely people. And there was no one-upmanship or posturing or 'Oh yeah? So when's *your* book coming out? Because *my* book . . .' And believe me, I've been at my fair share of those sorts of competitive yokes over the years and this was nothing like them.

I was having such a great time that the hours *rattled* by and before I knew it, it was four o'clock and I had to leave to ketch my flight to 'jet' back to Dublin (*definitely* 'jetting'), and as I was leaving I had a little chat with Lucy Mangan and, to be honest, I was afeerd of Lucy Mangan because she's such a passionate defender of the poorest and most deprived people in Britain that

I thought she'd dismiss me as a fluffy eejit airhead. But! Would you believe that we talked about shoes! Yes! We both have abnormally small feet and we bonded over what a pain in the arse it is to never be able to find shoes to fit.

Then off I went, and because everyone was so great and because it's not that long since I was so mad in the head that I couldn't even get out of bed, it was one of the best days of my entire life.

mariankeyes.com, October 2014.

FRIENDS AND FAMILY

This section contains bits and pieces culled from various newsletters written over the years, which will hopefully give you an idea of all the lovely people in my life.

Various Family Things

Tadhg and Susan are getting married! This is extra wonderful because Tadhg has always insisted he would never get married, and not that people need to be married or anything to show their commitment, but a wedding can be a great day out. (Also a reason to have a nervous breakdown if you were planning one anyway.)

The only condition Tadhg (which, incidentally, is my favourite man's name in the whole world and I'd love to write a hero called Tadhg but no one outside of Ireland would be able to pronounce it) . . . anyway, yes, the only condition Tadhg has put on things is that he doesn't want the big, traditional wedding, and this is fine by me because they're planning to get married abroad and we'll all get a holiday out of it.

Initial talk was of the Caribbean, but some older members of the family began cribbing about long flights, so that plan has been abandoned and now Italy is the word on the street.

I've never been to Italy, so I'm extra thrilled, but then yesterday my mother came up with some nugget of information that Irish people have been banned from getting married in Italy because they've been causing ruckus and commotion. I don't know if there's any truth to this rumour, but in fairness there might be because a reliable woman I know says that at any Irish wedding the most important question you must ask is 'What time does the fight start?'

Then, on Saturday 28th, baby Gabriel was born to Caron (partner of Chris, Himself's brother). This is thrilling, thrilling news. (I may have already told you that they're the parents of the beautiful Jude – two and a quarter) and there are celebrations all round. You can't beat a new baby for cheering everyone up.

Then, a couple of weeks ago, we had an unexpected visit from Ema (almost seven) and Luka (five). Niall and Ljiljana had to come from Prague for a funeral, and Himself and myself were put on childcare duties while they went to the funeral. And of course it's a bad business to profit from someone else's misfortune, but we had a lovely time.

I had great middle-class plans for a brisk bracing walk down the pier, pointing out educational things ('Did you know 4,000 tons of rock were blasted to build Dún Laoghaire harbour?' and other such boring facts), a healthy home-cooked lunch, educational games in the afternoon, followed by ten minutes of Nick Jr, if they'd eaten all of their organic beetroot.

Sadly, it didn't work out that way. First of all, Ema tried on all my shoes and went away with a pair of my very highest and later I got into trouble with Ljiljana about it, then she tried on all my lip glosses and later I got into trouble with Ljiljana about that too. Then, after Luka nearly killed himself messing on the treadmill (Ljiljana doesn't know about that, but if she had I would have got into trouble with her about that also), they watched *Monty Python and the Holy Grail* and learnt many new words (notably 'fuck').

Then we got into the car and went – yes! Where else? – to McDonald's, where they had – yes! – Happy Meals, with crappy toys, then Ema put a bag of excessively smelly fries into my Balenciaga handbag (which she had commandeered) and we traipsed desultorily around Dundrum shopping centre, buying things we didn't want and didn't need (except for my jacket, see below), then we went to see *Meet the Robinsons* and bought loads of sweets. This, I suppose, is the modern way.

In fairness I had a GREAT time and – of course – got a new jacket. I'd been looking for a jacket and had drawn a blank and then there it was! It's very nice. Navy, mid-thigh, canvas. My only anxiety is that it has two rows of buttons and I look a bit like Sergeant Pepper.

However, it is very nice, so nice that when my dad saw me in it he said, 'That's very nice.' Which was highly unexpected because he is a) blind as a bat, and b) a man. He called my mother into the hall in order for her to admire it alongside him, and she looked at me doubtfully and said, 'Has it an awful lot of buttons?'

Then Niall and Ljiljana came home from the funeral, and Ljiljana and I sat on the couch for about ten hours and discussed all the different vitamins and supplements we take every day. I know it sounds odd, but it was HUGELY enjoyable.

Then they went back to Prague and – I suppose triggered by the funeral – Mam and I got into a discussion one night about *her* funeral. She is incredibly specific about what she wants. She listed out a whole load of yokes – she doesn't want earrings while she's 'laid out'. She does want lipstick but she doesn't want blusher. Or maybe it's the other way round. Christ! I was meant to write it all down and she'll come back and haunt me if I get it wrong.

Honestly, there was a load of specifications: she wants to wear blue and white; she wants her 'good rosary beads' wound through her fingers; and she doesn't care what shoes she wears, because apparently your feet are covered, so no one will see. She doesn't want a biodegradable coffin because she's afraid it would be too flimsy and that while she was being carried down the aisle it might give way and she might topple out on top of the mourners and the shame of her bare feet would be there for all to see.

Although she is a humble woman, she was quite definite that she wanted 'a decent coffin'. Not necessarily made of 'endangered species', she said, but something 'decent'. THEN we had a discussion about who she wanted to carry her down the aisle. She thought the undertaker's would have 'lads' to do it, but I suggested that having family members doing it would be nicer. We tussled a little and then I got to use words that you don't often get to use in their correct context, which are, of course, 'Well [heavy sigh], it's your funeral.'

I know it sounds horribly morbid, but it was actually very funny. 'Uplifting' was the word my mother used. Odd, no?

Then, on the 17th, I was on *The Paul O'Grady Show* and it was FABULOUS. I love that show and he was so nice and funny. I have to tell you something. Dad watches Paul O'Grady and loves, loves, *loves* Buster the dog. I also (even though I fear dogs) love Buster the dog. (Buster the dog is Paul O'Grady's dog.) Anyway, when I heard I was going on the show I said to Dad, 'And I'll meet Buster!' 'Yes,' he sez, 'and the other dog.' 'What other dog?' I asked. And he said, 'The other dog, there's another dog that's on sometimes.' 'Is that right?' I said, suddenly going patronizing and like I was talking to a small child. That is because poor Dad sometimes gets the wrong end of the stick; that and the bad eyesight made me conclude that 'the other dog' was a figment of his elderly imagination. So on I go to the show and I'm telling everyone behind the scenes that Dad is a great fan of Buster and then someone said, 'But it's not Buster who's on today, it's Olga.'

'Olga?!' I said.

'Oh yes,' they said. 'There's another dog. Olga.'

The mythical second dog! I was rightly humbled! Rightly! Dad was right and I was wrong.

mariankeyes.com, April 2007.

France en Famille

At the start of May, we went to Euro Disney. I will list the cast
members: me, Himself, Mam, Dad, Rita-Anne, Jimmy, Caitríona
and Seán (who had come from New York), and Ema (seven),
Luka (five) and Ljiljana (not exactly sure, something in her thir-
ties), who had come from Prague.

I had worked round the clock before we went in the hope that
I'd finish the first draft of *This Charming Man* and therefore
would be able to kick up my heels with great relief in the com-
pany of Minnie Mouse, Tigger, etc., but sadly it was not to be. A
small but challenging portion still remained to be written and
hung over me like a guilt-making, anxious-making cloud as we
boarded the Minnie Mouse Express.

But never mind! Have you ever been to any of the Disney
places? Now, I wouldn't blame you for curling your lip in a sneer
and saying, 'You'd never catch me in any of them places. It's
nothing but a money-making exercise!' Well, I agree with you
that it probably IS a money-making exercise, but not JUST a
money-making exercise, because it's GORGEOUS.

There were a few hairy moments, such as when Dad overdid it
on the teacups and got 'a reel in the head' (Irish phrase meaning
'dizzy') and had to be led away, weaving all over Main Street USA,
bumping into small children and knocking their Mickey Mouse
ears off their heads, and he had to be reinstated in his hotel room
by my mother. It was her I felt for really because she'd got a

253

gleam in her eye and had fashioned plans for the Aerosmith ride which now came to naught.

And speaking of which, the Aerosmith ride is just TOO funny. It's a roller coaster, like other roller coasters, except that they play Aerosmith songs, so there you are doing loop-de-loops and hanging upside down and singing 'Walk This Way' and doing the 'nerdiddynerdiddyner' guitar bit.

Another hairy moment was on The Cars ride (or indeed *Les Voitures*) when I got chastised by an outraged Disney employee as I flicked the Vs at Himself, as Ema and I drove past Luka and Himself.

Then we went to Paris! Yes, for two days! Where Niall (father of Ema and Luka) joined us and the thing was, and none of us knew it, but Seán Ferguson had planned to ask Caitríona to marry him! Yes! In Paris! How romantic!

But everything conspired against him. She got a sore throat (oh yes, she is a Keyes, no doubt about it) and refused to go out in the cold for a romantic walk, where he had planned to find an ultra-romantic spot to pop the question.

So he shelved his plans until after dinner that evening. But guess what! We put on the news and there was a big newsflash saying, '40,000 rioters expected in central Paris this evening!' Because of the election, you see? That right-wing bloke Sarkovy, or whatever his name is, had been elected instead of the lovely Socialist WOMAN, and people – specifically the Algerian-descended youths in the outer suburbs whom Sarkovy had called 'scum' – were flooding into the Champs-Elysée to demonstrate their displeasure. As it happened, we were staying two feet from the Champs-Elysée, and the restaurant we were going to for our dinner was approx eighteen inches from the Champs-Elysée.

As we went out for dinner the fuss was beginning, but after

dinner, when we emerged from the restaurant, preparations for the riot were in full flow. There were riot police EVERYWHERE and sounds of shouting and general chaos.

I love the French so I do: if they're not striking, they're rioting. As a nation, they really *care* about things.

At this stage Seán Ferguson was a sweaty wreck but nothing would divert him from his plan, so somehow – and God knows how exactly he managed it – he persuaded Caitríona to go down to the Seine. Himself turned to me, extended a gentlemanly arm and said, 'Care to take a stroll up to view the riots?'

Well, being an old lefty, as indeed Himself is, I couldn't think of anything nicer. Sadly we couldn't get very close, what with barriers and armed police and all that, but as luck would have it, we were standing outside the very apartment block where Sarkovy was having his celebratory dinner ('may it choke him' – Irish phrase meaning 'Well, yes, I hope some of your dinner gets lodged in your oesophagus because I don't like you') and there were 4 million television cameras waiting outside, so we waited too and every time one of the citizens of the building came down to put out his bin or leave a note for the milkman or give his dog his last walk of the evening, the crowd thought it was the right-winger and alternately cheered and booed (me and Himself booed of course. I also shouted, 'Shame on you, you smelly right-winger. You can't go round calling people "scum" then refusing to apologize for it. Also it is VERY WRONG to wear a double-breasted blazer with jeans').

So by the time we got back to the hotel, the deed was done, the question had been popped, the answer had been in the affirmative, a ring had been produced, the most beautiful diamond, very, very pretty, very Caitríona, and all the Keyesez were sitting in the lobby of the hotel drinking champagne! *Fantastique!*

mariankeyes.com, May 2007.

Sickest Family in the Whole of Ireland

I find that the best way to enjoy December is to say no to 99 out of every 100 party invitations which come my way. In fact, saying yes but then simply *not turning up* is even better. That way no one badgers me to change my mind and all the other guests get so scuttered they don't even notice that I'm actually at home, tucked up in bed, eating Pringles and watching *Strictly Come Dancing*.

Sometimes I even think about pretending afterwards that I was actually *at* the knees-up and saying things like, 'God almighty, you were in TOP form there on Saturday night.' And because there is such a pervasive sense of shame about everything everyone does in December, they'll think, 'Christ, I don't even remember meeting her, I'll really have to knock off the sauce come January.' But I am a kind person, one who has experienced plenty of shame herself, so I refrain from that sort of cruelty.

At Christmas, inevitably all the Keyesez got sick, and I know I'm always telling you about our familial ill health, but this is a real blockbuster of a story and nothing short of hilarious. First I have to give you the list of characters: Mam, Dad, Niall, his wife Ljiljana, their daughter Ema (seven), their son Luka (six), my sister Caitríona, her fiancé Seán, my sister Rita-Anne, her husband Jimmy, my brother Tadhg, Himself and me. (Tadhg's fiancée Susan was in Gorey, Co Wexford, with her family.)

Okay, so there are thirteen of us and it all kicks off on the Thursday before Christmas when Dad suddenly started puking his guts up. The puking continued round the clock and when Mam suggested ringing a doctor, Dad begged her not to, as he said he was obviously SO VERY SERIOUSLY ILL that the doctor would immediately summon an ambulance and send him to A&E, where he would have to lie on a trolley for a month and compete for the nurses' attention with stab victims and those sporting gunshot wounds and no one would care whether Dad lived or died as he is an oul' lad anyway and is bound to croak sooner rather than later. (And they wonder where I get my dramatic hypochondriac streak from?)

On Friday night the Praguers arrive to stay in my parents' house, and on Saturday Dad returns from the brink of death, only for Ljiljana and Ema to fall foul of the lurgy and spend Christmas Eve thrun in the bed, competing for puking space in a basin.

I should also stress at this stage that every bed in the house was full, as the four Praguers and the two home from NY were staying with Mam and Dad, and as Susan was away Tadhg also likes to stay (but he had to sleep on the couch because, despite my mammy's fondness for collecting beds, there wasn't one for him).

However, miraculously, everyone is well for Christmas Day . . . but on the following day Caitríona is struck down.

The next day – the 27th – Himself and myself go to John and Shirley, his parents in England, and it is the mercy of God that we did, because we would surely not be alive to tell the tale otherwise.

Parallel to all of this is that Himself had been badly injured tending to his reindeers. For the past God knows how many years he's had Rudy on the porch roof, a beautiful electric reindeer, to light people's way. But this year, Rudy got retired and two beautiful new reindeers (as yet nameless) arrived and took their place on the porch roof. But they kept falling over and Himself kept having to lean out the window and pick them up again, and in one of those leaning-out sessions he badly bruised his rib and is still not able to cough or laugh without intense pain.

At John and Shirley's everything was well and civilized and peaceful, and when I rang home on the 28th for a little chat, I discovered that all hell had broken loose in Ireland. They were being felled like ninepins, *ninepins*, *mes amies*. Caitríona was still sick, Dad had relapsed, Seán had succumbed, Rita-Anne had it so bad that Jimmy had to cancel his flight to Cheltenham to see his family, then when it seemed that R-A was well enough for Jimmy to leave, Jimmy was struck down and had to catch the plane dry-retching and carrying a bag to throw up in. Then Niall got it and had to cancel their New Year family trip to Dunmore East.

But worse, far worse than the puking, was the cabin fever. There were ten of them in a house designed for far fewer people, and competition for bed space and puking opportunities was intense. I have it on good authority that they all 'turned' on each other.

In the midst of it all, my mother and Rita-Anne deserted the place and moved in down the road to my house, where they savoured the peace and quiet and germ-free air with much relish.

Also, oh I totally forgot about this – I LOVE this, this is my very favourite! On Christmas night Luka accidentally drank a bottle of cough mixture (he thought it was Lucozade, which doesn't make any sense to me) and he had to be forced to drink gallons of water, which made *him* puke.

In one of my phone calls home I asked how Tadhg was doing, as no one had mentioned him for a couple of days, and there was this startled little pause and they said, 'Tadhg, God, you know, now that you mention him, we haven't seen Tadhg in a while.' But no one was particularly worried as it was assumed that his disappearance was drink-related, and sure enough, didn't he turn up in Siam Thai on the evening of the 29th, tucking into a beef curry and acting as if nothing was untoward.

So there we are – is that not impressive? I am upgrading our title to Sickest Family in the Whole of Ireland.

mariankeyes.com, December 2007.

Caitríona and Seán's Wedding

With Caitríona's wedding and all, there have been millions of people in the house for what feels like months and months. First the Praguers arrived, and because we've got a Wii yoke they took up permanent residence; meanwhile, we'd had the lovely, lovely Dylan staying with us, and none of this is to say that it was unpleasant, because it was delightful, but chaotic, you know. Ema being eight and Luka being seven and Dylan being three months, it was all go.

The house was permanently filthy and you couldn't go two steps without stepping on a baby alarm, or kicking over a glass of milk abandoned by Luka, or breaking your neck skidding on all my shoes, which Ema had taken out of my wardrobe and strewn throughout the hall.

Then people started arriving for the wedding – Anne Marie and Jack (nineteen months) and Caitríona's friend Denise.

Meanwhile, many other people from New York were billeted nearby, and our house became Pitta-Bread-and-Hummus Central (it was all I was able to concentrate on in the supermarket – pitta bread and hummus is always safe. And quiche. And fecking Ben & Jerry's, more of which anon).

We had the hen night in the Powerscourt Hotel, a very glitzy, de luxe joint, and the next day we went to the spa, which I was very interested in because so many Irish spas are crap. (It's a feminist issue: because they're mostly used by women there's an attitude of 'Ah sure, give them any oul' shite, any crappy oul' rub with a bit of lavender oil and they'll be delighted. Call it sixty minutes, but only give them forty-three, fling around the words "pamper" and "deserve" and make sure you charge them a fortune.')

But this one (it's by Espa) is the real thing. Expensive, yes, undeniably expensive. I feel it's unseemly, going to a fancy-Dan spa in these credit-crunchy times. All I'm saying is that although it's costly, you get what you pay for. *More* than get.

Then we had a week of rehearsals and hair and make-up trials and fake tan and pedicures and a rehearsal dinner with forty-five of us, then the day itself, which was truly miraculous and it didn't rain and Caitríona looked STUNNING, like Grace Kelly and Gwyneth Paltrow, only far more beautiful, and it was all really great.

Then I sort of thought that everything would go quiet, but it didn't, because although the wedding was on the Saturday, we were still overrun with people (I'm not saying it wasn't lovely, because it was) until the Wednesday, and I was so knackered from toasting pitta breads and I'd slipped way, way off the sugar-free horse and was eating rings around myself, shoving ice cream into my clob at all hours of the day and night – you see, the thing is normally I wouldn't have ice cream in the house because it would drive me insane and I'd have to get up in the middle of the night and eat it simply to stop it badgering me, but because of the visitors the place was full of all kinds of lovely grub and between the high emotion and the tiredness, I couldn't resist. I'm fecking HUGE and struggling to get back on the straight and narrow, but it's hard work.

THEN I went to Austria and Germany on a book tour. And although I was destroyed before I even started, I had a wonderful time. I LOVE Germans, I find them warm and polite and – yes! – punctual. Nothing wrong with being punctual, the world would be a far nicer place if people were ON TIME and didn't make fun of poor Virgos such as myself for wanting to puke if I'm ten minutes late for something.

Which brings me neatly to my birthday, which was on 10 September. I started the day in stunningly beautiful Hamburg, then on to Mannheim, which not many people have heard of but it was a nice place, and at that night's reading, everyone sang 'Happy Birthday' to me, which made me happy.

It was an uplifting and rewarding tour – there were five of us travelling together – and even though we were working and travelling a lot from city to city, we had a (well, I did anyway) gorgeous time, and on my birthday, on the train to Mannheim, a man carrying an icebox full of Magnums arrived in our carriage. Isn't that the most amazing thing you ever heard? Like, they weren't *free*, you had to pay for them, 2.5 euro a go, but we all had one and afterwards my German companions said that they'd never before heard of such a phenomenon, a man laden with Magnums on the Hamburg-to-Mannheim train. Which made me wonder if I'd dreamt it, but if so, we'd all had the same dream.

On the Friday we went to London, because Himself was going to Tadhg's stag do in Brighton and had to drink forty pints and lie on the couch all the next day, roaring for a bucket, then on the Saturday was Suzanne's fortieth birthday, also Seán and Caitríona were back from their honeymoon in Italy, so we all met up.

THEN, when we got back to Dublin, both myself and Himself had massive dental work done. THEN my dad took a tumble and cut his face and broke his glasses and got a terrible fright. THEN myself, Himself, Mam and Dad all had to go to Newbridge to look for Mam's mother-of-the-groom rig-out for Tadhg's wedding (she would go nowhere else but Newbridge, even though there are hundreds of shops in Dublin, but shur feck it, what harm is there in indulging her).

Dad was going round with his cut face and crooked glasses offering his styling services to other customers, and I'm sure the people in the shop thought I was guilty of elder abuse and that I must have pushed him and broken his glasses, because I kept shouting at him to sit down and stop helping the other shoppers.

THEN on the Friday night it was Susan's hen night.

THEN on the Sunday it was Dylan's christening.

And as I write, it's going to be Himself's birthday on Saturday, also his father's eightieth, so we're going to the UK for that, then back for Tadhg and Susan's wedding.

Himself is after doing something to his back and he's not able to sit in his chair, he has to type his emails while kneeling on the floor, and last night in bed he couldn't lie on his right side because his back hurt, then he couldn't sleep on his left side because his back hurt, then when he lay on his back, his back DIDN'T hurt but it triggered his persistent cough, so in the end he had to get up and go downstairs and sleep sitting up on the couch. For the love of God!

I made him go to the doctor because I'm sick of it, and I expected much resistance because even if his head has fallen off his shoulders and is rolling around on the floor, bumping into the legs of chairs, he always says, 'I'm fine, I'm GRAND, what could a doctor do for me?'

THEN Himself and I had a scrap about the meaning of 'persistent'. As in me saying, 'While you're at it, talk to the doctor about your persistent cough.' And he said, 'What persistent cough?' And I said, 'That cough of yours that has persisted for the past week,' and he said, 'It's a cough, I grant you, but it's not persistent,' and I said, 'But if it has persisted for a week, which it fecking well has, then it's PERSISTENT.'

Of course all of this was just delaying tactics by him to get out of going to the doctor.

But he WENT to the doctor and got a prescription for Solpa-dol. Do you know it? A delightful codeine-based painkiller. I had it last November for a throat infection and, *mes amies*, I was OUT OF MY HEAD on it. Extremely pleasant, so it was. Well worth the sore throat!

Luckily Himself is a stoic and fears painkillers, thinking if he takes more than four Anadins a year he's in danger of being 'addicted'. Amateur. Therefore I ferried away his lovely packet of tablets to my medicine press (as big as other people's walk-in wardrobes) and I planned to fob him off with Nurofen, which is grand but nothing like as nice as Solpadol, and he will never know.

Meanwhile, I was wishing for something painful to befall me so I'd have a legitimate excuse to lie in bed OUT OF MY HEAD, mildly itchy (that's the codeine) but otherwise in great form.

But then Himself approached me and ASKED – yes, ASKED – for some Solpadol. He claimed to be in terrible pain. I turned down his request. I said that he wasn't meant to take lovely tab-lets on an empty stomach, so he did something unprecedented, he said he would *eat something even though it isn't a mealtime* (he is very, very, oh yes, VERY different from me). I will give you his exact words. He said, 'I will have a Solpadol sangwidge.'

In the guise of concern, I snapped two caplets out of their foil and gave them to him with a glass of water, in the hope of obscur-ing the fact that I was fobbing him off with Nurofen. He'll be grand.

Anyway, he's going to see a specialist soon. He must have slipped a disc or something, God love him.

mariankeyes.com, September 2008.

Various Family Events

We'll kick off with Himself's ongoing health debacle. He was sent for an MRI scan, and while we were waiting for the results he was in absolute agony and my old friend Solpadol wasn't even touching the sides of the pain, so I flung myself on the mercy of the neck pain specialist (because it's always easier to do it for someone else, no?) and he gave Himself some (to quote the pharmacist) 'very potent painkillers' – MORE potent than Solpadol!

But even they didn't do the trick. It was late Friday afternoon and we were in Dundrum with baby Dylan, and Himself was grey and sweaty and glazed-eyed with the pain, and I thought, 'Cripes, we can't go into the weekend with him in this much agony,' so I rang the specialist again but couldn't get him, so I rang the local GP and they had to see the 'potent painkiller' prescription before they'd do anything and it was all very messy.

But at the eleventh hour, just before the chemist shut, the scrip was faxed through and the receptionist scored a NEW scrip for (and once again I quote) 'opiate analogues', even stronger than the ones that were stronger than Solpadol, and if they didn't work, the next step was to admit Himself into hospital and put him in traction and on a morphine drip.

God, it was horrific, but I was convinced at this stage that Himself had slipped a disc and that it would all be fixable, but it turns out that no! No disc was slipped! The result of the scan shows he has some sort of degenerative condition where some bone in his

neck is growing against 'a bundle of nerves' and that's what's caus-
ing all the pain.

We looked it up – it's called Cervical Spondy-something or
other. I wish I could tell you more, but every time I tried to read
it I thought I was going to faint and had to stop before I toppled
over and crashed face-first into the keyboard.

It's horrible when someone you love is in pain. I wish I could
take the pain from him and feel it myself. (Of course it's very easy
for me to say that, as such a transaction is impossible and if it
WAS possible, I'd probably waste no time trying to give the pain
back fairly lively – 'Take it, take it, for the love of Christ, take it!')

He had to embark on a variety of anti-arthritis pills and madzer
painkillers and wait for two long, horrible, agony-riddled weeks
for a series of steroid injections. I was convinced that the steroid
injections would fix him entirely, but no, when the day rolled
around and he got the injection, the specialist said that physio
was the next step and if there wasn't an improvement, Himself
would have to go under the knife and have the offending bit of
sticky-outy bone removed (i.e. sawed off).

Meanwhile, TONS of stuff was happening. Including poor Him-
self's birthday, which he shares with his dad, and it was his dad
John's eightieth birthday and we went to Saffron Walden for it, and
I suppose between this far more dramatic celebration and Him-
self's agony, Himself's birthday was somewhat overshadowed.

THEN no sooner were we back from England than we repaired
to County Clare for Tadhg and Susie's wedding! In Gregans Hotel
in the wilds of the Burren. It rained so much on the way down
that the roads were impassable (honestly). *Father Ted* was filmed
in Clare, and you know the episode where a priest gets trapped in
Craggy Island Parochial House because the bad weather meant
'they've taken in the roads'? Well, it was a bit like that.

Himself, maddened by the cocktail of drugs he was on, took a notion to go some bizarre back route known only to him and his fevered imagination, and because I forgot that he was out of his head and stone mad, I let him, and by the time we'd been driving on a single-track boreen for half an hour, getting precisely nowhere, it was too late.

Anyway, we eventually got to the hotel, and the biblical-style rain ceased for the day of the actual wedding and it was blue and blustery and very beautiful. (I LOVE County Clare.) Susan looked stunning and everyone was very happy and it was all great fun.

Newly-weds Caitríona and Seán were over from New York, and Niall, Lilers, Ema and Luka were over from Prague, and apart from the hand-to-hand combat that ensued as we all tried to get a go of Dylan, we had a great time. (Dylan is now nearly five months! And the most sweet-natured, smiley, squashy creature you could hope to meet. And he has gorgeous bright red hair!)

mariankeyes.com, October 2008.

Himself's Health Improves

Well, the great news is that Himself is much improved. Things were bad, bad, bad and he continued to be in appalling pain or out of his head on painkillers or both, and there was no let-up, and I know that it wasn't my agony so I've no right to whinge, but like I said last month, when someone you love is in pain, it's horrible to witness, and suddenly I remembered all those articles I'd read about people living with chronic pain, people who've been in car crashes or are cursed with bad arthritis, and I realized that for every day of their life they're in agony and their main purpose every day is to manage that pain, and suddenly I was wondering what 'manage' meant.

It made me realize how very lucky he and I'd been previous to this. That we'd been going along, not realizing how very beautiful our lives were, simply because we were living each day without pain.

Mam is forever saying 'Your health is your wealth', which usually generates much mockery from me and the rest of her children, but the older I get the more I'm inclined to agree.

The funny thing is that every night I try to write a gratitude list and one of the things that regularly appears is 'Today no terrible disasters happened to me or anyone I love', so in a way I HAD been grateful for the luxury of ordinariness and I was desperate to return to those halcyon, pain-free, anxiety-free days.

Then! Unexpectedly a corner was turned! Himself went back to his physio, who did some fiendish jiggery-pokery on the place where the nerves and his spine intersected, which released him from much of the pain, and he came home armed with a set of exercises, which the physio claimed would be a great help.

He's meant to do them for ten minutes three times a day, and in solidarity I am his coach and timekeeper and I wear a hoodie and sweats and carry a stopwatch. First of all he has to nod his head vigorously and while he's doing that I shout, 'Yes! Yes! Yes!'

Then he has to shake his head vigorously and I shout, 'No! No! No!'

Then he has to waggle his head in a strange, inconclusive way and I shout, 'I don't know! I don't know! I don't know!'

Then he has to do rotating movements with his head, like I used to do in the warm-ups in the aerobic classes I did in the 1980s, and I shout, 'Round we go! Round we go! Round we go!'

At this point he tries to look at the watch and I say, 'It's only been four and a half minutes, keep going,' and he objects and says that it must be at least seven minutes, but I shout, 'Funky chicken! Funky chicken!' and I hide the watch inside my hoodie.

Defeated, he commences doing jutting movements with his head (like he's doing the funky chicken), and I sing Earth, Wind and Fire songs to get him in the funky chicken mood.

Then he has to do some funny business with a ball and a wall, where he sort of headbutts the ball against the wall using his neck muscles. I am still looking for the best song to accompany this, but 'Saturday Night's Alright for Fighting' has been my default thus far.

Meanwhile, Christmas looms. God, what a wretched business it is, and hard to believe that this time last year we were swanning around, so bounteously laden with worldly goods that we were altruistically giving each other goats on behalf of communities in the developing world.

This year, seeing as the world economy has gone into melt-down, it's more like, feck the Ethiopian farmers and where's me Body Shop gift basket! I am, of course, joking! All I'm saying is that things are very different this year. Lots of people won't be buying anything – goats OR Body Shop gift baskets.

I am getting Himself a yearly subscription to Sheridans Cheese Club for his Christmas present. It's what I got him last year and he says it's the best present anyone's ever given him, and what it entails is that on the second Wednesday of every month a foul-smelling parcel shows up at the front door (usually flung by the postman, who yells, 'For the love of God! The stench in the van!').

When the foul-smelling parcel is unwrapped, it is found to contain four different cheeses and a long biography on each of them: the farm they grew up in, their nationality, age, favourite member of Girls Aloud, all that business. I couldn't be bothered myself, cheese is cheese, but Himself gets a great kick out of it.

Regarding the worldwide economic meltdown, Himself says that if there's any way that people can, we should continue spend-ing. This causes me to narrow my eyes suspiciously at him and conclude he's after buying a load more CDs. 'It's basic Keynesian economics,' he keeps saying, and I keep replying, 'What the hell would you know?' And then I remember that actually he has an MA in Economics and, wrong-footed, I shout, 'Time for your exercises! Dance! Boogie Wonderlaaaa-aaand!'

mariankeyes.com, November 2008.

Nephews

There are several 'clusters' of nephews in play, in my life. I will commence with the Redzers, who are Dylan (four) and Oscar (two), who are the children of my sister Rita-Anne and her husband Jimmy. Anyway, myself and Himself went with them on a little mini-holiday (Friday to Monday) to the Powerscourt Hotel. Now, I make no bones about it, I am besotted with the place. It's odd: when it was first built in the heyday of the Celtic Tiger I withheld my judgement, I decided I wasn't going to be easily seduced by it . . . and then I went there . . .

Oh God, where do I start?

Well it's only half an hour's drive from my house. So in thirty minutes I went from crowded Dún Laoghaire to the mountains and the trees and the greenery and the lakes and the peace of Wicklow. No airports, no planes, no seven-hour drives, just thirty minutes in the vehicle.

We parked the car and already my shoulders were loosening and lowering.

Rita-Anne and the Redzers had also just arrived, and in we went and the welcome we got was lovely. The staff are so nice – a lot of 'foncy' hotels offer 'Snotty Disdainful Service' under their list of amenities, but not here. They're very warm and they even have a little 'pretend' check-in for nippers, so they don't get bored and start flinging themselves around, roaring and shouting, while the real check-in goes on.

Then we went to our lovely rooms, with views of the Sugar Loaf, and in the Redzers' room they'd put in a 'special' (that's what he kept calling it) roll-out bed for Dylan and a cage (i.e. cot) for Oscar, only he *is* a bit of a wild man, so that's why you could easily visualize him in a cage. Also, for 'the younger guests' there are mini-bathrobes! And biscuits! And free milk in the fridge.

Then it was time for everyone – even the younger guests – to put on their togs and bathrobes and go for a swim. And, oh my God, the pool! It's all mood-lit and almost womb-like.

In general, I fear the water. Not fear it, in that it might *drown* me; I fear it, in that it might *wet* me. You couldn't pay me to have a bath. I DO, I must stress this, I DO know my duties as a member of society, so of course I have plentiful showers. But I forced myself into this beautiful pool because I knew it would calm me. And it did.

Then it was time to watch the Redzers eat their tea! Despite his tender years Dylan has already been to the Powerscourt Hotel (we went for Dad's eightieth back in March), so he knows all about room service and he thinks it's the most wonderful thing ever invented!

I had a quick (and I do mean quick) shower and changed into my nightdress and went in my bare feet with Himself to watch the tea-eating. (This information becomes relevant very shortly.) Jimmy (husband of Rita-Anne) was after arriving and then in came Tibor with the grub – Tibor is Mr Room Service, he's from Hungary.

The chip-eating began with gusto – then the most godawful racket started up. It was the fire alarm. It was one of those noises that make you feel like your head is going to explode with the vibrations – they probably use them in Guantánamo Bay – but like the Irish people we are, we calmly continued eating our chips. 'Just a drill,' one of us would say, from time to time, while our heads started to judder and melt. 'Are you eating your gherkin? Can I have it?'

All of a sudden, it dawned on us, as one, that maybe it wasn't a drill, that maybe there *was* a fire. Giving the few remaining chips a wistful farewell glance, the six of us hurried from the room, three of us in our jim-jams (Dylan, Oscar and me).

'Don't go back for anything!' somebody shouted, and out in the corridor other people (all of them, sadly, fully dressed) were pouring from their rooms. Instinctively we made for the lifts – and then we remembered everything we knew about lifts and fires, so we recoiled and started hurrying down the stairs, Dylan and Oscar being carried. It was high drama, my amigos, high drama.

We emerged into the Sugar Loaf Lounge, which is in the lobby, and there was no alarm going off there. Instead there were a load of civilized people wearing chinos or nice frocks and sipping glasses of wine and looking in alarm at our ragged barefoot band. 'Fire alarm,' I said weakly, pointing upwards, suddenly aware that I didn't have any make-up on. But we weren't allowed to go back to our rooms – the noise was still clanging away up there and a load of men wearing belts full of tools were heading upstairs with purpose. So we settled ourselves on a couple of couches and when a lovely member of staff offered us a drink, we said, 'Feck it! Why not? We're on our holiers!'

The strange thing was that it felt very homey. Apart from the worry that some random stranger might catch sight of the soles of my hideous feet, we were all quite relaxed and happy there. No one – certainly not the staff – behaved as if there was anything untoward in the sight of a grown woman sitting in the lobby of this lovely foncy hotel in her nightdress. (May I stress that my nightdress was my usual long-sleeved, high-necked, floor-length, stripy jersey item from Marimekko; at least it had the virtue of being very modest.)

We all had a lovely time and then two weeks later Himself and myself went to Englandshire to visit his parents, his brother Chris, his partner Caron and their two boys, Jude (seven) and Gabe (five). Our visit coincided with the annual Cambridge Folk Festival, which is nothing like as bad as it sounds. For a start it's not just folk music (although there *was* some 'As I roved out one dewy morn, I spied a maid all fair and square', etc.). And it's not like a festival in that people aren't falling around scuttered drunk. It's all very mellow.

People spread out rugs and read the *Guardian* and eat falafels and buy jester's hats made of felt and occasionally go to one of the three music tents to hear some music.

Now, I readily confess to not being a music-lover. I'd be quite happy to be described as a music-hater. Nevertheless, it was all fine. The sun shone on the Saturday and then, from Stage 1, I heard the oddest noise. It was music . . . but I liked it. 'This I have to see,' I said and pushed my way through the crowds – the great thing about being in a place full of *Guardian* readers is that no one feels they can chide you for pushing – and I got right up near the front. My information was that this was the Keb' Mo' band, and I swear to God, I spent the next forty-five minutes transfixed, goosebumps all over my body. The Keb' Mo' man was singing sort of soul, and sometimes he was more bluesy; he has the most captivating voice, like melted chocolate, and the charisma was rolling off him like a sea mist.

When I got back to base camp, everyone fell on me and gave me a right scolding. 'We were worried!' they said. 'We didn't know where you'd gone!' Then, when they heard I'd gone to see a band, they were even more worried.

Nephews

Keb' Mo' was *almost* the highlight of the Cambridge Folk Festival. My two actual highlights were 1) Jude 'cycling' me a smoothie – do you know of such a thing? He hops up on a special bike and cycles like mad and the energy generated powers a blender. And 2) Gabe holding my hand when we went to get ice cream! It's the little things, isn't it . . .

mariankeyes.com, August 2012.

Redzer-Sitting

Right! Rita-Anne asked me if I'd mind the Redzers and I was keen – yes, keen – to help because they are two little balls of delight, but knew that I alone would be insufficient for the task, for they are full of vim, but Himself couldn't help on account of going to Watford for the football and especially on account of Watford having done so well this season and, as we speak, definitely in the play-offs, which is very good! Yes!

So I asked Gwen if she'd help and Gwen said yes, and oh, my amigos, this was great, great news as Gwen is officially GWN (good with nippers). She really has the gift: she has a handbag full of stickers and just has a great 'way' with childer. Whereas I do NOT have a great way with childer, because somehow they intuit that I've no natural authority and am a total pushover and therefore they do NOTHING I ask them to.

So anyway, yesterday I arrived at Redzerville and Gwen had already been there for two hours and I expected the house to be bedlam because whenever the Redzers come to me they zoom through the house like a pair of red-haired tornados, rearranging everything, and we find the oddest things in the oddest of places for months afterwards. (Do not get me started on my beloved home bingo kit is all I will say . . .)

But no, as good as gold they were, sitting at the kitchen table, doing colouring.

Then we left and proceeded to the nearby shopping paradise

of Dundrum, where we aimed for MaccyD's. The Redzers don't often go to MaccyD's, so this was a big, big, big treat, which they'd been looking forward to for ages. I will digress slightly here and tell you that Oscar (Redzer No 2), who is super strong-willed, would only wear his Cheltenham Town football outfit for the visit, which is slightly (quite a bit) too large for him, and red socks so long they went up to his thighs. He cut a dashing figure.

To get to MaccyD's we had to go through House of Fraser, and the thing is I wanted to get Gwen a little present because Gwen is a really good person who has been incredibly kind to me in a multitude of ways and I knew Gwen was looking for a Clinique Chubby Eyes Stick in Bountiful Beige and her fella had tried and failed to purchase it in Manchester and in various duty-frees.

So, as I discovered myself to be actually *passing* the Clinique stand in House of Fraser, I brought our cavalcade to an abrupt halt and asked of the lady, 'Have you any Bountiful Beige?'

'No,' says she, 'and we won't be getting any until the end of April.'

Distressed, I exclaimed, 'There's a world shortage!'

'Yes,' she replies, 'and it's all your fault for tweeting about it.'

For some reason that made us all fall around the place laughing, even the Redzers, who are young and innocent and who know nothing of Chubby Eyes or tweeting but who are essentially upbeat souls who enjoy a good laugh.

All went well in the McDonald's, including the Happy Meal toy, which the lads were very excited about. Oscar didn't finish his chips, but Rita-Anne had warned us this might happen and under no circumstances were we to leave them behind because he'd be looking for them later, so we wrapped them up in a napkin into a little parcel which he insisted on carrying himself. Oscar, it has to be said, is a great man for carrying things. Oscar always has something in his hand.

However, unbeknown to either myself or Gwen, Dylan had stashed half his hamburger in his pocket. (This detail becomes important later.)

Out in the Dundrum concourse, I put it to the lads that we go to Harvey Nichols to 'look at make-up'. The lads, who are always positive, seemed happy enough to 'look at make-up', even if they had no idea what it entailed.

But the thing was, I had an ulterior motive. See, I had a plan to try to get something nice for Gwen, seeing as the Chubby Eyes were embargoed till the end of the month.

So in we went and I strong-armed her to the Hourglass counter (I would have brought her to the Tom Ford counter but that is only in Brown Thomas) and shoved her at the lovely lady and said, 'My friend here needs a foundation. Will you look after her?'

Next thing poor Gwen is 'taking the stool' and the Redzers were left in my sole care, and the thing is that even though there are only two of them, it feels more like a hundred and I am a poor figure of authority at the best of times.

They were *extremely* interested in the make-up, the pair of them, EXTREMELY interested. And full of zip and vim after their lunch. They were grabbing lipsticks and scribbling on their faces and sticking their fingers into eyeshadows and thinking they were like finger-paints and putting stripes of colour everywhere, and I was racing around trying to control them but it was like herding weasels and they were slipping like mercury from my grasp and thinking it was all hilarious and I could feel the aghast looks of the other shoppers, that is to say, the *real* Harvey Nichols shoppers.

Oscar had managed to procure a pile of Chantecaille eye-shadows, a collection worth about a thousand euro, in his squishy little paws and was all set to depart for home with them, and

Dylan was trying out the new Hourglass illuminating powder, which isn't even officially launched yet, and it was absolute mayhem and poor Gwen was up on the stool, being done, and in all fairness the Harvey Nichols staff remained cool. Which was good, because there was worse to come. Oh, much worse.

Gwen eventually agreed to let me buy her something (an Hourglass primer), mostly because she just wanted it all to be over, I think, and she came down off the stool and tried to put a shape on the lads but it was too late, the damage was done, they were wildly overexcited and in fairness who would blame them? I too get very excited around make-up, especially new stuff.

I went to the till, and Gwen had the bright idea of taking the boys to look at the fish in the tank at the Crème de la Mer counter, and in fairness the fish *did* have a calming effect because the shrieks died down for a while.

Then Dylan produced the hamburger half that he'd put in his pocket for 'later', and of course Oscar had his leftover chips, so they took a notion to sit on the floor and have an impromptu picnic, right in the Harvey Nichols doorway.

Which, even writing about it now, is still making me laugh. And I think everyone came out of it well. The Harvey Nichols employees were really nice, no one made us feel anything other than welcome, and the Redzers' *joie de vivre* and their total unselfconsciousness and ability to be spontaneous and in the moment was lovely to behold.

mariankeyes.com, April 2013.

Novena-Max

Not so long ago, I decided to do a reading/Q&A/meet'n'greet-style event in the Pavilion Theatre in Dún Laoghaire. And I was absolutely thrilled because it's my local theatre and I'd been there many times in the past few years to see other authors – the lovely Kate Mosse, the magnificent Joseph O'Connor, the wonderful Kate Atkinson, the hilarious Armistead Maupin, the wise Ruby Wax, the beloved Paul Howard aka Ross O'Carroll-Kelly, and I *think* (but can't be certain, because my memory isn't what it was) the delightful Alexander McCall Smith (I saw him *somewhere*, it *could* have been the Pavilion).

And at all the yokes, I'd be sitting there and enjoying the show, but there was always a bit of sadness because I'd have loved the opportunity to do something similar myself, but it couldn't happen because of me being too mad in the head and not able to for the excitement/stress/having to talk.

But suddenly I was well enough to be doing it and I can't tell you what it means to me. The plan was that I'd read from my new book (*The Woman Who Stole My Life*) and then the most lovely person, Maria Dickenson, would interview me. And then it'd be over to the audience, who could ax me anything. And I mean ANYTHING!

Following the axing, we would have a GLITTERIN' raffle! My beloved niece Ema and beloved nephew Luka would be there to make sure everyone's names were in the Salad Spinner of Happiness.

I'd have loved the Redzers to be there too, but it'd be past their bedtime. But Mam announced she was coming, so I decided to ax her if one of the prizes in the GLITTERIN' raffle could be to win one of her novenas, because her novenas are POWER-FUL STUFF – novena-max! You'd be sure to get your intention.

But when I put it to her she visibly recoiled and straightened herself in her seat and her cheeks went a bit pink and she said, quite stiffly, 'No, Marian. Sorry, but no. That wouldn't be right. That wouldn't be respectful.'

So I had a little think about it and said, 'I suppose you're right, Mammy, I suppose you're right.'

Then she brightened a bit and sez, 'How about I say a prayer for EVERYONE'S intentions?'

And yes, I thought, that would be nice.

Then . . . oh yes . . . *then* I could see the wheels in her head turning and she opened her mouth to speak and I thrust my palm at her and said, 'No, Mammy! No leading the entire audience in a decade of the rosary!'

'But –'

'No, Mammy, not even if it's one of the Glorious Mysteries.'

'How did you know I was going to suggest a Glorious Mystery?'

'Because I just do, Mam. I am intuitive.'

Then she muttered some things under her breath and I'm sure they weren't complimentary about me and we sat in huffy silence for approximately three minutes, thirty-seven seconds, until she exclaimed, 'I need you to buy something for me.'

Immediately she was raging with herself for 'breaking' first, but see, because she doesn't know how to work the interwebs I have her over a barrel when it comes to website purchases. She refers to my tablet as 'the Magic Yoke'.

So she produced some quare little booklet that had been put

through her letter box and points out a GANKY-looking press and sez, 'Should I get this one? Or . . .' Then she thumbed a few (obviously very well-perused) pages and pointed to an equally ganky-looking press: 'Or this? Which one should I buy?'

'Neither of them, Mammy,' sez I. 'That's which one you should buy.'

'Which? One?' And she went a bit steely, so I said, 'Right, that one.' (I picked the first one, because really what difference could it make, they were both SHOCKEN.)

Then we were friends again and she said, 'Will that man be there at your yoke? That man that you like?'

'Tom Dunne?'

'Yes. Him.'

'I doubt it, Mam. Anyway, Tom has to work in the evenings, his show starts at 10 p.m.'

'I thought he was on in the mornings.'

'They've changed him. He's on in the evenings now.'

Another little silence followed, then Mam said, all casual like, 'That husband of yours is a great man. A GREAT man. God was looking out for you when he sent Himself to you. The day you met Himself was the luckiest day of your life. You were STEEPED in good luck. STEEPED, I'm telling you. STEE–'

'All right!' sez I. 'I get the message! I LOVE Himself! He's the only man for me, ever, and the Tom Dunne thing, it's only a bit of harmless fun, like looking at pictures of houses on sale in Killiney. Or Balenciaga coats in Brown Thomasez.'

'Grand,' she said. 'Fine. Good.'

'Yeah!' I said. 'That's right. Fine! Good!'

'All the same,' she murmured, 'I wouldn't mind getting a look at him.'

'Well, you won't.'

Then the bus drew up outside, bringing Dad home from the day centre, and we had to go to attend to him and convince the poor divil that this was where he actually lived and that neither of us were his sisters, thereby bringing our tense little chat to an abrupt (but merciful) end.

mariankeyes.com, October 2014.

Madeira

I made a rash promise on the Twitters that I'd do a diary of my holiers in Madeira, the way I did when I was on my holiers in Antarctica. However! I had not factored in that it was a walking holiday I was on in Madeira and at the end of every day I was absolutely SHATTERED and in no fit condition to be writing my name, never mind a diary.

However. All was not entirely lost, because I'd written the below while I was on the two planes flying to Madeira (from Dublin to Lisbon, from Lisbon to Funchal), and it seemed a shame to decommission it entirely. It's not about anything much, except the previous night's Friday Night Dinner over at Mam's, but it might be better than nothing.

Here is a diary of my holiers in Madeira! However, as I'm on the plane on the first leg on the flights, flying to Lisbon, I don't have much but minutiae to report. So I will report said minutiae!

Well, I rose at 8 a.m., readying myself for a 9.30 a.m. departure from the house. I donned my Fitbit and this is only my second day of the fecker but it is already tyrannizing me. I decided I needed to do a quick skite to Ronan the Chemist, because I suddenly became worried that the three crates of medicaments that I'd purchased earlier in the week wouldn't be enough. And although Ronan isn't far away, I usually go in the vehicle, but with one eye on my 'step-count' I decided I'd – yes! – WALK to Ronan!

But then, after a discussion with Himself, I realized that actually I DID have enough medicaments and that I was just doing the panicky pre-holiday thing that I always do, and I abandoned all plans to visit Ronan.

I 'took' my breakfast of porridge and enjoyed it tremenjussly, but I was brimming over with pre-holiday giddiness that had no outlet, so I had to eat fifteen cinnamon and apple 'diet' biscuits in order to calm myself. Then I hated myself. And that was grand, business as usual, you might say.

I will backtrack slightly to yesterday, where we had the Friday Night Dinner at the mammy's. Turnout was low because all four of the Praguers were 'otherwise occupied' as they prepared for their holiday in Madeira with myself and Himself. Present were: Me, Himself, Mam, Dad, Anne Marie (visiting from UK), Rita-Anne and the Redzers.

It was a joyous occasion because the Redzers had just returned from wrecking New York and I'd missed the little blighters while they'd been away, things had been eerily quiet. I interrogated them on what they'd done while 'Stateside', and Redzer the Elder said they'd gone swimming. And Redzer the Younger said, 'The pool was in the outside.' So I assumed it was the local baths in the park opposite Caitríona and Seán's apartming in Brooklyn.

But no! It transpired that the Redzers had gone swimming in the roof-top pool in the Soho House! And I nearly got SICK from the laughing. I'm sure you know, but the Soho House is a foncy members' club – I'd been in that self-same New York one a few years back and around the pool is *profoundly* intimidating – many, MANY slender beauties in elaborate bikinis and ginormous sunglasses lounging around, being aloof and soignée and icy and drinking foncy elegant cocktails in misty glasses with tiny white straws – the time I was there I was a cringing ball of fear and unworthiness. And the thoughts of the Redzers in their goggles and armbands, doing energetic water-bombs and wild shrieking and splashing, had me in convulsions.

'Then we had pancakes,' RTE (Redzer the Elder, aged seven) said.

'No, we didn't!' RTY (Redzer the Younger, aged five) said. 'We had BRUNCH!!!!'

'Yes,' RTE said, in a rare display of agreement with his brother, 'we had brunch.'

And that started me off with the laughing again, and it made me think of the scene in *The Blues Brothers* when the two brothers go into the foncy restaurant and make shows of themselves, flinging food across the table into each other's mouths. I had to check with Rita-Anne, but yes, the Redzers really DID have brunch in the Soho House. 'We had HASH BROWNS!' RTE said, and clearly the hash browns had made a big impression on him.

Next thing, Tadhg's car drew up outside and we all rushed to the window because a) he'd been vague about whether or not he'd be coming over at all, and b) and far more importantly, he hadn't given a definitive yes when we'd asked him if he was bringing over baby Teddy. And being quite honest with you, no one has much interest in Tadhg these days, unless he's accessorized by baby Teddy. 'He's getting out,' someone says. 'He's out. He's on his own. No, no! He's getting something else out of the car!' Then, in disappointment, we saw that it was only a bag.

'Awwwww, it's only a bag,' RTE said.

'But why would he need a bag?!' Mam asked. 'Tadhg isn't a "man-bag" type. He'd only need a bag if he was bringing –'

'BABY TEDDY!!!' we all chorused, and then we saw Tadhg

opening the back door of the car. 'He's opening the back door! He's opening the back door! There he is!!! THERE HE IS!!!!' And sure enough, there was baby Teddy in his little chair, being led up to the house.

Everyone thundered out into the hall, and as soon as the door opened we were all pawing at baby Teddy. Mam yelled, 'Don't be UP in the craythur's face! Don't be UP in his face!'

Out of the corner of my ear, I heard Rita-Anne say, 'When did Mam start saying that saying?' 'While you were away,' Mam replied, 'and you can't make fun of me because it's a real saying, I checked. So don't be UP in baby Teddy's face.'

But we couldn't help ourselves. We were UP in baby Teddy's face, and it's a good job the poor little divil is as easy-going as he is, because a lesser child would have been terrified.

Details on baby Teddy: he was six months yesterday. He is FABULOUSLY squishy – he has the squashiest thighs you've ever seen. He is SUPER-smiley. He loves dogs, and his best friend is Tadhg and Susie's boxer, Katie (named after Katie Taylor).

I hadn't a hope of getting near him, so I went into 'the room' and had a little chat with Dad, who greeted me by saying, 'You look very dirty.'

'That's my fake tan,' I said.

'What's that?' He asked. I attempted an explanation, but I'd have made more headway with baby Teddy.

'And why do you put them colours on your nails?' he asked.

'Because I like them,' sez I.

'So do I,' sez he. 'Are you married?'

'I am,' sez I.

'Well, I wish someone had told me!' he declared.

Then it was dinner time, and this week it was mine and Himself's turn to get the grub and I'd gone off-piste. Usually we get them big pasta yokes from Marks & Spencer, but I'd been up in Stillorgan and airily I'd said to Himself that I'd 'pick up' some dinner from Donnybrook Fair because I liked that picture of myself, of a woman who stands at a delicatessen counter, chatting with a white-attired chef/server person about the various different salads and things.

And I'd got – what I considered anyway to be – a FABLISS array of summery things: potato skins, lemongrass chicken, coleslaw, something called 'summer salad' and garlic bread, and ontra noo I'd only fecked in the garlic bread at the last minute because I sensed there might be a mini-revolution if I didn't.

And let me tell you that it was the mercy of God that I DID get the two garlic breads, because when I dished up the lovely off-piste dinner, there were wild cries of disappointment – where were the pasta yokes? Why were they being fobbed off with this shite? Nervously I strove for airiness: 'I thought we'd try something new!'

'New?' they cried. 'Why would we want "new"? We like the pasta yokes!'

'But it's summer. These are summery things.' Then I played my trump card. 'They're from Donnybrook Fair.'

'I don't care if they're from Fossett's Circus,' Mam said. 'I want the pasta yokes.'

'Are these hash browns?' RTE poked at the little cubes of chicken in deep-fried batter.

Sensing I could potentially form an alliance that would serve me well, I said stoutly, 'Yes, YES, Redzer the Elder, they ARE hash browns!' So he shoved about six into his mouth, gave a little chew, then spat them out again – and that was the moment that I knew I was sunk.

They divvied up the garlic bread among themselves and, giving

me baleful looks, placed their allotted tiny slice on their other-
wise empty dinner plates and ate in resentful silence. Even Dad,
who under usual conditions would eat the leg of the chair, refused
to partake of my lovely summery food. 'Well, feck yiz,' I said to
them. 'Feck the lot of yiz!'

'Feck you,' Dad said, 'feck you right back.'

But then it was Magnum time and the mammy took everyone's
orders and while the rest of us went into the sitting room and
flung ourselves on the couches, Mam went into the kitchen and
began burrowing around in the freezer and now and again she'd
come back into the room with bits of hoary frost in her eyebrows
and say, 'Where's Oscar? Here's your Mint Magnet*. And Rita-
Anne? Here's your Pink one.' And someone would say, 'Where's
mines?' And Mam would say, in shrill tones, 'I'm going as fast as
I can! There's only the wan of me!' Then back into the kitchen
she'd go and we'd hear the funny scraping noises that are made as
a mother moves around bodily inside a freezer, burrowing her
way into cardboard Magnum boxes and emerging with the cor-
rectly flavoured Magnum and bursting joyously to the surface
with it held between her teeth.

'The tea might have been a wash-out,' Tadhg said, 'but we'll
always have Magnums . . .'

The flight was uneventful, which is probably the best kind, and
then we landed in Lisbon, and despite my great love for José
Mourinho I've only been to Portugal once and that was donkey's
years ago, but I remember being struck by how LOVELY the
people were. On that previous visit, myself and Himself spent
about four days in a place called Sintra, which is atmospheric
and sort of spooky and had lots of fabliss houses that – if I'm

---

* Explanation in 'Guilty Pleasures', p. 314.

remembering correctly and I mightn't be – Byron and his pals used to be taking drugs and stuff in, and there was a funny well and lots of overhanging trees and, like I said . . . atmospheric.

After four days in Sintra we went to stay in Lisbon, and when I asked the 'man' in the hotel what tourist things he recommended in Lisbon, he said, 'You must go to Sintra! Sintra is the best thing about Lisbon. We will organize for you a car and a driver-man for to take you there – José! Fetch the hotel car to take Missy Keyes to Sintra, for she will love it! Byron went there, Missy Keyes. Off his nut on laudanum the whole time he was!' And it was the mercy of God that I found my voice in time to tell the 'man' to stand down his vehicle, that wasn't I only after *arriving* direct from Sintra, and that delightful as it had been, I wanted to spend a bit of time in Lisbon.

But the man was glum and downcast and could hardly bring himself to unfurl the map of the local area on to the counter and stab at our current location with a blue biro, so Himself and myself elected to go exploring on our own and these are my abiding memories of Lisbon: custard pies, a furniture shop run by a man called Senor Toucan, quare-flavoured Magnums, difficulty finding a public wees-facility, kindly people, custard pies . . . Oh! And custard pies!

And now we are on the quare little plane, flying to Madeira-land, and they have come around and given us FREE hang sangwidges and 'drinks' and they are SO nice and smiley and warm and friendly and I'm quite – still! – giddy! I mean, it's nice when people are nice, no? Why can't we all just be nice?'

. . . and there I'm afraid, my Madeira diary ends . . . I know! I know! I'm sorry! Tanken yew for all your kindnesses to me, and now I will sign off as I have to go and make the tay.

PS: I nearly forgot! I love this, so I do – on Friday at dinner time, I rang Mam's from Madeira, just to see how they were all getting on, and Rita-Anne came on the phone and over the shrieking and crashing noises in the background managed to tell me that when she was driving the Redzers over, Oscar (Redzer the Younger, who is only five) said, in sudden high alarm, 'What if Auntie Marian is doing the dinner again this week?!' And it took a good bit of TLC and effusive promises that I was far away in another land before he calmed down.

mariankeyes.com, July 2015.

THINGS I LOVE

Autumn

As the poet so eloquently put it, autumn: season of new boots and jackets. At least the poet *would* have so eloquently put it, if the poet had been a woman.

I love autumn. It might be because my birthday is in September (oh, poor maligned Virgo) and I associate it with presents and cake and lots of attention. But the shameful truth of the matter is that I'm not really a summer person. All right, all right, go easy! I know this won't go down well. I know saying you don't like summer is like saying you don't like dolphins, or Michael Palin, or Crunchies.

My 'issue' (I'm not at all sure I like that word) with summer is that everything's too bright and glare-y and exposed and hot. My clothes are all wrong and summer brings me into a head-on collision with my lumpy upper arms. I'm *tormented* by them. What should I do? Reveal them, looking like sausage skins stuffed with cauliflower florets, and endure the mortification and sniggers of others? Or keep them under wraps and swelter? And if I elect to swelter, then I have to deal with skinny, smooth-armed types, who've never known a day's lumpiness in their life, goading me. 'Why are you wearing your fleece? You look so hot! Look at her, everyone! She's *melting*. Stupid woman.' While I'll have to insist – even though my face is the colour of raw steak and sweat is sluicing down my back – that I'm 'fine, a little chilly even'.

Then, of course, there's the personal hairiness question, something that requires constant and meticulous vigilance. Almost as much as the sunblock situation – skin *and* hair. Not to mention keeping on top of my fake tan. The bodily running repairs demanded by summer mean there's always something that needs doing – I can never relax! (I'm not the only one who feels like this, just in case you're interested. There is a small but dedicated band; we call ourselves No TO Summer! NOTS! (With risible lack of imagination, our enemies call us NUTS!) There is also a break-away schism group who are a little more extreme, called People Happy Entering Winter! PHEW!

Autumn is *far* nicer than summer: moss-green cardigans; copper-coloured knee boots; jeans. Everything pleasingly covered up. I feel safer in autumn, I can breathe properly. I can straighten up and look the world right in the eye without having to recoil from the sun bouncing off too-bright pavements and blinding me.

While I'm at it, I might as well go for broke and add that I like the back-to-school feel of autumn. All that lounging around the whole summer long, in Cornwall or the Hamptons or wherever it is people go, is well and good, but it's not *real life*, is it?

The start of autumn feels like a mini New Year – Christ! Calm down! Obviously nothing like as terrible! We're not so poor or fat or cold or guilt-ridden. Nevertheless, autumn feels like it's about change and fresh starts and commitment to self-improvement. And yes, I admit this appeals to me.

Older readers will remember when autumn was about more than good new series starting on telly, when autumn used to be about evening classes. But – I'm not wrong, am I? – evening classes are over. A thing of the past, like nosy neighbours and Vesta curries and political agitation. It makes sense: the only reason anyone ever went was to meet a man – the cliché was that the

Car Maintenance classes were always jammers with ladies on the prowl – but now if you want to meet a man, you simply go online. (If you were particularly lonely and had no friends *at all* – male or female – magazine agony aunts encouraged you to try an evening class; nowadays if you have no friends, you simply go on SSRIs. You still have no friends, but you don't mind as much.)

A long time ago – alarmingly so: it feels like only ten months have elapsed, when in fact it's over twenty years – I shared a flat with two other girls and whenever we were dumped by a man, there was a definite 'recovery arc'. The craziness, the weight loss, the drunken one-night stands with unsuitable types . . . and then – the nadir – the talk of evening classes. Tearful, drunken defiance, 'I'll get over this, and next time he meets me I'll be strong and . . . and . . . interesting. I'll do an evening class! I'll learn to speak Italian and the class will be full of ridey Italian sex-gods.' (And obviously no one was unkind enough to point out that the thing about ridey Italian sex-gods was that they could already speak Italian and had no need to attend basic introductions to it.)

Sometimes we'd even ring the man who'd dumped us, to advise him we were about to do an evening class (usually during one of those 'I'm just calling you to tell you I won't be calling you any more' calls) and to expect us to be dazzling and fabulous the next time he met us.

Good times, good times . . . Well, actually they weren't in the slightest. But all this talk of autumn has really fired (autumnal pun) me up. It should be along any day now. Unless we get a NOTS! worst nightmare, an Indian summer . . .

First published in *Marie Claire*, August 2007.

My Perfect Life

You know the way sometimes a fabulous famous woman tells us about her average day? Well, this is what I wish I could write . . .

Every day I wake at 6 a.m. on the dot. I've no need of an alarm clock or any of that nonsense, my body knows when it's had all the sleep it needs, and simply wakes of its own accord. I'm lucky enough to have several homes – an eighteen-roomed apartment on the Upper West Side, a four-storey house in Primrose Hill, a charming cottage in the Stockholm archipelago and a light-filled, over-water modernist glass cube in Sydney.

There was a time when I had a tendency to bite people until I'd had eight capsules of Kazaar Nespresso, but these days after three glasses of the special sulphur water I have imported specially from Pompeii, I'm raring to go – straight on to my deck, which juts far out into the ocean, for my morning BarreConcept. A Russian dance master used to coach me, but it got a little embarrassing when I became better than him, *and* he was charging me £375 an hour and calling me 'veak end lazy', so we said our farewells . . .

After fifty minutes of *pliés*, I step into my outdoor, rainforest shower, then a gentle knock on my bedroom door tells me my breakfast tray has been left outside. My staff are amazing – so thorough – I never have a moment when I look at the remote control and think, 'Christ ALIVE, when was the last time this thing was cleaned?' They're also discreet enough that I never see them scrubbing my kitchen floor so I'm spared chronic, gnawing guilt.

Breakfast might be miso broth or an egg-white omelette, and yes, I used to think egg-white omelettes constituted cruel and unusual punishment but now I understand it's all about simply *deciding* that egg-white omelettes are delicious. I have mine with 35g of plain kale and perhaps an avocado smoothie. The days when my ideal breakfast involved me lying on the floor and pouring Sugar Puffs straight at my face are long in the past. Especially because I keep my daily net carb intake under 15g.

Of course, I love sweet things, but find them so filling – I think mini-Magnums should be rebranded because actually, they're *huge*. And when I look at pick'n'mix stations, I don't see pretty, irresistible jellies that I want to cram, handful after handful, into my mouth until I feel pleasantly queasy – no, I see toxic little balls of death. A fizzy cola bottle? Why not just give me a cyanide capsule?

Before I start work, it's time for the DHL man. I once met Miuccia Prada and she thought I was 'delightful' and as a result I get deliveries of next season's Prada or Miu Miu a few times a month. They're always gorgeous – I mean, it's Miuccia! – but sometimes even the sample sizes are too big for me. And if it's not stuff from Miuccia, it could be cripplingly expensive skincare like Natura Bissé or the Tom Ford make-up range. (Tom loves me too. You know he's started doing womenswear now? Well, he sent me the entire collection. I said, 'Tom, you bad man! There was no need to send the handbag in *every* colour!' But he said, 'Marian, the thought of you wearing my clothes makes me happy.' And who am I to deny Tom Ford his happiness?)

I have a husband and we have huge amounts of astonishingly inventive sex; after all these years, we still can't keep our hands off each other. Like teenagers, we are.

Then it's time for work! I write novels that are huge bestsellers *and* get critical acclaim, so not once have I been insulted at a party by people asking, 'Just how many of your bonkbusters do you churn out a year?'

I sit at my keyboard and instantly the words start to flow. I never stare in despair at an empty screen or slam my head off my keyboard and shout, 'This is a load of sh°t,' or delete an entire day's work because it's rubbish, or announce to the four empty walls, 'That's it! I'm retraining as a nail technician!'

I don't stop to eat for the simple reason that I don't get hungry, and under no circumstances do I look at the clock at 9.35 a.m. and wonder if it's too early for lunch. But at 3.30 I force myself away from my desk, then I go for a run. I don't jog – I *run*. I haven't an addictive bone in my body, except maybe when it comes to exercise.

When I return I meditate for thirty minutes, managing to still my mind into blissful silence, and no way do I think, 'Oh Christ, I'd better make that dentist's appointment, I can't keep putting it off for ever.' Or 'Why the hell did I invite those people over tonight? I just want to slump on the couch and watch eight hours of telly.'

Evenings vary. If it's not my night to volunteer at the soup kitchen or my Movie Club (we're currently exploring Yugoslavian cinema under Tito) we have an eclectic group of talented, beautiful friends round for dinner. I'm a calm, skilled cook and don't find having to have the stuffed pheasant ready at the same time as the kohlrabi at the same time as the quinoa stressful enough to warrant a Xanax. We sit at our twenty-foot-long limed-oak dining table and chat and laugh late into the night and no one gets messy drunk and follows someone else's boyfriend into the downstairs loo.

When I get into bed, I don't lie awake for several hours, my head whirling like a washing machine, wondering how I can con my doctor into giving me some delicious *verboten* Stilnoct. I fall asleep as soon as my head hits the pillow and *never* wake at 4 a.m., feeling like an imposter and a failure and that all my teeth are going to fall out. My life is in perfect balance.

Yes, well . . . I no longer eat the Sugar Puffs. It's a start.

First published in the *Sunday Times Style*, August 2015.

Beachhouse Banjo

Right, here we go – my name is Marian and I have a hobby. And I feel *really* weird saying it, because I think the whole notion of hobbies belongs to the olden days, before we had box sets and Twitter and online shopping. Back then (I'm picturing the 1950s) people had to have hobbies because – well – *there was nothing else to do*.

Until recently, if someone told me they had a hobby I'd automatically think, 'Trainspotter! Who has difficulty making friends!' And start backing away.

But for years Himself was 'at' me to get an interest, because as he often said, 'All you do is work, sleep and watch telly.'

'And buy shoes,' I'd always remind him. 'Buying shoes is an "interest". I watch telly, I eat chocolate and I buy shoes. This is the modern way. I have a full and rounded life.'

Eventually, to shut him up, I gave something a go and even now, several years later, Anne Marie will occasionally say, 'Do you remember that time you tried to get a hobby and you made a clock?' Then she'll start weeping with laughing. 'A clock,' she'll say, wiping tears of mirth from her face. 'A . . . a . . . *clock*!'

And yes, all credit to me, I *did* make a clock. Which sounds far more impressive than it actually was – basically I went down the town to the art-and-hobby shop and bought a kit, where the clock-mechanism bit was already assembled and all I had to do was make the clock face and numbers out of Play-Doh. I didn't get much enjoyment out of it and decided I wouldn't be repeating the exercise.

But Himself kept at me because he was convinced I needed something to help me to relax. However, the thing is you can't just go out and 'get an interest'. You have to be – well – *interested* in the thing, and that's something you've no control over.

However, there *was* something . . . I'd long nurtured a secret little kernel deep in my heart that, given the right circumstances, I might be an UTTERLY FABLISS artist. This was something I'd kept to myself because I am EXTREMELY bad at drawing things. I remember being mocked in art class at school for a drawing I did of a running dog – the teacher thought it was a tractor.

Nevertheless, I thought I'd be a good painter – but it would have to be abstract stuff. No dogs. Or tractors. Or anything that had to look like a 'thing'. I'd decided I wanted to work in oils – no namby-pamby watercolours for me – and I'd use GINORMOUS canvases. I had visions of myself in a paint-streaked smock, wearing a fake moustache and flinging pots of paint around a canvas the size of a wall, then borrowing someone's bicycle and cycling it over and back a few times, and when I had enough 'pieces' created (I thought a week should cover it) an exhibition would be held of my work and I would be LAUDED with praise.

In fact, I decided I'd paint under a pseudonym, so that the art critics would have no preconceived notions about my work. Then, when they'd given me tons of praise, I'd whip off my false moustache and shout, 'Surprise! 'Tis me! Chick-lit scribbler! And now ground-breaking artist-person!'

Fired up with zeal, I went back down to the art-and-hobby shop, but things didn't work out as planned. The canvas was the first problem: the art-and-hobby shop only had titchy ones, and words began to be bandied about, about 'stretching' canvases and nailing them to 'frames', and I knew I was in over my head. I wasn't a DIY person, I hated hardware stores – too cold, too strange, too full of ugly-looking things that I didn't understand – and there was no way I could get involved with nails and hammers and stretching. Suddenly I got why artists needed to go to artists' college.

Next thing to disappoint was the paint: it only came in tiny little tubes and I'd be needing gallons of the stuff to bring my unique artistic vision to fruition.

However, the man in the shop mentioned they did evening art classes and when – all agog – I pressed him for details he said, 'It's just the basics, really.'

'Basics?' I was a little worried. 'Would I have to draw a dog?'

'Maybe,' he replied. 'Or perhaps a still life.'

'Like an apple?'

'Or maybe a tomato.'

'But I want to do abstracts.'

'Abstracts aren't on the curriculum.'

'I see,' I said. And that was the end of that.

Then life changed and I went totally bananas and suddenly I started baking like a demon, which came as a massive surprise because I'd never been domesticated or 'crafty'. But it had become fashionable for modern women, many of them proud feminists, to knit or embroider or make cupcakes. So I was very zeitgeisty. Also stone mad.

For eighteen months, I baked like a maniac. It was an absolute compulsion and I simply couldn't stop. Nor could I stop eating the cakes I'd made, and I tripled in size. Then, almost as suddenly as it began, the baking urge vanished and I needed another hobby to fill the void, preferably one where I couldn't eat the end product.

But there was nothing I was interested in – until I realized that

I had to do some reconnaissance. (If only there had been a magazine called *What Hobby?*) It was like the quest for true love or the perfect job – it doesn't just appear on your doorstep, saying, 'Hello there. I'm the answer to all your prayers.' Effort has to be put into finding it. This seemed counter-intuitive to me – I thought that if I loved something, surely I'd know it? But what if I hadn't 'met' the right thing yet?

So I gave various activities a go and learnt that, just as with true love, you've to kiss a lot of frogs before you find your prince.

I did evening classes in pottery – that sounds like a total cliché, but yes, *I actually did evening classes in pottery*. Sadly, it didn't 'take': I couldn't work the wheel-thing and I couldn't bear the feel of the clay on my hands, and you should have seen the state of the little bowl I made – lopsided, bokety and awful in every way.

Next I gave jewellery-making a go and found it too fiddly. And card-making – too sticky.

Then Rita-Anne made a passing comment about 'chalk paint', and even though I wasn't aware I knew the first thing about it, some whisper of something must have reached me on the breeze, because I had an immediate sense of YES! I googled it and found there was a place nearby doing a course *that very weekend* – it was a sign! Even though I don't believe in signs!

So along I went with Ljiljana and it was love at first sight. Chalk painting is *perfect* for the likes of me – lazy, slapdash and all about instant gratification. Nothing needs to be sanded or 'stripped back' or anything else dull and responsible. You're just straight in, slapping colour on, making everything look lovely.

The day before I even did the course, I'd visited a second-hand furniture shop and bought a crappy little brown cabinet for thirty euro. Then, the very moment the course ended, I bought paint and brushes and wax and spent the rest of the weekend transforming the crappy little cabinet into a charming blue thing that was fit to grace even the most high-end of homes. It was FECKEN lovely!

I know it's unseemly to boast – good manners dictate that when we're praised we should say, 'Ah no, no, God no, it's *awful*. Look at how streaky it is and see all the bits I missed here.' But when it comes to my upcycled furniture, I actually egg people on, drawing their attention to features they might have missed. 'Isn't it fantastic?' I say.

I'm excellent at getting obsessed with things – I've always got some fixation on the go – and overnight, my obsession shifted to chalk paint. I was perpetually online, purchasing the stuff, and every time I thought I'd accumulated enough colours, I suddenly needed more. Barely a day passed without a new delivery of paint arriving – blues, turquoises, pinks, more blues, a white because you'd always need a white, a green, although that was a mistake (gank), and another turquoise. I couldn't find any lilacs for sale in Ireland or the UK, but I found a US company doing it – at a very reasonable price. Well, it *was* reasonable, until the day it was delivered and I discovered I had to pay about an extra £8,000 on import duty, but shur, we live and learn!

One of the techniques I'd learnt on the course was 'distressing' – by going over certain areas of the painted surface with sandpaper, you make your piece of furniture look wrecked, but 'good' wrecked. Not just cheap, crappy *bad* wrecked, but charming wrecked, like it had spent the last forty years being bleached by the sun, in a delightful beach house in New England, three doors down from Martha Stewart.

Now, a little aside here: the Keyes siblings co-own a holiday home in Lahinch, County Clare (west coast of Ireland, on the Atlantic, lovely spot, salty air, full of surfers), which had been furnished on the *extreme cheap* – brown melamine left, right and centre. I decided I would go there with a carload of blue paints and utterly transform the place into a billowing-white-muslin-curtains, lime-bleached-floorboards, shell-strewn, dreamy seaside home that might appear in an interiors magazine. (Apart from being prone to obsession, I am also prone to delusion.)

Because the term 'Shabby Beach Chic' already existed, I decided to invent my own name and settled on 'Beachhouse Banjo'. ('Banjo' being Irish slang, meaning wrecked, broken, in smithereens, hungover, in rag order, etc., etc. I thought the two words together were euphonious and 'catchy' – it would be sure to lodge in the minds of the editors of the interiors magazines. I had vague plans that I could take this thing 'global'.)

Then, looking for dust sheets, sugar soap, white spirits and other exotic items, I – *voluntarily* – went to a hardware store, which was like visiting a foreign country: they spoke a different language and the men were very flirty. (Honestly, if you're look-ing for love and you're not too choosy, hang around a hardware store, fingering the screws.)

At this stage, I'd spent about a million pounds on brushes and waxes and paint and more paint and knobs (a whole other subsec-tion of obsession), yet I was still feeling delightfully thrifty and 'make-do-and-mend'.

I had the most wonderful few days in Lahinch, Beachhouse Banjoing™ every stick of furniture in the place. As it transpired, I was on my own for a lot of the time because Himself was away up a mountain or something, and although the Redzer family were there at the start, they went off to Cork, visiting friends of Jimmy. I had no telly, no phone, no internet connection and no one to talk to, yet I couldn't have been happier. I was totally at peace, immersed in a world of blue upon blue.

The way I'm constructed is that I'm never fully at peace. Down in my depths, something's in perpetual uneasy motion and I've spent fifteen years trying and failing to calm myself with meditation. Mindfulness is another thing that baffles and tyrannizes me. But when I'm painting furniture, I lose myself entirely and I'm fully in the moment. Hours can pass by without me noticing and mostly I'm utterly at peace. All I'm focused on is the paint and the colour and the brush and the wood.

Stuff unravels in my head and if I find myself remembering painful patches of my life, instead of my usual knee-jerk attempts to escape (like jumping on Instagram or eating something sugary) I do what any expert would advise: I stay with the feelings.

The soothing back-and-forth of the paintbrush enables me to examine whatever it is until eventually the discomfort subsides. I can honestly say, I've (dread phrase) 'worked through' more of my issues while painting lopsided drawers bright pink than during any other of the (many, many) therapies and fixes I've tried over the years.

For me, painting is like meditation except that at the end I have a colourful piece of furniture.

When I ran out of stuff to paint in Lahinch, I left. And although I understood that the house wouldn't be featuring in any interiors magazines (the silk purse/sow's ear thing), I'd made my peace with it.

Home I went to Dublin, where I continued to Beachhouse Banjo™ anything I could lay my hands on, and suddenly there was nothing left to paint and I started to get EXTREMELY twitchy. I was all set to go to the second-hand shop but I had to go over to Mam and Dad's (a mahogany wonderland, crammed to the gills with mahogany cabinets and nests of tables and console tables and telephone tables and hall tables and all kinds of other furniture), to spend time with Dad while Mam went to bridge. Before she left, I insisted on getting out my phone and showing her pictures of all my Beachhouse Banjoed™ handiwork and she oohed and aahed and made suitably impressed noises. 'That's lovely, Marian. Good girl, Marian. Great girl, Marian.'

Buoyed up by her encouragement I said, 'Well, while you're out, I could paint your hall table pink.'

'No!' she all-but-shrieked at me. 'No! Stay away from my good furniture with your horrible paints!'

I drew myself up to my full height (not very high). 'I see,' I said stiffly. 'Well. The truth will out.'

So I started haunting the second-hand furniture shops in my local area and kept buying dressing tables and painting them pink, then gifting them to people even though they didn't want them and they had no room for them. And I literally couldn't look at anything without wanting to paint it – at a funeral, I was jolted from my grief when I found myself eyeing the carved pew-ends and thinking, 'Heliotrope. With a dry-brushing of Silver Pearl.'

Visiting my parents became exquisite torture but Mam refused to surrender anything so, in three separate instalments, I stole a small nest of tables from her sitting room. (In fairness to me, when I'd made them far more beautiful, I offered them back. However, she declined. What can I say? Her loss.)

And then I got a commission – oh yaze! One of the tables I'd purloined from Mam's 'nest' I'd painted a spring green with coloured butterflies stencilled on them. I brought it over to Mam one Friday night (where the Keyesez gather for our weekly dinner) and Redzer the Elder lay immediate and passionate claim to it. Right away Redzer the Younger started bellyaching that he wanted a table too and Rita-Anne said, 'Auntie Marian will paint another table exactly the same for you.' And I said, 'Auntie Marian will *not*!'

Rita-Anne looked a little shocked and I explained, 'Redzer the Younger is his own person with his own tastes,' and I invited the young man to sit down beside me for a 'clee-yong consultation'. I asked him what colour he wanted his table painted and he shouted, 'Black!' And I had to say 'I'm very sorry, my clee-yong, but chalk paint doesn't come in a true black, it would be more of a charcoal, and I'm not sure that's what you're "feeling".'

At this stage, RTY had hopped off the couch, run into the kitchen, kicked the freezer door, thumped back into the sitting room and stood on Redzer the Elder's head, and I suggested, in only slightly strained tones, 'What about blue?'

'Yeh!' he yelled. 'Blue!'

'What kind of blue?' I asked. 'Light blue? Mid blue? I can put together a mood board? Or would you trust me to choose on your behalf?'

'I want a Mint Magnet!' he declared.

'You've to eat your dinner first,' Rita-Anne said.

'Blue,' I said, putting a tick on a receipt I'd found in my bag. 'To be chosen by me. And what about a pattern?' I was considering the stencils I had. 'Might I suggest an animal print?' 'Seeing as you're a bit of an animal yourself,' I was thinking, but didn't say. This is how it is with commissions from clee-yongs – diplomacy must be your watchword. 'How about leopard print?' I suggested. 'Or zebra?'

'Which one kills the most people?'

'Probably leopards,' I said.

'Yeh, LEOPARD.'

'Very well,' I said. 'I think I have a good grasp of your sensibilities. A blue table with blue metallic leopard print.'

'No! A black leopard.'

'I don't have black paint. You're getting blue.'

'It can't be for girls.' He cast a scornful eye on the butterfly table that his elder brother had laid claim to. 'Not like that one that Miss Dylan has.'

'It won't be for girls. It will be specially for you.'

So I went away and painted his table, and I really put my heart and soul into it because even though he's only four he's a contrary live-wire with strong opinions. He can take agin something for the most capricious of reasons and I really wanted him to love it. And he did!

Because he has such a short attention span (probably age-related) he'd completely forgotten I was doing a table for him, so when, the following Friday, he arrived at Mam's and saw it and realized it was for him he went all red and shy and seemed like he might be on the verge of crying, and I swear to God, it made me feel fantastic.

Since then I've been 'swamped' with commissions. Well, I've had three. And everyone keeps saying, 'You could set up in business doing this.'

However, the thing is I couldn't. I spend a fortune on supplies, particularly the knobs, which I 'source' from around the world, at outlandish prices (made more outlandish by the inevitable import duty).

And if I set up in business, not only would I be bankrupt in a matter of days, but my hobby wouldn't be my hobby any longer. And I really love my hobby . . .

From an article first published in the *Sunday Times Style*, April 2015.

Guilty Pleasures

We all have our guilty pleasures, but as I'm focusing on mine to write this piece I realize that a disproportionate number of them involve food. I have zero restraint around anything containing sugar so I can't keep any in the house, but if I'm having people over, well, *of course* I have to get them something nice for dessert – to offer them a satsuma would be the height of bad manners!

So I go out and buy something fabulous, like a triple-chocolate cheesecake, and from the moment it enters my house I never stop thinking about it. When my guests arrive and I open the fridge to get drinks, the cheesecake winks at me and says, 'Come on, you know you want to.' As I dish up whatever dinnerly food I'm providing (and really I've no interest at all in that side of things), I'm thinking, 'Cheesecake, cheesecake, cheesecake.'

So the night proceeds and we're all chatting away and I'm becoming tighter and tauter as I watch the others savour their lamb tagine and a voice in my head is shouting, 'Eat faster!' Then they ask for more lamb tagine and I suspect they're only doing it to be polite but as their hostess I'm obliged to fulfil their request and as my access to the cheesecake is deferred even further I become somewhat enraged and shrill, then I fall into despair and become surly and eventually monosyllabic.

Until I hit on a magical solution: whenever people are coming over to be fed (did you notice how I refuse to say the dread words 'dinner party'?) , I have my dessert *before they arrive*. Yes! I have a fine big slice of the cheesecake about fifteen minutes before kick-off, then I am calm and happy and at peace. I can go about my hostessing duties with charm and zeal – *nothing* is too much trouble. Seconds of the lamb tagine? Of course! Why not make it thirds? Would they like a lengthy break between their main course and dessert? They should take as long as they like – what's the hurry?

And when the time for the cheesecake eventually arrives, in the privacy of the kitchen I cut several slices and rearrange them on the plate to disguise the gap. Then I feign a will-I-won't-I attitude of indecision about having any and eventually say, like I'm making a big concession, 'Okay, just a tiny slice.' (Which always impresses people, especially other women.)

As I said, because of the powerful hold sugar has on me, I can't keep any in the house. But as luck would have it, I live five minutes' drive from my parents, which is Trans-Fat Central – if you open a cupboard in their kitchen, you're in very real danger of being brained by an avalanche of biscuits, and their freezer is so jam-packed with Magnums I sometimes worry that when I open the door the ice creams will explode at me, like chocolate-coated bullets.

Oftentimes, while I'm out and about in my car, I think, 'I'll just pop in and say hi to Mam and Dad. They'd like that, a visit from their eldest daughter. And I'd like it too, because at some stage they'll be dead and I'll be grateful for the memories.' So I arrive at their door and my poor mammy eyes me warily and says, 'Are you here to steal more of my furniture?'

'Not at all,' I say heartily. 'I'm here to see you. I'm creating memories for –'

'– when I'm dead. Yes, I know.'

So we go into the sitting room and I lie on the couch and put my feet in her lap and we chat for – oh, thirty seconds or so – then I say, '. . . any Magnums?'

Because I've somehow convinced myself that if I haven't personally bought the Magnums, they don't count.

Mam gets to her feet. 'What flavour do you want?'

'What flavours have you got?'

'All of them.'

And to be fair, she does. Which brings me to another guilty pleasure: Redzer the Younger has a charming approach to certain words, he unilaterally changes them, and he's adamant that 'Magnums' are called 'Magnets'. So every Friday, when the Keyes clan descend on my parents for dinner, I'm just DYING for it to be time for Redzer the Younger's Magnum. And because Rita-Anne (mother of the Redzers) knows I get a kick out of it, she tells him to ask me.

'I want a Mint Magnet,' he says.

'A what?' I ask.

'A Mint Magnet.'

'A Mint what?'

'A Mint MAGNET.'

'A mint biscuit?'

'No. A MINT MAGNET!'

'I can't hear you. Say it louder.'

'I WANT A MINT MAGNET!'

. . . and then I kill myself laughing. Wrong of me to take pleasure from the foibles of a small child? Well, I do feel guilty. A little bit.

Walking

Fresh air – funny stuff. Smells . . . of *stuff*. And brings sensation to your face and hands and other exposed body parts. Between ourselves, I've never been a fan.

It was the way I was brought up – the only childhood memory I have of a window being opened was after the bedrooms had been repainted and the painter managed to convince Mam that we'd all be poisoned if we didn't let some air in. To this day I don't like opening windows. Even when the sun is splitting the stones I'm happy to keep the windows closed, and once they're open I always feel anxious and on edge till they're shut again.

I don't think I'm alone. It's definitely an Irish thing – maybe it's down to our epic rainfall. Over the centuries, our DNA has been re-hardwired into recognizing the value of a closed window: it lets in the light – no problems with that – but keeps at bay the air and the wet and the damp and the mist and the rain and the general misery of 'out there'.

I think it's our biggest difference with the English. The English are divils for opening windows, they're at it non-stop. And they're mad for their gardens – any chance at all and they're out there, 'taking' their breakfasts in the morning sunshine and admiring their lupins.

I admit I have a garden, it's mostly gravel and bamboo and low-maintenance stuff, but it's nice. I like to look at it. From inside the house. On the odd occasion when there's no good ads on telly. The only time I've ever been in it is when there are visitors over and they insist on going out there – it usually involves young lads wanting to kick balls. But I have never – and I genuinely mean *never* – sat out there by myself.

Now and again, when the weather is roasting (almost never, I need hardly add), Himself and I entertain wild plans of having our dinner in the garden. There's a little table out there, ideally situated to catch the evening sun. 'It'll be like being on our holidays,' I say. But at the last minute, as I have the plates of food in my hand, I waver. 'Are we really going to do this?' I ask. 'I don't know,' he replies.

Then he considers the fact that we'd have to sit opposite each other. And talk to each other. And not be able to watch telly. That makes his mind up. 'No,' he says. 'Let's do it the usual way.' So we sit on the couch and eat our dinners on our laps in front of Bryan Dobson and we are happy.

Of course, Ireland is a beautiful country with much fresh air to partake of, and that's nice for the tourists. For us locals, it was enough to visit Glendalough once a year, usually on a bank holiday Monday, admire the lake for seven to ten minutes, then proceed to the Mr Whippy van.

So I'm at a loss, *a total loss*, as to how to explain how I've taken up hill-walking in Wicklow.

There *are* some mitigating factors. Fact one: Wicklow is on my doorstep. Fact two: Wicklow, like lots of Ireland, is very beautiful. Fact three: Wicklow, unlike lots of Ireland, has actually marked out some walks. (I have visions of debates in county-council meetings around Ireland where councillors are genuinely baffled by the benefit of laying out way-marked walks through their beautiful countryside. 'Enough of that nonsense, lads, let's get back to granting planning applications for eyesore buildings in places of stunning natural beauty.')

And it's not like I've never gone for the odd walk in the past. The first time Himself and myself met Rita-Anne's future husband Jimmy, we went for a walk where the weather was so shocking that the wind actually blew away one of my contact lenses, but because I barely knew Jimmy, I had to pretend it didn't matter, the way if you accidentally break your ankle in front of someone you don't know well, you can't let on you're in paralysing agony. 'Ah no, I'm grand, I'm grand. No, I'm grand!'

But anyway, a while back some of us started going on regular walks, every two or three weeks. This is the cast of characters: myself, Himself, Posh Kate, Posh Malcolm, Hilly and Mark the Communist. And we all have roles: Himself plans the walks (oh, he loves it, consulting his maps and his special book and whatnot); Posh Malcolm takes the photos; Hilly and Mark give reviews of all the latest films (they see everything); Posh Kate provides condensed versions of *The Late Late Show* (also she talks about her cat, which is nice for the cat-lovers in the group); as for me, I'm not sure what I bring to the party, except maybe to make up numbers.

Then there are the sangwidges . . . Sangwidge-making 'rotates' from person to person and there is definitely sangwidge one-upmanship. Posh Kate is grand because her egg and bacon on granary bread is legendary. But the rest of us try very hard to delight. Posh Malcolm is gifted at showcasing sandwiches featuring horseradish or basil picked from his very own garden. Mark the Communist (or is he Mark the Socialist? I must check, these things are important) recently wowed us with a batch of 'Iberian ham and Manchego cheese'. (He even told us where he'd bought the ham – some lovely shop on Camden Street.) And Hilly always makes us go 'OOOoooh!' because she's so inventive with the bread – recent examples are bridge rolls, pitta pockets and focaccia.

I must admit that when it's my turn, I fret terribly – should I go for a profoundly traditional (and easy) cheese and tomato, which could perhaps be passed off as a retro treat? Or would everyone see through my lazy-arse ruse and should I do Kobe beef, where I actually cooked the beef myself? And where could I get some blaas, seeing as they are a delicacy only available in Waterford, and Waterford is a three-hour drive away?

But sandwich-anxiety aside, I'll readily admit that beforehand I never want to go on the walk, but I feel a duty to the others. So I go and afterwards, no matter how tough it's been, I'm always glad. Who knew there were so many great walks half an hour from Dublin? Mountains and lakes and forests and streams. Did you know there's a Seamus Heaney walk (featuring quotes on benches)? And a densely forested valley called the Devil's Glen, dotted with spooky magical sculptures and strange, hilarious sentences carved into the stone? (For example, 'When we find the ring, I'll propose.' And in front of a moss-covered bundle of rocks that looks a bit like a staircase is: 'I must clean these steps.')

The six of us have kept up the walks while one of us went through cancer and chemo, another of us (me) had a nervous breakdown, and another of us had to endure the death of their mother. Maybe it even helped us, who knows? During the worst of my madness, I was advised to take a 'mindfulness' approach to my walking. Mindfulness? Are you familiar with it? It's (allegedly) a method of treating depression by urging a person to stay in the moment. (Many people swear by it.) So I'd be walking along and saying to myself, 'There's my foot on the ground and I'm looking at a leaf and it's very green and the stream running beside me is making a right racket and there's my other foot on the ground and . . . God, I'm sick of this mindfulness shit!' So I gave up on it and went back to discussing *The Killing* with the others and it seemed to work just as well.

Obviously, living in Ireland as we do, the weather doesn't

always work in our favour so we have to take the attitude that there's no such thing as bad weather, just the wrong clothes. Over time, we've gradually accumulated technical raingear and proper walking boots and suchlike.

When we first started walking, you'd hardly ever see anyone else, and if you did it would provoke great consternation. 'Oh Christ! People.' It would take everything in my power not to jump behind a rock and wait till they'd gone – because the Walkers' Greetings Etiquette was a tricky one.

Initially the only people who said hello to us were beardy Germans or Dutch, and you could tell they were longing to stop and exchange a bit of guff. Or rather, they were longing for *you*, the Irish person, to provide the guff and they would listen and marvel at your beautiful, colourful, curlicued sentences and perhaps even write it down in a little notebook to report to their pals when they returned to Dortmund or Rotterdam.

But when we encountered other Dublin people, we'd all put our heads down and blush a little and shuffle past in silence. We were a bit mortified because this new outdoorsy business was uncharted territory for us all and we didn't know the rules.

However, things have changed . . . As the recession deepened, the numbers of people out walking increased and there was a sense that we were all in it together. So these days we smile, we speak, we say hello, we comment on the day, we admire people's dogs, we warn of boggy bits ahead or congratulate people on how far they've come and tell them the worst is nearly over (even if it isn't, but that is the Irish way. We are a nation of liars).

Sometimes – it's always the men who do this – we will enquire about a bit of kit, perhaps a fancy-looking walking pole. But it's more out of politeness than actual interest – the way a woman would admire another woman's nail varnish.

Walking people have lovely manners: say you're going at a gentle pace and you're aware there's a group behind you who are gaining on you, you don't slow down to annoy them the way you might (only *might*, I'm not saying you would) in a car. Instead you move out of the way to let the faster people past and everyone smiles and is nice.

And nice is so . . . well . . . *nice*. This walking business brings out the best in people. It's no wonder I love it.

First published in *Irish Independent*, August 2012.

ON. THE. TWITTERS!!!!!

It's happened! It's real! I am. ON. THE. TWITTERS! It happened on Friday. Himself set up an account for me, and I hadn't a clue what to do, so he said that I should start gently, begin by 'following' people I love, see what they're saying, see what people are saying back and generally observe how it all works.

But being me, I wanted to get going immediately, and I asked, 'How do I get followers?' 'We'll put it up on your website,' sez he.

'Well, do it so,' I said.

Very calmly and firmly he said, 'You're not listening to me. You're going to follow other people first and see how it works.'

And I was a bit disappointed, but he was right because I DO have a tendency to race into things and get overexcited and oftentimes mess it up and do it wrong.

So anyway, I picked out seven people that I 'admire' (i.e. am obsessed with) to follow. Tom Dunne from *Newstalk*. India Knight, author and journalist. Davina McCall, needs no introduction. Katy Perry's blue hair, but as that wasn't an entity in itself, I had to follow Katy Perry the person. Claudia Winkleman. Zayn from One Direction (I need to explain this, I'm not really a One Direction fan, being about seventy-nine years older than their average fan, but when they were on *The X Factor* I was MAD about them and him in particular, the strop he threw at his audition; also, he reminds me of my nephew Luka. But since the year's *X Factor* finished I sort of forgot about them. But my head had gone blank when I was trying to think of people I love, in order to 'follow' them, which is strange because I love so many people, and I'd just read a piece in Friday's *Guardian* about how One Direction have gone down a storm in the US, so I said, 'Right, I'll "follow" Zayn').

Then I *tried* to follow Louise Moore, my very fabulous editor, but she's not on the Twitters, nor is Liz Smith (also from Penguin).

Then I tried Jason Schwartzman (I adore *Bored to Death*. And Jason Schwartzman wrote the theme music, which is the ringtone on my phone). But he wasn't ON the Twitters. Nor was A. A. Gill. Or Mark Cagney from *Ireland AM*. But even as we were typing in Mark Cagney's name, Himself was laughing and saying, 'No WAY will Mark Cagney be on the Twitters. Mark Cagney would think the Twitters was a stupid waste of time.' And Himself was right! Important note here: both Himself and I LOVE Mark Cagney. He has always been very, very, very, very nice to me, he has a big heart, he's a great interviewer, and although he has – he'd be the first to admit it, I'd say – mildly curmudgeonly tendencies, they just make him extra funny and interesting. Big love for the Cagney from this household. Himself even more than me, I suspect.

So I managed to 'follow' seven people (I can't off the top of my head remember who the seventh was) and wasn't exactly sure what to do next. Nothing, I realized. And THEN! Someone tweeted me! And not just anyone! But Tom Dunne from *Newstalk*! Tom Dunne, whom I love with a passion dangerously close to obsession! Both myself and Himself were SCREAMING with excitement. We really were! And it was a very pertinent tweet, it was about how the bins hadn't been collected on Wednesday night (something to do with St Patrick's Day, I suspect). We were BESIDE ourselves.

Then India Knight tweeted, asking if it was really me, and I checked and I was, so I tweeted her back and she did something with a hashtag (FF? Follow Friday? Still quite at sea in this strange new world) and suddenly people were FOLLOWING me. Something like 163 in the first half-hour; 270 by the end of the first hour.

Himself and myself were glued to the screen, watching as the numbers kept rising. At this point I became a bit overwhelmed and had to go out for a while, so I went down to Dún Laoghaire and bought *The Hunger Games*.

The youth who sold it to me had obviously sold about 473 copies already that day. When I asked where it was, he had clearly pointed at that same spot in the shop many, many times. (Can I just say how thrilled I am that there's now a section in bookshops called Dystopian Fiction. Since *The Road*, I've been more and more drawn to this sort of thing, both in books and films, and am thrilled it's officially a category.)

When I came home, Himself opened the front door and said, 'It's over a thousand now.' It was sort of like watching a presidential election, as the numbers kept rising. Then Grace Dent 'followed' me and the honour nearly floored me.

I still hadn't tweeted anything to say hello, and the more time went on, the more frightened I became. I wanted to set out my stall with something funny and witty. Also something that encapsulated my gratitude for all the love I was being shown. But I had performance anxiety. Then it was five o'clock and priorities shifted. Caitríona and Seán had come home from New York earlier that day (for Dad's eightieth next weekend) and they arrived, jet-lagged and looking to be fed. As did the Redzers and the Praguers. The house was overrun for several hours and everyone was brought into Himself's office to admire the tweet from Tom Dunne.

By close of business on Friday the number of followers stood at over 2,000 and still I hadn't said hello. The next day was Saturday, and Himself went off at 6.20 a.m. to go to the UK to the football (Watford v. Coventry, nil all) and I was ALONE with the Twitters. So I chanced it. I said hello.

Two seconds later I tweeted that it was St Patrick's Day and it wasn't hailstoning and what had we done to offend the gods? Then people start tweeting me from around Ireland, with their hailstone stories. At this point I had to go to a meeting and I was late and I am NEVER late. As soon as I came back, I started on the Twitters again.

I DID manage to do, actually *do*, the Davina exercise video, instead of just sitting on the couch watching it, but I spent the rest of the afternoon, into early evening, tweeting. For some bizarre reason that made perfect twittery sense at the time, I decided to do a hailstone watch and collate accounts of hailstones from around Ireland.

I even had a mild spat with a woman from Limerick because I'd accused Limerick of having hailstones when apparently the sun was splitting the stones, but I'd MISUNDERSTOOD. See, another person had tweeted saying that 'It's splitting the stones here in Limerick.' I thought she meant the bad weather was splitting the stones, not the GOOD weather.

At this point I had to collect my poor mother and bring her to Teach a Céilí in the National Concert Hall, and I was late. AGAIN. Second time in the one day! I am a pitch-perfect Virgo who is NEVER late. Blame the Twitters!

Mick Hanly was playing in the Teach a Céilí, and my mammy, as a young woman, used to be 'in digs' (that's what it was called when you were lodging with someone) with Mick Hanly's family in Limerick, before she got married. And he dedicated a song to her from the stage on Saturday night! She was nearly as excited about that as I was about the tweet from Tom Dunne.

When I woke up on Sunday morning, I felt hungover, I literally actually did. Not from drink, mercifully, but from the Twitters. And all I wanted to do was start again! There we are – full-blown addiction in action for you.

But we were going to my lovely friend Judy's lovely grandson Jack's christening. All the same, I started tweeting, even though I had nothing to say; all I wanted was to tweet about how much I love tweeting.

Then Himself caught me and told me to get ready for the christening. Also he said that I should only tweet when I had something to say, not just tweet about how much I love tweeting.

So fair enough. I'd started reading *The Hunger Games* and God, I loved it. LOVED it! So yesterday I tweeted that.

In the meantime I started watching the trailers for *The Hunger Games* film, and DESPERATELY wanted to go, so I looked up the times – it starts here in Dublin on Friday. But on Friday, the entire Keyes family (there seem to be several hundred of us at this stage) are going away to a hotel for the night to celebrate Dad's eightieth birthday, and even though I was trying to convince myself that I could just about manage to get to the first screening of the day and still be in time for the birthday high jinks, it wasn't really adding up.

And then! Something wonderful happened! Just now! Himself walked into the room and said, 'Do you want to go to see *The Hunger Games* today at four o'clock?'

'How?' I said. 'It doesn't start until Friday. Today's only Tuesday.'

He said, 'Lovely Maria Dickenson saw your tweet about the book! She thought you might like to go.'

How lucky am I? I know times are so hard and it really doesn't seem fair that the likes of me get to go to a free movie, and I really am sorry that the world isn't fairer. What I'm trying to say is, I'm not gloating, I'm just grateful, very grateful.

And it's all thanks to Twitter!

mariankeyes.com, March 2012.

Sleep

Oh Sleep, how much do I love you? A lot, oh a huge lot! But for most of my life, it's been like a shy, almost-mythical beast that is occasionally sighted through a thicket of trees and skitters away fearfully when it realizes it's been spotted. It is nervy and fragile and will only approach when it is shown how much it is loved. Every day I must begin anew to win its trust, trying to lure it towards me with mint tea and valerian tablets and dim lighting and boring books.

Insomnia, on the other hand, is a thuggish bruiser who barges in whenever it feels like it, putting its dirty boots on my coffee table and hogging the remote control and breaking out the good wine that I'd been saving for Important Visitors. I plead with it to leave, and sometimes it does, but always with the swaggery proviso, 'You ain't seen the last of me, gel,' just like Nasty Nick Cotton in *EastEnders*.

It is a difficult way to live, my amigos.

I crave sleep – I mean, don't we all? My head is a whirry, busy place, filled with anxieties and to-do lists and peculiar memories, and I like to escape from it once in a while, the way rich people helicopter off from the hustle and bustle of the city for their peaceful weekend retreat.

Without sleep I spend the following day feeling queasy and borderline psychotic, and there is no greater misery than lying awake, staring into the darkness, worrying about all the important things I have to – *have to* – do when morning arrives.

There are many varieties of insomnia: there's the one where sleep refuses to show up at bedtime; there's the one where I'm awoken abruptly at 4 a.m. and that's my lot for the night (with that version, the sound I dread the most is the first bus – it means the night is over and there's no more chance of sleep). Then there's the 5.15 a.m. version, when – oddly – I eventually tumble back into sleep, ten minutes before the alarm goes off, and I wake up feeling like I'm coming round from a general anaesthetic. I'm prone to them all.

Every day, my preparations for sleep begin about twenty minutes after I wake up. I have my lone daily permitted cup of coffee and instantly wish I could have twelve more, but I chide myself, 'No, no! Think of the caffeine! In fifteen short hours' time, you'll be desperately trying to fall asleep and you don't want to scupper all chances by flooding yourself with stimulants. So I'm sorry, but no.'

'They' say that lavender is the insomniac's friend – that if, at bedtime, I drench my pillow in lavender mist, I'll tumble easily into eight blissful hours of oblivion. But surely I can't be the only person who thinks that lavender smells gank? Because, yes, I bought the spray and drenched my pillow with it, only to wake in the darkness-of-the-night, thinking, 'Christ *alive*, what's that *horrific* stench?' And I was only able to get back to sleep by putting the ruined pillow outside the front door and borrowing a smell-free pillow from the spare room.

A long soak in a hot bath is another frequently recommended sleep-lurer. But I hate water, I hate getting wet, and if I had one great wish for the human race, it wouldn't be something worthy like us all being able to live in harmony, but that we could be 'self-cleaning' – that we'd have no need to ever wash ourselves.

Nevertheless, during a recent bad bout of The Awakes, I gave the hot-bath thing a go. But when Himself looked in on me, and saw me sitting bolt upright, among the bubbles, anxiously watching the clock, he said sadly, 'I don't think you're really getting the best from this experience.'

'Grand,' I said, eagerly clambering out. 'I tried, I failed. *C'est la vee*. Pass me the towel.'

I usually 'retire' before Himself, hoping to be asleep before he arrives, because he nods off in two seconds flat and I lie staring into the darkness, feeling like a lonely failure.

If I'm still awake when he comes to bed, we have a little snuggle, but if I feel stirrings in his nethers, I have to say, 'No. No! Not now. Leave it till the morning and I'll see you right, but not *now*. Now I need to concentrate hard on going to sleep. Goodnight, goodnight, sorry, but goodnight.'

I'll tell you what *does* work with insomnia – tablets. Yes. Sleeping pills. They are *lovely*. Ambien, Stilnoct, Zimovane, those sorts of things. They do all the hard graft, they welcome me on board the *Sleep Express* and soon enough they've whisked me away to merciful oblivion. But after a while they stop being lovely, and higher amounts of them are needed to achieve the initial blissful effect, and then I find myself in my doctor's, begging for more and being told to hop it, that they're addictive and only intended for 'short-term use'. Also, there are countless reports of people doing very strange things while under the influence of sleepers – eating the entire contents of the fridge and remembering nothing about it, or more sinister stuff, like driving and crashing, and really, I don't want to do that. So actually, sleeping tablets are very *bad* news.

Over time I've learnt some tricks to help me sleep – regular exercise is one of them. (I realize this isn't exactly breaking news, but when you're in a queasy insomniac fog it's hard to muster the will to exercise, so you never get to find out that actually it really does help).

And all that blah about having no electronics in the bedroom is also true. As is reading an extraordinarily detailed biography of an army general.

Lists, too, they're handy. Each night I list all my jobs – from 'google Gucci nail varnishes' to 'lose two stone' – then the notebook has to be placed outside the bedroom door because otherwise I can 'feel' it at me all night, disturbing me with its countless demands.

Next I do some sort of gratitude list; it doesn't have to be a *War and Peace*-length opus, but it's good to write three or four things I'm grateful for (e.g. a lavender-free pillow, the gift of sight, the fact that the cold sore on my lip didn't burgeon across my entire chin, that sort of thing).

Most importantly, I do a scan of my day, seeking unpleasant emotions that I tried to gloss over at the time: shame is usually a biggie – shame that I didn't stand up for myself, or shame that I *did* stand up for myself. I try not to bury any negative emotion, because it'll burrow up through me and emerge as awakeness at 4 a.m.

Even so, there are still some nights when I literally don't sleep at all and I feel like I'm going insane.

Himself says I should just admit defeat and get up and go to the spare room and read. But I lie in bed in the dark, raging to myself, 'Sleep is a basic human instinct. It's like hunger and lust and the desire for lovely shoes. I am *entitled* to it. It is my *right*. I'm not moving, I'm staying right here in this bed, where I deserve to be, and I am not leaving until my needs have been met!' I'm on the verge of singing 'We Shall Overcome'.

There is no loneliness like the middle-of-the-night loneliness, and recently I actually did go to the spare room and into the emptiness of cyberspace I tweeted, 'Is anyone awake?'

But nothing happened, and I felt very sad.

Then my tablet made a little noise – a tweet had arrived. One word, 'Yes.' So someone else *was* awake! Next thing another tweet arrived: 'I'm awake too.' And then more: 'I've been awake since two'; 'I'm breastfeeding my baby'; 'I'm still on LA time'; 'I had a bad dream and I'm afraid to go back to sleep'; 'I've got a big presentation tomorrow and I'm catastrophizing.'

And suddenly there were dozens and dozens of us, all of us awake at the wrong time – then I felt really happy and sang 'Message in a Bottle' at the top of my voice: 'Seems I'm not alone in being aloooonnne. Hundred million castaways looking for a HOOOOOOMMMMME!'

And from the next room, Himself's voice shouted, 'Quieten the feck down, I'm trying to sleep in here.'

First published in the *Sunday Times Style*, December 2014.

Yoga

Did I ever tell you about the time I decided to become a yoga instructor? Only a couple of years ago, it was.

Well, like all women of my age, I'd 'dabbled' over the years, I'd done my fair share of 'experimenting'. Yoga used to be a thing that only hippies did, but about fifteen years ago a new mutated version of yoga started doing the rounds. This yoga wasn't an adjunct to meditation but a new way to get hard-bodied. It was *cripplingly* difficult. So difficult that it was okay for even rugby and GAA players to do it. (Although I believe they've stopped now.)

This new yoga pretended to be 'spiritual' like the old yoga, and every class would begin with a wafty speech from the instructor about how you should listen to your body and how you shouldn't be in competition with anyone around you and it was 'your practice' and no one else's, and everyone would nod in agreement. But in reality I found it horribly competitive and there were times when I'd be holding a pose and the sweat would be pouring off me and I'd feel like I was going to die but I was damned if I was going to give my screaming muscles a break and topple on to the floor and let the girl beside me with the fake-serene look on her face snicker up her sleeve.

People – oh, they can deny it all they like, but it's true – were even competitive about their mats: every now and again someone would show up with a springy new mat in a beautiful colour that you couldn't get in Ireland and they'd be swanking around, acting all 'Oh this old thing?' about it, and everyone would be sickened with jealousy and stare at their own curly-edged old blue mat with hatred but then they had to get all spiritual and 'rise above it'.

I hated yoga. In fairness, I hated all exercise but regarded it as a necessary evil. Yoga, however, was the most awful – I think it was the cod spirituality that made it difficult to stomach. A spinning class might be hell, but at least no one makes you think positive thoughts about people you dislike – you think about your thighs and that's all.

So with yoga, I'd go for a while, then I'd stop. Then I'd read another article about how yoga builds core strength and gives you lovely long lean muscles *and* gives you peace of mind into the bargain and I'd start up again for a while, but always lapse.

I never got the serenity that people talked about. Then, when it all went to hell with me, mental-health-wise, and I flailed around, looking for a lifebuoy, I somehow started doing yoga again and to my great surprise I'd get moments at the end of a class when my tormented head would settle down and I'd have a brief spell of feeling like I could cope.

Yoga, I decided, was the answer. Yoga would save me. Yoga would give me *a new life*! I couldn't write and I needed a job, so why not become a yoga instructor?! I had great plans: I'd open each class with beautiful inspirational readings; at the end I'd talk people through glorious visualizations and I'd cover them with pink cashmere throws – I spent the best part of a day on the Designers Guild site trying to decide which blankets to buy. I wondered about venues. And how much I should charge people. And other mad stuff.

Then I found a yoga school! Over the course of a year I'd do twelve weekends of practical and theoretical yoga and at the end

I'd do an exam and, assuming I passed, then I'd be a yoga instructor. Earnestly, I began my 'study'. I bought a fabulous jealous-making purple mat. And a notebook. But there was one thing I hadn't factored into the equation: I didn't look like a yoga instructor. Yoga instructors are lean and long and lithe and limber and lissom. They can do headstands and handstands and itch their eye with their big toe, and if they aren't born that way, they get that way by starting to practise yoga at a young age and doing it all day, every day.

I was the wrong side of forty-five. Throughout my life I'd exercised sporadically at best. I was short and stout and my joints had already started to seize up – my right hip was gammy and my right knee was banjaxed.

Worst of all, I had the wrong kind of feet. Yoga instructors' feet are as soft and pink as a baby's cheek. My feet look like the Burren – my soles are insulated with layer upon layer of grey stony stuff. I went to a woman who promised to burn off the limestone, which she duly did, but the skin underneath was a startlingly bright yellow. It was hopeless, *hopeless.*

And to be honest, by then I was losing interest. It was too hard – I was expected to do a yoga class every day. And there were too many Sanskrit words: Savasanas and Padmasanas and Pranayamas. Reluctantly I admitted to myself that I'd have to find salvation and a new career elsewhere, and after the second training weekend I tiptoed quietly away, leaving my good purple mat behind.

Easons.com, August 2012.

First Aid

Recently, I fulfilled a long-held ambition, something I've wanted to do for years and years, a dream that I've nurtured for as long as I can remember but the time just never seemed right. Anyway, last Saturday it finally came to pass – I did a basic first-aid course!

. . . and now I sense I've disappointed you. Maybe you thought I was going to say I saw the sun rise over Angkor Wat? Or I floated in a hot-air balloon across the Serengeti? Don't worry, you're not the only one to think that way – now and again, usually when I'm promoting a book, I get wheeled out from my Dublin suburb to do interviews. And a question that's often asked is, 'So what's next for Marian Keyes?' (Because they talk this way, interviewers. Especially if they're on the telly.) I usually mumble something about hoping to write another book, because I like writing books. But they press their case, 'What's on Marian Keyes's bucket list?'

Shamefaced, Marian Keyes has to admit that, apart from the first-aid course, she doesn't really have a bucket list – which perplexes the interviewers no end. 'What if Hollywood comes a-calling?' So I explain that actually Hollywood *did* come a-calling and flew me over there and introduced me to lots of smiley, tanned people and showed me buffet tables groaning with food, which we all stood around and admired, but which none of us actually ate from, and everyone was really, really, really lovely and clearly we were best friends for ever, but bafflingly when I got home I never heard from any of them again.

'Well, surely there must be something,' the interviewers insist. 'How about swimming with dolphins?' (*Always* the poor dolphins, who must be exhausted from the endless swimming they're having to do, as they help millions of people tick off the number-one item on their list.) Then I have to explain that I have the 'Keyes Ear', which means myself and my siblings get infections in our right ear at the drop of a hat and I was told by an ear specialist that I must NEVER get water in mine. So swimming is out. Also, I have to admit that I don't exactly ... *trust* dolphins. They're just too nice. I can't stop myself from thinking, 'What's their game? What are they up to? *Where's the catch?*'

At this point, my inquisitor is openly contemptuous of me – because the rule is that we're meant to have aspirations, five-year plans, things to aim for. We have to be improving constantly, 'moving closer to our goals'. To stand still is to regress.

But here's how it is: I spent my entire life in a state of yearning. During my (very ordinary) childhood, happiness belonged in the far-off future and the markers kept being moved. I'd be okay when I became a teenager. No, when I left school. No, when I got a degree.

My twenties were a decade of suspended animation – before I could declare my life open for business, I needed the right man, the right job, the right flat, the right hair, the right legs and the right lifestyle (Heal's, jogging, Barcelona).

Unaccountably, everything remained wrong. Until, through a small amount of rare proactive effort on my part, coupled with a huge amount of dumb luck, I ended up getting a book published. *And* I met a nice man. I got almost everything I yearned for (not the legs, nothing can be done about them, not until bone-lengthening is invented), but to my great surprise, I was not yearn-free.

Even as I was writing the first book, I was already worried

about the next one – what if I couldn't write it, what if it was awful, what if everyone hated the current one and it all became irrelevant anyway? Those worries never went away, to the point where every book that I was due to write in my lifetime I yearned to have already written, so that I didn't have to worry about them, if that makes any sense?

But I don't want to live in a state of yearning. I don't want to move through my days not touching the sides. I don't want my life to be deferred until everything is perfect, because that will be never. Instead I want to want what I have. Whatever that is.

I'm at my happiest when I want nothing. Even happier when I realize that I'm *entitled* to nothing – but that I've been granted so much. It's only an accident of birth that I live in a country that's not at war; somewhere in a refugee camp made of endless rows of tents is a Syrian woman the same age as me – we might even share a birthday – trying to accept that her home has gone for ever. When I think that way, I'm filled with wonder at the water that flows from my kitchen tap and the electricity that works my lamp, so that I can read at night. I'm grateful that I can read. And that I have a book. And that I can see . . . And then I'm no longer yearning. Instead I'm giddy, almost queasy at my good fortune.

So anyway, my first-aid course. You know if you're on a plane and someone announces, 'If there's a doctor on board, can they make themselves known'? Well, I wanted to *be* that person. Basically, I wanted to be a doctor but without having to do the seven pesky years in university, followed by three years of 72-hour shifts in A&E departments.

And because I come from a family that enjoys bad health, and gets no end of peculiar ailments, I felt I'd had a great medical schooling. To be honest with you, I felt I already *was* a doctor in all but name.

But on the course I discovered that being a doctor is harder than I'd thought. And having to save lives – that's a big responsibility.

Still! At least now I know and I can tick it off my list.

First published in the *Sunday Times Style*, June 2014.

SOUL-SEARCHING

Therapies

You know, I was *always* a bit odd. Growing up in dull-as-anything Catholic Ireland I was convinced that I was adopted and it was only a matter of time before my real – much more glamorous – parents showed up and whisked me off to start my real life. Aged about nine, I fell in love with Donny Osmond, and during the sermon at Mass I'd disappear into my head and fantasize about our thrilling life together in Salt Lake City – then I'd get the ferocious guilts and do a great deal of kneeling by the side of my bed, saying decades of the rosary.

After I grew up a bit and moved into disposable-income territory, I did all the obvious stuff – drinking too much, eating too much, spending too much, exercising too much, working too little, looking at every man as a potential saviour, visiting dodgy 'psychics' and buying an unholy quantity of shoes.

But in recent years I stepped up my game and moved into 'second tier' fixes (basically more expensive ones). Despite being ludicrously lucky in having a lovely job and a lovely husband and a great family (they turned out to be not dull at all) I always felt . . . I suppose the best word is *afraid*. Afraid and incomplete. So I did rehab, sobriety, counselling, craniosacral therapy, meditation, reiki, reflexology, sugar, no sugar, sugar, no sugar and 'good deeds' (basically offering lifts to strangers standing in the rain at bus stops – they never accepted but I got the warm glow of having done 'a good thing'). And when all else failed, I bought more shoes.

Then! I moved on to the hard stuff. Convinced that some forgotten trauma was generating my feelings of 'wrongness', I started hypnotherapy, looking to retrieve repressed memories. But because I'm an outrageous people-pleaser, I used to pretend I was 'under' when I don't think I was really, and went along with the therapist's suggestions, speaking in a faint 'hypnotized-style' voice, as we searched for the one bad event that had broken me. However, after seven months I reluctantly admitted that actually nothing terrible had happened to me. It was a bad blow. Then I got back in the game and embraced acupuncture, persuaded that my meridians (whatever they may be) were out of whack. And I threw 'chakra yoga' into the mix (a strange form of yoga that involves – horrors! – singing).

I did a week in the Golden Door, a well-fancy holistic spa in California, where I was looking for spiritual enlightenment, but all they seemed to care about was that I lost weight. But I escaped for a day and had a fabulous time in the local branch of Anthropologie, so it wasn't all bad.

Next, I found an angel-channeller, a lovely, lovely woman, who kept cocking her head and listening to messages of encouragement from my own personal angels, who had nothing but FABULOUS news. However, it was so silly that I used to have to suck my tongue really hard to stop myself from sniggering.

I had my astrological chart done by a truly creepy man who delighted in telling me that I was transitioning into a time of great disaster in my life and that I should consider moving to Peru.

Continuing my search, I stumbled across a crowd called the Art of Living and did a weekend course with them, which consisted – mostly – of doing funny breathing. The breathing bit was nice (and is something I continue to do, probably the only useful thing I've learnt in all my questing, apart from the fact that I love

Therapies

Anthropologie). But, well meaning as they were, they were vaguely cult-like and I was expected to meet up with other members and bring 'pot-luck' dishes and we'd all do our funny breathing together, and because the phrase 'pot-luck' makes big smacky-rage rise up in me, I made my excuses and left.

In the last nine months, something has changed: I've grasped that happiness is not the single 'correct' feeling and that all other feelings must be wrestled into submission. Happiness is simply one of countless emotions I'll feel in my lifetime.

These days I'm consciously grateful for every good thing. More importantly, I'm accepting that I'm always going to have 'a hole in my soul' – that every human being has it, to a greater or lesser extent. Sometimes the volume is turned up high and other times it's quiet, but like a stone in my shoe it's always there, and it's absolutely fine. I'm not doing anything wrong, I am simply a human being.

Today I do NOTHING to fix myself (except obsessively buying second-hand furniture and banjoing it). I've been reading a lot about ayahuasca and there was a time when I would have thought, 'Quick, quick! Sign me up immediately!' But not any longer.

These days I won't even read my horoscope. I don't want to know what's coming – I want to live in today and focus on what I have rather than what I haven't.

I finally accept that there's no cure for the condition of being human – feeling incomplete is *central* to it. And if this isn't peace, well, it's something very similar.

First published in the *Sunday Times Style*, October 2014.

Sorry

Can I tell you about a time I behaved very badly? Well, one Saturday afternoon I booked a spa appointment in a lovely hotel which had whispery candlelit rooms, fragrant whirlpools and, best of all, 'ample parking'.

On the drive there I was full of happy expectations. (But as a wise person once said, 'Expectations are merely disappointments under construction.') As I got closer, the streets started to teem with men and from their regalia I gathered an international rugby match was on nearby.

The men-crowds became ever denser, and when I reached the hotel it had about a million people standing outside. Then – disaster! – a heavy metal chain blocked me from entering the hotel car park. I was completely – as my friend Posh Kate would say – *bouleversé* (a French word meaning 'knocked for six', all-at-sea and entirely without coping mechanisms for this unprecedented situation). A big, bouncer-type man appeared and gratefully I rolled down my window.

'Hotel is full,' bouncer-man said. 'Rugby fans. You park over there.' He pointed to an underground multistorey across the road, which was a bizarre tight shape and descended countless layers, drilling straight into the earth. It was like driving down a spiral staircase, and if hell has a car park, that would be it.

But in the lovely hotel there were empty parking spots – lovely, wide, above-ground ones, shimmering invitingly, like the last parking spaces left in heaven. 'Hotel is *not* full,' I told bouncer-man.

'Parking for residents only.'

'I'm a resident.' Sort of. 'I've an appointment in the spa.' (Even now I cringe a little reporting those words – the *haughtiness*.) 'And I'm not parking over there.'

Strange shifts were going on in my emotions – later, with the benefit of hindsight, I'd identify them as disappointment and fear – but at the time I eyeballed bouncer-man (we'll call him Hans) mutinously. 'I'd better cancel my appointment.'

Certain that we were just playing a little game of brinkmanship, I rang the spa and said I couldn't come because Hans wouldn't let me in. I said the last bit very loudly so that Hans would hear. The spa receptionist said, 'What about the car park across the road?' And, in fairness, I *did* consider it, but by then the whole business had become a battle of wills.

So – in an open-and-shut case of cutting my nose off to spite my face – I cancelled my appointment. Even then I was hoping that Hans would lift the chain and say, 'Ah go on.' But he just stood there, as solid and silent as a Smeg fridge. So I stuck my head out of the car window and said in scathing tones, 'Thanks for a lovely afternoon, Hans.' Then I screeched away, scarlet with rage.

At home, I told Himself the story and embroidered it a teensy bit by saying that Hans had shrugged, 'Your spa appointment is not my problem.'

Then I rang Posh Kate and we agreed that Hans was a power-crazed bully and I said, 'I was actually afraid of him.'

A while later my sister dropped in and I beefed up the 'Afraid of Hans' theme even more, and by the sixth or seventh retelling

I'd embellished things so much that I had Hans kicking my car door and shouting, 'You snotty bitch!' after me.

Every time people sympathized, I liked it. But my self-righteous ire had begun to drain away and a little voice was whispering that Hans had only been doing his job.

With each, ever more elaborate, retelling of the story I was trying to conceal my shame. But it was like the time Mammy Keyes did up the bathroom on the cheap by painting over the fish wallpaper. No matter how many coats of paint she put on, the fish kept breaking through and reappearing.

By the following morning, I understood what had happened: my happy expectations had been thwarted and I'd been disappointed. On top of that, I was afraid of hell's car park. But Hans wasn't to know and I was awash with shame. And the thing is, I can't afford shame. Well, I should say I can't afford any *extra* shame – for whatever reason, I'm already full-to-bursting and in an attempt to quell it I try to balance the cosmic books by doing things I don't want to do for people I don't like.

I've done terrible things in my life – not *terrible* terrible, I'm not like Osama Bin Laden or similar – but I once cheated on a man I loved. And I was disloyal to a boss who'd been very good to me (and my punishment is that even though it was over twenty years ago, I still dream about it). But as well as the big-ticket events, there are countless smaller items.

Like, once I spent an afternoon at a barbecue addressing a friend of my brother's by the wrong name (by the name of another man, who had in fact stolen the first man's girlfriend). And the thing was, I *knew* something was off, so I tried to fix it by saying his (wrong) name more and more, because I'd read somewhere that to engender intimacy it's good to address a person by name.

I couldn't tell you how many times I said, 'Isn't that right, X?' When all along his name was Y.

I only realized my error when I was leaving and bumped into X, who had deliberately showed up late because he had his new girlfriend (i.e. Y's ex-girlfriend) in tow and he was hoping to avoid meeting Y. I should have gone straight back in and apologized to Y, but I was too mortified, and the memory still makes me cringe, like lemon juice on an oyster.

I've made countless similar mistakes – okay, no one died, but they're like paper cuts to my soul. I want to be a good person, but despite my best intentions I do bad things – because I'm a human being and therefore flawed to my core.

The only way I can help myself is to stop adding to my already-colossal reservoir of shame, and that means apologizing. Which I find very difficult. My ego doesn't like admitting that I made a mistake. Also, I was brought up to be 'a good girl' and I've never shaken the fear of 'getting into trouble'. By saying sorry, I'm admitting culpability, so for a long time my motto used to be 'When in doubt, lie.'

But I've learnt that humbling as apologizing is, it's better for me in the long run. So I drove back to the lovely hotel and parked (plenty of spaces that day). Hans was guarding the front door and when he saw me approaching he looked wary. But I maintained steady eye-contact and, even though I was quaking, I delivered my rehearsed speech. 'Hans, I'm very sorry about my behaviour yesterday. It wasn't your fault there were no parking spaces.'

He nodded stiffly. 'Just trying to do my job.'

'Just trying to do your job,' I agreed eagerly. 'And I'm sorry I made it difficult for you.'

We eyed each other, and for a split second I thought we might have a Hollywood moment and share a hug. But it passed. 'Well, grand, thanks,' I said. 'Um, goodbye.'

'Bye,' he said.

Then I returned to my car and, feeling a little bit lighter, off I drove, back into my life.

First published in the *Sunday Times Style*, January 2015.

Saying Goodbye

My life would be so much easier if I never had to say goodbye. I'm not talking about the big goodbyes – like break-ups and moving jobs and people pegging it – because, horrible as they are, there is no way round them, and it's best to just strive for acceptance. No, I'm talking about the small goodbyes, particularly those that happen at the end of a night's socializing.

Like, say I was at a dinner party (although does anyone, these days – other than newly-weds keen to showcase their new plates and napkin rings – have something as irredeemably grim as a dinner party?) . . . *any*way, let's just say that I was, and I was having a nice time and all that, you know how it is – these things can happen. Then, without warning, I hit my saturation point and I've had enough and I want to go home. No. I'll be more specific – I want to BE at home.

But first I must say goodbye to everyone present, and frankly I'd rather swim across a crocodile-infested river. It's the lengthy small talk that accompanies all valedictions that I find so daunting and exhausting: 'We must do this again soon' and 'Stay well' and 'Text me the name of that place' and 'No, please, don't give me any buns because I'll only eat them and then I'll hate myself.'

It's unfortunate that goodbyes happen at the end of an encounter, when most of my chat and liveliness have been used up, because last impressions count. Giving good goodbye is a real art, and when I leave a group of people, I'd like a rosy glow to remain in my place.

I can't tell you the number of hours I've wasted, sitting at a table, afraid to get up, my face aching from the lactic acid generated by holding a fake smile, because I simply can't summon the vast amounts of emotional energy that a decent departure requires. I eye the door and yearn to be on the far side of it, having wrestled with all the obstacles in my path and made good my escape.

What makes things worse is that I'm always the first to leave anything, which is a source of great shame. (According to a personality quiz, I'm an extreme introvert, which means I can only handle other people in small bursts of time. Also, I have a very short attention span. And I don't drink. I'd make a top-notch recluse.)

So I can't tell you how overjoyed I am on those rare, rare occasions when someone 'goes' before me. Suddenly I feel as debauched as Keith Richards – a stay-out-late, round-the-clock party animal. Better still, if a person is leaving, they've also given me permission to leave and often I try to 'bundle' my parting in with theirs, so that in the flurry of farewells, I make my exit almost unscathed.

But mostly I'm first to go, probably by several hours, so round the table I go, kissing people goodbye, and because of my mortification about my premature departure I overcompensate by complimenting everyone. However, due to giddiness about my forthcoming escape, my bon mots always end up being a little strange: 'You have a lovely nose' or 'Stay away from sudokus, you're obviously a left-brain thinker.'

But then I'm free to go and I skip out into the street, happy as can be.

However, things aren't always that simple because sometimes a departure involves waiting for a taxi. And now I'm going to use a metaphor: there's a thing in hill-walking called the false summit, where you're staggering up the side of a mountain, gasping for breath, your legs trembling with exhaustion, and you manage to keep on climbing because the end is in sight. In a few more minutes, you'll be on the top of the mountain and you'll feel fantastic. You're nearly there, nearly there, your lungs are bursting, your legs are like jelly . . . but you're nearly there. Then, due to the curvature of the earth and the funny angles of mountains you make a shocking discovery: hiding behind the summit you're looking at is the REAL summit.

So when my hostess ends the call to the taxi company and says to me, 'Twenty minutes, maybe half an hour,' that's my false summit. To all intents and purposes, my night is over and I just want is to sit on the stairs and sob quietly. Instead, I have to resume my place at the dinner table and dredge up anecdotes from an empty well, while my every sinew strains to hear the beautiful sound of the taxi.

When the half-hour mark passes, panic rises and grabs me by the throat and next thing I'm on my feet. My hostess tries ringing the taxi company again but can't get through, and I grab my bag and say, in a shrill, tight voice, 'It's fine, it's fine. I'll just . . .' Stand out here in the snow. 'If I start walking, I'll probably hail one on the street. Blizzard? Hardly a blizzard, just a few snowflakes.'

So what I'm asking is, is there any way round having to say goodbye? Manners morph over time, don't they? Look at how the rigid protocol of Victorian times has been largely dismantled. Surely we can move into a new way of taking our leave?

What I propose is a coin system – colour-coded to mean different things. So a person could tiptoe from the room, making vague

'I'm going to the loo' gestures, but in fact leave the building. The only sign that they had actually gone would be the little pink coin they'd left in their place, of which the general gist would be: 'Thank you, I had a lovely time but I'm all used up now and have to go home.'

And it could work the other way also. When you want to get rid of rowdy guests who show no indication of leaving, you could slap a large black coin before them which implies: 'Thank you for coming, you've been a delight, I particularly enjoyed your story about the chipolatas but you've overstayed your welcome by five hours and I've called you a cab.'

What do you think? Is anyone with me on this? Anyone . . .?

Previously unpublished.

Tipping

Hotels. Oh God, I love hotels. You can throw your pillows on the floor and someone else will pick them up. Fresh towels are yours every day (if you can overcome the guilt of the card that pretends to care about the environment but is really just a cost-saving measure). Sometimes you even get free foam slippers.

But there's a serpent in every paradise. Because there I am in the taxi, all happy, getting closer and closer to the hotel and wondering if I'll get a free weather forecast left on my pillow in the evening, when I suddenly think, 'Christ! Tips!'

And then it's too late, because the taxi has drawn up outside the hotel and they're *all over me*. Swarming like hungry ants, attached like leeches. A bloke has opened the car door with one hand and his other hand is opening and closing like that plant that eats things – but frankly he can get lost, I'm not tipping someone for opening my car door, even *my* guilt doesn't extend that far. Some other bloke is hoisting my suitcase out of the boot – and he has to be tipped at the same time as the taxi driver has to be paid, and in the confusion I sometimes mistakenly give the taxi driver's tenner to the suitcase boy, who can't believe his luck and then goes all suspicious, like he's afraid I want to sleep with him. Then there's the bloke who brings my suitcase up in the lift to my room – a *different* bloke from the one who took the case out of the car, so he has to be tipped too. Sometimes there's even another layer: a bloke, entirely separate and distinct from the suitcase bloke, will escort me to my room to show me how the taps work and will linger and linger and linger, pointing out more and more features of the room – the windowsill, the carpet ('look at the beauty of the weave, please, come down here and have a look') – until I've found a crumpled thousand-zloty note in the bottom of my bag.

It's awful! It's not that I begrudge them the money – mind you, it all adds up – it's the anxiety. How do other people do it? How do they know how much to give each person? Where do they get the right denomination cash? How do they manage to always have enough change to tip everyone? And where do they keep it? In their hands? In their pockets? In a special sack? Ideally I'd like a jacket covered entirely with plastic, see-through pockets, like those shower curtains which have compartments for your sponge, shampoo, razor, etc.

Rich posh people don't tip. It doesn't even occur to them. In their natural arrogance, they assume everyone is there to do their bidding. But it's different for people like me. I have no natural arrogance, nothing but a strong, strong fear that if I don't tip, everyone in sight will spit in my food, misdirect my phone calls and blacken my name ('Stingy bitch').

But why should we tip people at all? If I write a column you particularly like, you don't tip me. (Or if you do, I haven't been receiving them.) If your doctor successfully diagnoses strep throat, you don't slip him a couple of quid during your farewell.

And it's not like you tip people for doing a good job (at least I don't). I tip them because I have to. I tip them even when they've done a very bad job. I have tipped hairdressers while tears have been streaming down my face from the disaster they've wrought on my head.

It's the lowest paid who get and need tips: tipping is an arbitrary way of supplementing their minimum-wage income. In fact, in many cases, tips don't supplement *but actually make up* the minimum wage. In other words, customers are assumed to have tipped a certain amount (even if they haven't), so management simply pay the 'balance' – just enough to bring the meagre pay packets up to the legal limit. Is this not terrible?

Recently I stayed in a hotel in Los Angeles where, with all room-service deliveries, there was 15 per cent service charge, a ten-dollar 'tray charge' and – a new one, this – 'for your convenience' a five-dollar 'gratuity charge'. I was delighted that I didn't have to start rooting around in my bag for a tip, but when I questioned the waiter (a knackered-looking middle-aged Hispanic man) about whether he actually received the five dollars, he said 'yes' so unconvincingly and fearfully that I reached for my purse and the fumbling began.

The swizzers! It's all so wrong. This is a mad notion, I know, but could we not just do away with tips entirely and simply pay people properly? Pinko Commie nonsense, some might say, but there are times when I've thought that I'd find it less wearying to organize a Marxist revolution and bring down the entire capitalist system than find three quid for the young man who's brought me my breakfast. 'Sorry, son, no tip. But as soon as I've had my coffee I'm going to overthrow the capitalist system in order to secure decent pay for you. In fact, I could do with a couple of comrades, will you join me?'

First published in *Marie Claire*, January 2005.

Negative Thinking

When life throws me lemons, I'm told I should hop to it and make lemonade.

But when life throws me lemons, making lemonade is the last thing I want to do – I just want to curl up on the couch, nursing my bloodshot eye and sore knee from where a couple of the lemons hit me, and thinking dark thoughts about all citrus fruits.

However, that's regarded as very poor form these days. The tyranny of positive thinking insists that I must instantly reconfigure every negative into a good thing, and be able to name at least one life lesson learnt.

In fact there's a school of thought that says I should be actively grateful for every disaster that befalls me because they're opportunities for emotional and spiritual growth. And while I can see the truth of this *in theory*, in real life it's very different. In real life I want everything to be LATT (lovely all the time). I want to never feel scared, jealous, angry, abandoned, overlooked, invisible, unfulfilled, worthless . . . I could keep going ad infinitum.

But in modern life, there's no room for self-pity. To the point that I sometimes fear it's only a matter of time before it actually becomes illegal. Which would be a great shame, because self-pity can be a lovely activity. For one thing, it's free, and for another thing, it's very enjoyable to fling yourself on your bed and wail, 'I'm the unluckiest person on earth!' And 'Sometimes I think there's a curse on me!' And 'What's the point in bothering with *anything* because nothing ever goes right!'

A few short years ago, the following exchange would have been regarded as normal:

'I hear you had your car stolen.'

'That's right, it was. Bastards.'

'Yeah, bastards.'

Nowadays, though, the conversation tends to run along very different lines:

'I hear you had your car stolen.'

'That's right, it was. But you know what, it was the best thing that could have ever happened to me. Now I cycle to work and apart from the ever-present terror of being knocked down and killed – no, forget I said that, please wipe it from your memory – I've never been fitter. And the exercise endorphins are great: they just about cancel out my fear of falling under the wheels of a bus – again, if you could delete that from your records I'd appreciate it. But yes, everyone should have their car stolen!'

May I offer an alternative view: sometimes a horrible experience isn't an opportunity for growth, sometimes a horrible experience is simply that – a horrible experience. Some things will never not be sad. No amount of talking it up can change it, and people shouldn't be made to feel guilty about it. It's hard enough to be coping with loss or shame or humiliation without being labelled a whiner into the bargain.

A close friend was diagnosed with breast cancer and – as is only to be expected – was plunged into profound shock. Then her treatment started and she found it rough-going: the chemo made her as sick as a dog; everything tasted horrible; all her hair fell out and she had no end of unexpected extras, like the fact that her nose streamed endlessly. But when she was asked how she was doing and she answered honestly that she was doing quite badly, people seemed startled. Anxiously they said, 'But it's given you a new-found appreciation for life, right?' And when she explained that, on the contrary, there was no pleasure in anything – chocolate and coffee tasted funny, she wasn't allowed to drink, she hated having no eyelashes – they seemed displeased. Even more so if she tried to voice her fears of death or of terrible pain. Instead everyone expected her to be fired up and brimming with zeal for 'fighting this thing'.

'It's exhausting enough to have cancer,' she told me, 'without having to go round waving pom-poms, shouting, "Rah, rah, rah, I'm going to kick cancer's ass!"'

And the unspoken judgement of all of this is that if a person doesn't get well, they simply didn't 'battle' hard enough.

Do you know the saying 'You can't heal what you can't feel'? In general I distrust aphorisms that rhyme – just because they rhyme doesn't make them true. (For example: 'Analysis means paralysis' – actually, no. 'Analysis' simply *rhymes* with 'paralysis'. And analysis can be very useful.) But I do believe that unpleasant emotions need to be felt before they can be 'worked through' (awful phrase – sorry). Healing is a process – we can't jump straight from discovering our car has been stolen to being delighted that we're now a cyclist.

However, holding on to rage or bitterness benefits no one. The Buddhists say, 'You won't be punished *for* your anger, you'll be punished *by* your anger.' So how I do it is, I let myself be bitter for a while, I savour it, I positively wallow in it and wish ill on whoever has hurt me. I wake in the middle of the night to have conversations with myself in which I best my adversary and mock them as they grovel before me. But at some stage, just before I go officially insane, I make the decision to move on. And it doesn't always happen immediately – I'm a gifted grudge-holder – and often I have to make the decision several times before the obsession finally lifts.

A couple of weeks ago my house was burgled and things precious to me were stolen, but the worst part was the sense of violation – that strangers had been in my home and had been through my most private things. First I was scared, then I was sad, then I was ENRAGED. I entertained fantasies of getting a private detective to track down the perpetrators, then I'd hire some 'muscle' to kidnap them and bring them to a deserted basement, where I'd have them tied to chairs and in a scary, silky voice I'd 'chat' to them, while meaningfully fondling a pair of pliers.

It was GREAT fun for a while, then I had to stop. I made myself focus on how horrible it must be to earn your living by breaking into other people's homes. I thought long and hard about it and kept thinking about it – and now I actually feel sorry for them. Sometimes . . .

First published in the *Sunday Times Style*, May 2015.

No Regrets

Regrets are going the way of carbs – soon, mark my words, they'll be outlawed. Because any time some icon is asked what they regret, they always answer, 'Nothing. Any mistakes I made (and actually there are none) have made me the fabulous person I am today.'

But I have millions of regrets. Millions and millions. Big ones, small ones, mortifying ones and those really horrible peculiar little ones, the paper cuts of shame, where the pain is disproportionately huge compared to the event itself. Example of one: 8,000 years ago, in another life, a colleague had just come back from a holiday in Turkey and she was radiantly aglow with the wonderful time she'd had, and next thing I piped up, all po-faced and self-righteous and a recently signed-up member of Amnesty International, 'I wouldn't go to Turkey because of their position on human rights.'

For the love of God! Was that necessary? Was that kind? Was it even effective? No, no, and no again. I mean, she'd gone, she was back, what was I hoping to achieve? But my punishment is the memory of her poor shocked face, which still triggers a full-body SOS (sweat of shame).

'They' say you only regret the things you don't do, which is total codswallop because there are no words to describe how much I regret that time I dyed my hair blonde. (It went green. And not in a good way. And I didn't have any money to get it fixed, so it stayed bad-green for a very long time.) In fact it's safe to say I regret every single thing I did from the morning I turned twenty to the morning I turned thirty.

However, one of the biggest regrets *is* something I didn't do: a newspaper editor asked me to fly to Bono's house in the south of France, to interview Alison Hewson (aka Mrs Bono) about her eco fashion label, Edun – and I declined.

I know, I KNOW! But can I explain my thinking? First of all, the words 'fly to the south of France' send most people into a frenzy; it sounds WILDLY glamorous, conjuring up images of private jets and champagne and pointy cypress trees and driving around hairpin bends in a convertible Maserati with an extremely tanned man in aviators.

But the reality is different. Oh yes. As a journalist, you're given a very modest sum to cover the flight, and because I was due to go the following day, I knew I was probably looking at a 27-hour trip via Murmansk, on Aeroflot's budget line, where, doubtless, seats cost extra. I'd be in the land of sun and cypress trees for approximately three hours before leaving for my gruelling flight home.

But the awful journey was the least of my problems. Because the next words the editor said were: 'She says she'll only talk about the worthy fashion label, but push it. Keep pushing it. Keep asking questions. And have a good look around the house.'

'No,' I said, very, very anxiously, 'no. I'd be all wrong for this.'

At the best of times I'm hopeless at asking impertinent questions, I just haven't got the self-esteem to barrel in and demand answers. And Mrs Bono struck me (and still does) as a very able woman. Considering how famous her husband is, she engages with the press very much on her own terms, popping up only now and then, looking serenely beautiful and coolly enigmatic. Her face looks entirely un-interfered with, and even though she's slim and has fabulous clothes, she's not X-ray skinny. I bet she really *is* one of those women who eats what she wants and I bet she *never* exercises.

When I asked the editor why he'd picked me instead of one of his usual brazen, brass-necked, shameless, door-stepping Rottweilers, he said, 'Because you're Irish, you're chatty. Tell her all about your disastrous – I mean, your . . . ah . . . *interesting* life, win her trust, and you'll be gabbing away together in no time.'

But I knew we wouldn't. Mrs Bono is no eejit and it's no accident that she's kept her private life very, very, very private. A lot of work goes into staying that far below the radar and to never popping up in the Sidebar of Shame, pictured *en famille*, wearing Mickey Mouse hats in Euro Disney.

I knew that when I arrived I'd be ushered into a featureless cell that gave no clues whatsoever about life chez Bono – no family photos, no smelly socks abandoned behind the telly, no evidence of a recent Pringles binge. If I asked to use the bathroom, Mrs Bono would calmly and firmly tell me that that wouldn't be possible but that I could use the Ladies in the hotel down the road when I left, thus depriving me of any opportunity to root through their bathroom cabinets and hopefully uncover all kinds of enlightening products such as – in my wilder imaginings – Anusol (but you knew I was going to say that). Or a little jar containing Viagra (and you knew I was going to say that too). I'd even have been delighted with a bottle of Gaviscon. ('Bono's pain: top rocker self-medicates his torment by drinking. Behind closed doors, U2 frontman regularly sits at his kitchen table and swigs from large bottles. Of Gaviscon (aniseed flavour). Full story on pages 4, 5, 6 and 7.')

I knew I'd spend an hour sitting ramrod straight, listening to reams of statistics about cotton yield in Burkina Faso, desperately failing to find my opportunity to cut in and somehow convince Alison to trust me and tell me EVERYTHING about being Bono's wife.

I knew that when I left, clutching the press release and – if I was really lucky – a dun-coloured super-worthy T-shirt, I'd be so afraid of telling the newspaper editor that he'd paid for a wild goose chase that when my return flight stopped off at Murmansk, I'd disembark, buy a warm hat and just never go home.

But these days I think I should have gone. So what if I'd left with no story? Surely, the shame and sense of failure would have died down eventually? I'd have been in Bono's house! I'd have met Alison Hewson, who, like I say, strikes me as a very fabulous person.

It'd be a story for the grandkids. Assuming I had grandkids, and that looks extremely unlikely seeing as I don't have children. But funnily enough, despite all the heartache my husband and I went through as we discovered gradually that we wouldn't be having nippers, that's one wound that's healed. So I don't regret everything. Which is just as well because, as I suspect, soon regrets will be no more.

First published in the *Sunday Times Style*, October 2015.

Turning Fifty

... this was written shortly before I turned fifty ...

My lower back has been giving me gyp lately – now *there's* a sentence I never thought I'd hear myself say – but it *has*. If I stand for too long, it starts hurting and I have to look for some place for a quick sit-down. I've never known what lumbago is, but all of a sudden I'm *interested*. Because later this year I'll have a birthday and it'll be my fiftieth one.

When I mentioned it recently, my brother-in-law Jimmy went pale and said, 'Fifty! My God, that's ... *ancient!*' And yes, it *is* ancient!

But Caitríona, who a) lives in New York, and b) is glamorous, has taken a different approach and is full of talk of a big, big party. The words 'champagne cocktails' have been mentioned more than once.

As for me, although I don't want a party, being fifty doesn't scare me at all. I know that most people will think I'm nuts, but for the last few birthdays – forty-eight and forty-nine – I've been impatient to get to fifty. Fifty feels welcoming to me. It feels safe, like a cocoon. 'Come on in,' it says, 'we're a lot happier in here. People don't pester us so much. They patronize us a little, but we're wise enough to not mind.'

By contrast I remember my twenty-fifth birthday, when I was in the absolute horrors. I felt as old as the hills and like my glittering future was long behind me and certainly, by all the ways we measure success in our society, I had failed.

I knew the things I 'needed' in order to be happy: a perfect man (good-looking but not so good-looking that I'd be a perman- ent nervous wreck waiting for him to run off with someone else), a well-paid job that involved travelling to places like New York, and a mortgage on a one-bedroomed flat where the wardrobe door closed properly and the cutlery wasn't plastic. And, of course, I needed to be a size 8 – or a size 6 preferably – and to be able to get my hair blow-dried three times a week and to buy enough shoes to qualify as an addict.

But my reality was very different. I was living in a rented flat with two other girls. We had milk in our fridge approximately once a year. I drank too much and spent my electricity money on lip gloss and wondered when exactly God was going to send the right man along, because despite all the teachings of feminism, I was convinced I'd never be happy until I had the perfect boy- friend. But as the unsuitable men and discarded relationships mounted up, I often jerked awake in the middle of the night, my heart pounding with fear, aware that time was racing by, that my window of opportunity was closing and that if something didn't happen soon, I'd be alone for ever.

My career wasn't exactly flourishing either. Although I had a law degree, I never did the necessary further studies to qualify as a lawyer. (I was a top-notch self-saboteur without even knowing the phrase.)

(However, may I say that I had a gym membership – that counted for something, right? I went to the gym an awful, awful lot. Which was good, because I also ate an awful, awful lot. Exer- cise bulimia, there was another thing that I was experiencing, without even knowing it existed.)

So there I was, on my twenty-fifth birthday, convinced that there was a secret formula which would guarantee that I'd be

HATT (happy all the time). That was the promise of movies and ads and magazines: get everything in place emotionally, financially and domestically, then put that happiness in a shoebox (a nice one, Sophia Webster does lovely ones, with little grosgrain ribbons) and put that box on a high shelf where it would never be disturbed.

Thereafter my life would flow along smoothly, with enhanced add-ons like holidays and happy family occasions, and I'd have a lovely, lovely time, until one day, in a faraway sunlit future, surrounded by loving friends and family, I'd die.

But I just couldn't find that secret formula. I seemed to be perpetually on the outside looking in, watching as others got their lives together. Eventually, I went to night classes to study accountancy, even though my heart wasn't in it, because I had to do *something*.

My thirtieth birthday – a milestone – was really quite tragic: I was alone and drinking. But within days I began, out of the blue, to write funny little short stories. A few months later, I went into rehab and got sober.

Then all kinds of wonderful things began to happen. I met a lovely man who was different from the poor creatures I'd tried to take hostage in the past. I wrote a book and it was published. I wrote another book and that was published too, and suddenly I had a career. In fact, you could say I was LTD (living the dream).

But guess what? I wasn't HATT! I knew I'd been extraordinarily, bizarrely lucky but I also knew that if I didn't work until I dropped, both on writing books and publicizing them, I'd squander the chance I'd been given. I was always afraid – afraid I wouldn't be able to write another book, afraid that it wouldn't be as good as the previous one and all that blah-de-blah worrying that I'm sure you'll just dismiss as self-indulgence (I would too, if I were you . . .).

I got married to my lovely man and we hoped to have a big family – in our more delusional moments we talked about having six nippers – but as it transpired, we weren't able to have any. And that was shocking and sad and put paid to any HATT-ness for a good while. But over time the grief passed, and I saw how much love and luck I'd been given and that no one gets everything and that I'd be happier if I focused on what I had, rather than what I hadn't.

Then I was forty, and I'll tell you something: forty was great! Years forty to forty-five were *very* nice. In my constant battle with sugar, I wielded the whip-hand and I was looking good, and when I say good, I mean, of course, *thin*. I was more secure in my job, I took the attitude that if I did my best that that was acceptable, and all in all, life was lovely.

Then things went a bit skaw-ways and I had a breakdown where a powerful truth was revealed to me: it didn't matter how hard I worked, I'd never be HATT. Up until then, I'd been thinking of being happy as the 'right' way to feel – in fact, the *only* way to feel. But now, as I near fifty, I accept that happiness is simply one of thousands of emotions any person will experience in a life.

Another delightful side-effect of my fifty-ness is that I'm a lot better at standing up for myself. I try to do it politely. But I do do it. I had a recent contretemps with a young woman in a hotel when both my electronic door keys failed and I had to traipse all the way back down to reception, where the keys were replaced without a word of apology. 'And you're sorry, yes?' I said. 'For the inconvenience?' The look on her face was priceless: she was *luminous* with shock.

Healthwise, with fish oils and yoga and whatnot, fifty is the new twenty-nine, and this is great. But the pressure is also on to *look* youthful, and honestly, I don't see anything wrong with looking not-young.

So what are my thoughts on cosmetic surgery? Well, I'm not going to say, 'Never say never,' because for some reason the phrase makes big smacky-rage rise in me.

I haven't had Botox, because my face is a bit lopsided and I depend on keeping everything animated so that people don't notice. Regarding Restylane, I had one disastrous go about seven years ago, where a lump, like a baby-unicorn horn, sat between my eyebrows for three months, so I'm not doing it again. Wrinkles-wise, my face isn't too ravaged. This I put down to drinking two litres of waters a day . . . and using *colossally* expensive skincare. Also, being tubby helps. This is not something I've chosen, I'd be delighted to give 'skinny and haggard' a go, but despite my best efforts, I can't shift my excess weight.

That's another thing about being nearly fifty – the way my metabolism has come screeching to an abrupt halt. I still exercise, but it no longer seems to have any effect.

For all of my life, it was the size of my arse that caused me the most hand-wringing, but in this nearly-fifty zone it's my stomach that's the problem. It seems to have broken free from its moorings and there's no knowing how far it will roam.

I've been fighting it for a long time, trying to make the clothes in the shops work for me, clothes that are catwalked by sixteen-year-old anorexic models. But I felt increasingly exhausted and – yes – foolish.

And I knew I'd crossed some sort of line when I homed in on NYDJ (Not Your Daughter's Jeans) and felt giddy with delight inside the high-waist-banded, tummy-supported set-up.

One thing I'm *not* giving up on is my hair: I can't even contemplate letting the grey get a look-in. 'They' say you're supposed to lighten your hair colour as you age, but I tried it and it made me look like I had malaria, so I went back to getting it dyed dark again.

Turning Fifty

Being fifty means that I'm probably more than halfway through my life, but I've no fear of dying – again, I know this is unusual. It's not that I'm religious – on the contrary – so I don't see myself skipping around on the sunny uplands of heaven in an afterlife that resembles *Little House on the Prairie*. Maybe gratitude for my own mortality is one of the happy side-effects of having chronic depression – which just goes to show that everything has a silver lining!

All in all, I can't wait to be fifty – although I draw the line at having a party. No one enjoys their own party: they're too busy trying to blend people from all the separate parts of their life and make them get along. And to be honest, I don't enjoy *any* party – all the screeching 'You look fabulous!', 'No, *you* look fabulous!' is *extremely* tiring.

These days, I'm getting better and better at doing as I please, so for my half-century I'm going down the road to Pizza Express with my nearest and dearest.

People say that living to fifty is an achievement – but actually it's a gift. A gift that at times I didn't want and would have happily left outside the local Sue Ryder shop, but a gift that I now accept graciously.

In my fifty years on the planet I've learnt that life is not a problem to be solved but a mystery to be lived. And I'm glad I'm here to live it.

Previously unpublished.

A YEAR IN THE LIFE

I used to write a newsletter every month and had to stop when everything went a bit pear-shaped on the mental-health front. Mercifully I am now 'greatly restored', but in the interim I'd discovered the joy that is Twitter and now I do all my news on that instead. So, sadly, no newsletters have been written in recent times. But when I reread what I'd written this particular year (2006), I realized how little I and my life and friends etc. have changed, so even though some things are different (e.g. Dermot O'Leary is no longer on *Big Brother's Little Brother*, in fact *Big Brother's Little Brother* no longer exists), this gives a very accurate account of my daily life. So I hope you will forgive the dated bits and enjoy the rest.

January

January gloom!
Soup!
Dermot O'Leary!

January: a shocking month for everyone. Myself, I didn't want to leave the house, I didn't want to speak to anyone and I didn't want to wash myself (although in fairness, I never do. Want to, that is).

All I wanted to do was make soup – sweetcorn chowder, curried parsnip, spinach and nutmeg, you name it, I wanted to make it.

I spent many hours fiddling in the kitchen, wearing a shower cap (to protect my hair from cooking smells) and liquidizing things and freezing the excess in Tupperware containers, just like a proper person.

On 12 Jan had to 'go outside' and fly to London to be on *Celebrity Big Brother's Little Breakfast* with the delicious, the adorable, the hilarious Dermot O'Leary. Himself and Suzanne came with me, and Suzanne managed to persuade one of the George Galloway supporters to give her his George Galloway rosette-style badge. However, after he'd handed it over, it transpired that the badge was not, in fact, his to give – it belonged to the production company and they wanted it back.

An 'incident' occurred. But Suzanne is nothing if not tenacious and held on to it and wore it with pride on the tube to work and then on the plane to Ireland (where she was going later that day).

The next day was Saturday, and the funny thing is that I hadn't been shopping for ages (as a result of the New Stinginess) and normally I couldn't be arsed dragging myself around the sales because I never get bargains, I only ever buy a load of shite which I convince myself is worth the reduced price and which I NEVER wear.

But, bizarrely, I found a lovely anorak in the Nicole Farhi sale at half price and seeing as the dry-cleaners melted my last one, which I used to live in, I snapped it up!

Then I nearly got a bargain! Long story. Ages ago Himself bought me some lovely, lovely underwear from Myla, dark blue silk with lighter blue polka dots and a discreet pink frill. (Man buys lady-underwear that isn't red, polyester or crotchless! Bizarre!) And I liked it so much that I decided to get my youngest sister Rita-Anne the same set for Christmas. Then, in Prague, Caitríona saw it and she wanted a set too, so I said I'd get it for her for her birthday (in Feb). But when I tried ordering it from the Myla site, they didn't have it in her size. So that was that, it seemed. Great disappointment. But then, when I was in Selfridges, didn't I see the Myla underwear, in the sale! At half price! In many sizes! Possibly including Caitríona's! The only problem was that I couldn't remember her bra size because my memory is gone to hell even though I'm eating a lot of oily fish, and I couldn't ring her because it was only 6 a.m. in New York and she works very hard and I didn't want to wake her at that time on a Saturday morning, even if it was for a cut-price Myla bra.

Then I remembered that she was the same size as Rita-Anne! All I had to do was ring Rita-Anne, ask her her bra size, then buy it! But Jimmy answered the phone and told me Rita-Anne was at yoga, and once again I thought, 'Ah well, that's that.' Then I had the strangest idea. It was a long shot, but it might just work . . . 'Jimmy,' I said, 'could you do me a massive favour.' Now, ontra noo, I wasn't holding out much hope because you know what mens are like, but it was my only chance. 'Jimmy,' I said, 'you are a man and don't notice these sorts of things, but at Christmas I gave R-A a lovely set of blue silk underwear –'

'I know it!' he said. 'Yes, I know it!'

God above! But then again, they're only newly in love really.

'Yes,' he said. 'She was wearing it last night!'

'Great,' I said. 'Great, great! Can you check the bra size?'

So he duly did and then I went and bought the set and they wrapped it specially because it was a present and I rang Caitríona (at a more sensible time) and told her the joyous news, but now I can't find the shagging thing anywhere! I don't know what I've done with it. I might have left it in London; I'm hoping to God I did, because if it's not there, it's lost for ever. You see, I have a bargain-repeller zone. Even when I find them, I lose them!

While I was in London, I must have done something to offend the god of water, whoever he or she is. On the night we arrived, the hot water wasn't working, so when I had to get up in the middle of the night (5.30 a.m.) to be collected for Dermot, I had to have a miserable cold shower, because I couldn't *possibly* be smelly for my beloved Dermot. Then the next day the COLD water was broken, so there was nothing coming out of any of the taps and we couldn't fill the kettle or flush the loo or anything, and normally I'm thrilled at a bone-fide, cast-iron opportunity to not wash myself, but when I had no choice in the matter, I didn't like it one bit.

Previously unpublished.

February

Detox!

Wedding-dress shopping!

Ready Steady Lose!

Other than a detox – in which I consumed over the course of twenty-four hours the juice of eighteen carrots, three whole cucumbers, six red peppers, three pears, six apples and a big lump of ginger – it was a fairly quiet month.

I began the month trying to work on the new book and in the grip of despair – worse than the despair I feel when I realize a play is three acts long (which is *acute* despair). I couldn't create a new character and I felt worthless and hopeless, but I ploughed on anyway and eventually got somewhere!

It was thrilling! I haven't much written, but I'm encouraged by the way it's going. This will undoubtedly change, it always does, but it is better to be facing into three months of touring feeling upbeat rather than bereft.

Last Friday, Himself, myself, my mother and Rita-Anne went wedding-dress shopping and it was wonderful. When I saw her in the first dress, I cried like a sap – my little baby sister was all grown up! We went to a couple of shops, then we went to Brown Thomas, which normally my mother refuses to go into because it's too dear, but no sooner were we through the doors than she sort of tensed and sniffed the air, like an animal scenting prey. 'LV bags,' she said, her eyes gone milky and blind, like she was having a vision.

Yes! We were indeed in the LV bag department, and she had sensed it rather than seen it. 'Wheelie ones,' she said. 'Little wheelie ones you can bring on a plane.'

I asked her if she wanted one, then she seemed to come to and said briskly, 'No, not at all, what would the likes of me be doing with an LV wheelie case. Some oul' yoke from Leather Plus will do me.'

Then I managed to talk them into coming to look at Missoni coats because, *mes amies*, I've had a great – cunning – idea. Because Caitríona and I are bridesmaids (well, I am matron of honour. Christ! A matron. Anyway), I have fashioned (pun) a great idea. Instead of the horrible meringuey dresses bridesmaids usually have to wear, why don't we wear Missoni coats?! Stylish, chic, practical, warm and – well, it's a MISSONI COAT!!!!

I thought my mother would hate them, just on principle, but no, oh no, indeed no. She was very, very, very taken with them and examined them in great, excited detail. (She didn't see the prices.)

Then, when we were on our way to get chips, we passed a mannequin that was miles from the Missoni bit but was wearing a Missoni dress, and Mam shrieked, 'Look! There's another one!' See how quickly she picked it up? It was EXTREMELY FUNNY.

We went to the café and Rita-Anne and I had chips and Mam reluctantly had chocolate biscuit cake but nearly didn't order it because it was seven yoyos ninety-five and she said it was far too dear. (Himself had a double espresso and went for a wander around the men's department and came back full of talk of a stripy Alexander McQueen jacket, but he knew he wouldn't be allowed to have it so he didn't press the point.)

During the second week in the month I went to London for work, and while I was there I took a strange notion that I wanted to see Kathleen Turner in *Who's Afraid of Virginia Woolf?*

Strangely we were able to get tickets – I thought it would be sold out – and on Friday night, after a long, awful, shameful week (more of which in a while), we went along and yes, I quite enjoyed the first half. You know, *grand*. Not great but not bad, I'm not saying it was bad . . .

But as we stretched our legs in the foyer, Himself noticed that we had not in fact just sat through the first half, but only the first THIRD. There were three acts, and honestly, *mes amies*, when I heard this, I just lost the will to live. I went quiet and wondered if I should fake an injury, like a cracked rib, or a ruptured spleen – something not too bad, that wouldn't arouse undue suspicion when we got home and I suddenly made a miraculous recovery.

In the end, I succumbed to a bout of honesty. 'Himself,' I asked fake-casually, 'have you ever walked out of a play after the first act?' Himself is no fool and realized that this wasn't a simple theoretical enquiry. 'You want to leave?' he asked.

Then he admitted that he wasn't exactly riveted himself and that life was too short and that if we wanted to leave, we should just leave and not feel guilty or apologize or try to justify it or anything. So feeling very guilty and apologizing and trying to justify it, we left.

While I was in London I began eating and didn't stop until I left. All the good work done by my '24-hour juice detox' was unmade in a matter of seconds and there wasn't a thing I could do about it, because it was work! Yes, work. Please believe me.

Afternoon tea with Waterstones, followed by dinner with WHSmith Retail, followed by lunch with Borders and Amazon, dinner at *Ready Steady Cook* (we'll get to that), followed by afternoon tea with WHSmith Travel, followed by dinner with Tesco buyers, followed by lunch with Penguin CEO. I'm the size of a house!

And now my hunger has woken up and I need to eat around the clock to satisfy the beast that is my appetite – I'm waking in the middle of the night and sneaking downstairs for bananas and all sorts.

Okay then, *Ready Steady Cook*. Christ, the shame! Unbridled, unmitigated. No doubt but that pride goes before a fall. You see, as result of being a gourmet-swot, I thought I should be able to hold my own on a cookery programme.

I couldn't help a mild swagger in my step as I arrived along to *RSC* (*Ready Steady Cook*) with my basket of goodies. Also, I was partnered with chef James Martin of *Strictly Come Dancing* fame, and everyone fancies him. Frankly, I thought we were an unbeatable combination. But no. We were all too effing beatable.

Nicholas Parsons – who is eighty-two, you know, and a very nice man, didn't gloat at all – was partnered with chef Paul Rankin, also a decent skin, and they *wiped the floor with me*. I was a liability. I didn't know where the garlic was, I didn't butter the ramekins enough, I got in James Martin's way, I tried melting butter over a gas ring that wasn't turned on, it was all SO HUMILIATING!!

I should add a couple of things. Ainsley Harriott is a lovely man and wasn't just lovely to me but also to Himself and Suzanne, who were drinking wine in the green room. Also, Nicholas Parsons' prize for winning was a cheque for £100 for the charity of his choice.

I – the loser – got a hamper full of goodies (Ainsley Harriott couscous, Ainsley Harriott balsamic dressing, etc.), which I didn't have to give to anyone but which was mine to bring home, so *who* is the real winner here? Eh?

As soon as I got back from London I began packing for the Australian tour. Himself was amazed I had left it so late. I've made many, many lists of all the possible outfits available to me, but I know that once I get there I will wear the same three rig-outs into the ground.

Also, I attended the optician because my sight has gone to hell. Not just the crippling short-sightedness, but worse! When I am wearing my contact lenses and thus able to see things more than two feet away from me, I am no longer able to READ. The print goes all blurry!

Suddenly, I am like an old person! I'll have to get reading glasses, which is a terrible realization as I had never believed before that such things were necessary. I'd thought they were mere affecta-tions used by people in order to seem more intelligent-looking. Or to add gravitas to a situation. People who wear reading glasses get asked questions and they look up from documents and take off their glasses and say, 'I'm glad you asked me that question, George.'

The whole glasses-removing thing slows everything down and makes everyone look at the person, making them the centre of attention. I have always suspected reading glasses to be mere props. Have I been wrong all these years?

And the sight thing is only going to get worse for me. I have inherited my father's eyes, and he has been afflicted with cata-racts over the years and at the moment is missing a lens (a real lens, not a contact lens, although the exact details of how this came to pass escape me) and isn't allowed to drive, and I can see (pun) that this is all ahead of me.

Truly, as a family unit we are bedevilled with ill health. Any-way, I went to the optician and had my eyes tested, then the lady tried me out with different lens strengths and I had to sit in front of a machine and she'd do a little click and a new lens would slot into place and I had to look at the letters on the wall and shout, 'Better!' or 'Worse!' like I was getting married. But the thing is that I was never sure whether each new click was making my vision better or worse, it was all happening so fast, but I felt I had to say *something*. So sometimes I said, 'Better!' and other times I said, 'Worse!' but was never entirely convinced. Then I got a horrible thought: do opticians ever get bored testing people's eyes? Do they ever just click the same-strength lens into the little hole and snigger away quietly to themselves as the person says, 'Oh, better, much better, much clearer this time' and 'Oh yes, better again, yes, crystal clear' and 'God above! That's fantastic!'

What else happened this month? Well, yes, *Brokeback Mountain*, it was really, really lovely. But long, no? Why are things always *so long*? Hours and hours seems to be the current length for films, and I have a terribly short attention span. After an hour and a half, I just can't take it. So yes, a beautiful film, very moving, very touching and all that, just – as I say – a little long.

Previously unpublished.

March

Australia!

The talking map!

I am back from the Australian tour, where I met loads and loads of lovely readers and the weather was lovely and I went UTTERLY BERSERK in the Alannah Hill shops.

Himself and I flew out of Dublin on 27 Feb and landed in Melbourne approx a week later – this time-difference thing is ridiculous! Surely something can be done about it?

No direct flight from Dublin to Melbourne sadly, but via London, then Singapore. I behaved myself in the London airport but by the time I got to Singapore it was after a fourteen-hour flight and I was badly gone in the head and seeking *something* – obviously some sort of spiritual balm, something to mend the hole in the soul – so I went to a chemist.

I love chemists at the best of times, but this one promised Chinese remedies and somehow, along with Korean ginseng and Tiger Balm rub for sore muscles – 'Not made with real tigers?' I asked the woman sternly, but she elected not to speak English at that particular moment – I bought a jar of powdered Siberian deer antler. (Cripes! Horrible thought! The balm couldn't *actually* have been made with tigers, could it? I mean, surely that's illegal? But after the deer antler situation . . .?)

Anyway, I don't know how it happened, but I ended up being persuaded by the lady to purchase the jar of Siberian deer antler powder. According to its highly dodgy-looking packaging, it serves 'as a remedy for weakness, memory loss and general aches and pains'. But guilt? The guilt about the deer? No. No remedy for that.

Back on the plane, landed in Melbourne, all sunny and warm. I had a few days to recover from jet lag before starting work and it was GLORIOUS. I've been to Melbourne before but never for long and only in the middle of frantic work, so I never had time to appreciate it.

It is *fabulous* and they were getting ready for the Commonwealth Games and they had all these beautiful fish sculptures along the Yarra (the river, handy thing to know if you are ever on *Eggheads*). Also really fabulous grub. Also shops. Bought things. Oh God, yes. Alannah Hill. Lovely.

Right! Injuries. Himself suffered a scratch to his eyeball in a bizarre contact-lens-applying incident and needed antibiotic drops. Me? My trusty black sandals, the sandals I've had for a long time and wear for walking about, buying clothes and general enjoyment, suddenly turned on me and gave me a footful of blisters! Fecking agony! And confusion! Why now? I've had them for a long, reliable time, and God knows they were bought for comfort, not beauty (black solid-looking wedge slides, really quite unattractive), and frankly if they don't pull their socks up, they won't be coming to Canada and the States for the book tour there.

Plenty more sandals in the sea!

I visited a chemist (the same one where I bought Himself's drops – by the end of the four days in Melbourne, myself and the pharmacist were on first-name terms) and bought special expensive blister plasters, but they didn't work! They peeled off, causing extra agony.

Back to the chemist, where I purchased antiseptic powder,

then I had to change into my 'good' turquoise Chie Mihara sandals in order to walk about Melbourne. Ridiculous. Those sandals were specially bought for being on the telly!

Right then! Work began in Hobart, Tasmania. I've always wanted to go, and although the visit was short I'd love to go back. People at the reading were great. Also, the food was very delicious.

Back to Melbourne, where hundreds of enthusiastic readers – the most wonderful people – turned up to the events, and walking home with Himself after a great night in the Victorian Arts Centre we crossed the bridge and they were doing a rehearsal for the opening night of the Commonwealth Games, with fireworks and some funny business with the fish sculptures, and I felt extremely blessed to be there for it and incredibly lucky and happy.

Next stop Brisbane, a great night in Riverbend Books, then up the coast to Noosa, more nice people, then the weekend in Sydney.

This is where it gets really, really good. I mean it was fabulous before, but wait till you hear! We were staying in the Four Seasons, which is my most favourite hotel in the world anyway. But not only were we staying in the Sydney Four Seasons, but a very beautiful, kindly employee of the Four Seasons – Kaarin Lindsay – upgraded us to a suite! On the thirty-fourth floor! With a view of the opera house! I mean! How lucky am I?

Oh God, it was glorious! Huge and beautiful and a bathroom full of wonderful things, including excellently roomy shower caps.

Regular users of hotels may have noticed how small shower caps tend to be – I have an abnormally small head and sometimes even I find them a squeeze – but you could wear a bucket on your head and the Four Seasons shower caps would still fit you!

Funnily enough, we were staying in the Royal Suite – and indeed being treated like royalty – and didn't the Queen arrive! Yes, the Queen of England! Not actually to the Four Seasons, looking to be let into the Royal Suite and being told to feck off, that it was already occupied, but to Sydney, to open the new bit of the opera house, before going on to Melbourne to open the Games.

It was gas! I was looking out of the window on the Monday morning and saw throngs of people sitting in rows by the opera house. 'What's going on?' I wondered. Next thing, some woman in a ginormous hat, accompanied by some lanky bloke, got up to make a speech. It was Queenie!

Anyway, she got her revenge on me for stealing her hotel room. See, all the roads had to be closed off for her, so the people of Sydney who were coming to my literary lunch at the Four Seasons were badly delayed. Nevertheless, when they finally got there, we had a great time.

However, being delayed by the Queen was just one of the many examples of the havoc Mercury being in retrograde in Virgo caused this month. And it went on for the whole shagging month, until the 25th. Examples include: me ringing my mother on 12 March and singing 'Happy Birthday' down the phone, when her birthday wasn't until the next day. Himself's electronic organizer dying and losing all info, so we couldn't phone people. Also, we couldn't send or get emails. Also, the alarm clock on it began waking us at random times – one morning I was out of the bed and showered and dressed before Himself managed to tell me it was only 4.35 a.m. and we weren't due to get up for another hour and a half! Feck! Oh, *mes amies*, feck! Sleep is a precious enough commodity on a book tour, without this sort of a caper!

Next and final stop, Perth. Two gorgeous reader events, with time for a visit to David Jones in between them.

And then home, where the garden is finally being 'done'. After living with what basically amounts to a bog for the past nine years, we have finally taken the plunge and are getting the whole fecking thing concreted over and turned into a car park. (Well, it'll involve gravel and a decking and that sort of thing, but it will be grass-free.)

With all the rain, it's like the First World War out there. Like the Battle of the effing Somme. Mud, mud and more shagging mud. A muddy walkway connects the front door with the kitchen, random men abound, and in an attempt to ward off any stress-generated illnesses, I've taken the powdered deer antler. (My reasoning is, what can the poor deer do about it now?)

Right, football! As you know, Himself's football team are called Watford and they never seem to do very well. But it's all different this season. They have a new manager (yes, yet another new one) – Adrian 'Betty' Boothroyd – who is young and keen as mustard and has brought together a team of young renegades and turned them into a winning machine. (He is like Spencer Tracy in *Boys Town*, only not ginger.)

Watford keep winning and it is *so lovely* not to be the fecking underdog, for once. It is delightful to be able to 'lord' it over other teams, it is *great* when dodgy ref decisions are in Watford's favour, it is glorious when the other team play their hearts out and still lose.

The bad news, however, is that Watford are in very real danger of being promoted to the Premeer Division, where they will have to knock heads with the likes of Chelsea and Man U, who have buckets of cash behind them, and they will be the underdog again and will have the shit kicked out of them all season, and we will be terribly despondent again and they will be demoted at the end of the season. Oh dear.

Finally, my mother. Remember about her and the Missoni coats last month? Well, I was barely home from Australia when she rang me, all agog, to tell me that 'that Missoni crowd' have brought out a perfume. Gas.

Also, I didn't tell you about her and the satellite navigation in the new car. The day we went into town to look at wedding dresses for Rita-Anne, Mam sat in front and was bedazzled – yes, quite bedazzled – by Himself's sat-nav. She simply couldn't get over it, she marvelled and marvelled at it, especially when it knew the name of her road and when it spoke to Himself, telling him that when he'd dropped Mam off, to turn right, up Ashton Park. 'It's like magic,' she kept saying. And then it was only one quick logical step for her to decide that it was proof of the existence of God.

Since I've got back, most of her conversations with me have been about what she calls 'the talking map'. She said she had met Anne O'Byrne at bridge and told her about it and actually Anne O'Byrne had 'heard tell of it'. Clearly a sophisticated woman, a woman of the world. She'd never *seen* one, mind, but she knew about it.

Then Mam wanted to know if Dad could get one for his car. And when we were talking about going to Aughrim for dinner, trying out the place where R-A and Jimmy are getting married, and I expressed anxiety about driving there as I was unfamiliar with the route, she screeched, eyes a-bulge at my stupidity, 'But what are you worried about? Haven't you got the talking map?'

Previously unpublished.

April

Book launch!
Idea for own chat show!

Busy month. Book (*Anybody Out There*) out in Ireland, then out in the UK. Doing much publicity and readings. All very nice, esp. as the book went to No 1 in both countries, thank you very much.

I had a 'fabulous' launch party in London in the Sanderson Hotel, which I was v. anxious about, as I hate having parties. I spend two hours before kick-off a nervous wreck, convinced that no one will come and that I have no friends, but lots and lots of wonderful people came – and the best bit! Bobbi Brown did goodie bags! Gorgeous, gorgeous stuff!

I got a BEAUTIFUL lip gloss in Rose (which Ema subsequently tried to steal from me in Prague, but we tussled for ages and eventually I won – not seemly to win a wrestling match with a six-year-old, I know, but I'm very fond of that lip gloss), also a magnificent blusher.

Then, the following night, at a reading in Waterstones, Bobbi Brown did makeovers and there was a raffle where the prize was one of their glorious train cases crammed – yes, CRAMMED, *mes amies* – with Bobbi Brown goodies.

It was my job to graciously hand it over to the lucky winner, and I almost didn't. In fact, I nearly gave her a shove, then broke into a run, heading for the hills. However, at the last moment, I managed to behave like an adult.

Then we all went to Prague, even Caitríona and Seán Ferguson came from New York, and Mags and Eileen came as well as the rest of the Keyes family and stayed at the (non-fancy but nice) Savoy Hotel: helpful staff, comfortable rooms and delicious breakfasts – at least the reports from those who were able to get up for them say so. (I didn't get up. I find hotel breakfast rooms a bit much, what with it being early in the morning. Just too many men roaming about with plates of scrambled eggs – or worse still, fried. I can't say why, but they turn my stomach. The smell, the yellowness. I'd rather curl up in bed and gnaw on a dry crust which I'd stolen from dinner the previous night and secreted under my pillow.)

Niall had his birthday party on the Saturday night in Lávka. (Famed nightclub, which was much patronized during Niall and Ljiljana's wedding some years ago, the legendary time that Suzanne 'broke' Tadhg. Basically she drank him under the table and at 7 a.m. he had to admit defeat and stagger back to the hotel, while she stayed dancing with the cleaning staff as they put the chairs upside down on the tables and mopped the floors. Even now, many years on, no matter what time of day it is, if we are passing Lávka, we say, 'Oh, there's Suzanne. Who's she dancing with?' Then we squint hard and say, 'Looks like the man who restocks the barrels.' And that sort of thing.)

Although we had much fun this time, we were shadows of our former, younger selves. No one broke their nose, no one needed assistance from the Irish Embassy, no one visited the Gastronomical Clock and saw the twenty-four Apostles, not like at Niall's wedding. (When all those things actually happened.)

Anyway, shifting gears quite dramatically, myself and Himself had a great idea for a chat show. It would be hosted by me (I know that sounds incredibly arrogant, but it's only a bit of a laugh) and would sort of be like other chat shows in that we'd have famous people on, flogging their new book or song or line of underwear.

But instead of just letting them sit on the bed and drone on (yes, it would be hosted from a bed, maybe not my actual bed, but a reasonable facsimile), I would endeavour to help them in all kinds of ways.

For example, I'd like to bring on Vilma, my lovely, lovely Lithuanian naturopath, to examine their tongue and diagnose stagnant liver chi (to name one condition). She could give them all sorts of advice on diet, supplements, lifestyle, etc. (She says I have a very nice tongue, not too thick.)

Or we could have one of those Colour Me Beautiful people, where they would hold purple squares of fabric up to George Clooney's face (yes, I wish) and tell him he is a 'winter' person.

Or with baldies like Ross Kemp (Grant in *EastEnders*) we could bring on a wig expert and try him with Louis XVI long, mad, waist-length, Elton John curly yokes or suchlike. The list of helpful experts could be endless. We could get the guests acupunctured, test them for food allergies or do a little reflexology.

Then we could have the Ordinary Plain-Spoken Woman – a non-expert but one with strong opinions – who would tell them about all their mistakes, because most celebrities only get told that they're fantastic; it would be a great wake-up call. It would be a great way to get to *really* know celebrities. I mean, you can't hide a poor lifestyle from Vilma. If it's there, she'll see it on their tongue. Or we could bring on a Freudian psycho-person to analyse the celebrities' dreams, or someone to read their palms, and we'd find out ALL KINDS OF THINGS that they'd prefer we didn't know.

I would also love to have a slot called Ailment of the Day,

where I would have a massive medical encyclopaedia and I would simply open a page at random and read out the symptoms of, say, jargon aphasia, or trimethylaminuria, or Paris syndrome (a psychiatric breakdown that tends to happen in Japanese tourists when the city of Paris doesn't live up to its romanticized image). (These are all real!) And then we could all suspect we have contracted it.

I think I would also ask my guests to bring along their favourite purchase from a chemist and discuss it. Himself would be an important part of the show; he would bring the guest in, offer them a drink (nettle tea, perhaps, or maybe a glass of milk, whatever we have in the house basically), then he would sit on a nearby sofa, doing hard sudokus and interrupting if he feels the guest is talking nonsense.

Another item, in an homage to *Top Gear*'s Star in the Reasonably Priced Car, could be Star in the Reasonably Priced Boots, where our celebrity would wear nice boots (or shoes) from a reasonably priced shop (Topshop or Clarks, for example) and give their verdict on walkability, nice leather smell, zip smoothness, etc.

Then we would have an agony aunt (Anne Marie Scanlon in a mammy wig and cat's-arse mouth), where a viewer would write in with a (hopefully) interesting problem (if they're not interesting and salacious enough, we'll make them up) and A-M would dispense brutal, unsympathetic advice, in the manner of Mammy Walsh.

Then we would end every show with me, Himself and the guests playing air guitars to a heavy-metal rendition of a song that the audience could ring in and request. Preferably they wouldn't be heavy-metaller songs at all, but something like 'Bridge over Troubled Water' or 'Tie Me Kangaroo Down, Sport' or 'Pie Jesu'.

The more unlikely, the better. In fact, we could offer a prize for the most ridiculous suggestion, and the prize could be the chance to lick that day's celebrity.

Now, our wish list of guests. George Clooney (obviously); Alexander McCall Smith (no looker but vay, vay, vay charming; at least his books are, as I've never had the pleasure of meeting him in person; I'm mildly obsessed with him); Kurt Cobain (such a shame he's been dead these past twelve years, as I have developed a sudden passion for Nirvana; I was always a late starter); Davina McCall; Dermot O'Leary (OBVIOUSLY); Bruce Springsteen (another sudden passion, at a loss to explain it); and my mammy (vay funny).

I still haven't decided if the unattractive black wedges which turned on me so fiendishly in Melbourne and gave me no end of blisters will be making the cut for the Canada/US leg (pun) of me book tour.

Obviously I don't want sandals which nurture black blistery treachery in their heart, but I *do* need a comfortable pair. Fact – interesting piece of info: these allegedly comfortable sandals, which were specifically purchased for comfort and not beauty, were not cheap. In fact they were dearer – yes, DEARER – than the Chie Miharas. They are made by an Italian company, famed for doing high but comfortable footwear. (I cannot name and shame them: maybe it's not their fault, maybe it's my feet that are to blame.) (Oh, all right then, it's Ruco Line.)

Perhaps I should have stuck to Clarks, but I was bedazzled by Ruco Line's Italian-ness. Hubris. Nasty, humbling, blistery hubris.

Himself went to London for the weekend mid-month and I stayed in Dublin with Mam and Dad, where I reverted to surly teenagerhood for three days. We went to visit my poor Auntie Maureen, who's in a home near Roscrea, and we were three crocks heading off in the car – my dad nearly blind, my mother half-deaf, and me with my bargain-basement bladder. (I had to stop every ten minutes to make my wees. I'm convinced many women suffer from the same problem, and if we talk more about it, maybe the government will build more jaxes. Hah! As if! You can always tell that men have designed and built hotels/conference centres/whatever, as there are 417 males' jaxes, while there are only two female ones, each with three cubicles, two of them out of order and 9,328 women queuing to use them.)

On the road trip to Roscrea (me in the back seat, whining that I needed to go to the wees), I kept trying to get them to do the three-monkeys thing, Dad with his hands over his eyes, Mam with her hands over ears, and me with my hands on my bladder – See no evil, hear no evil, wee no evil – but although Mam was game, Dad wasn't. (Himself only makes his wees once a week. On a Saturday evening, after the football results are on the telly. There are times when I even have to remind him. I have to say, 'Isn't it time, dear, for your little . . . ?')

But I'll tell you something gas. For many years I've had this frequent-wees-making trouble and have to 'go' many times during the night. AND in the daylight hours, and long car journeys are a problem. Also short ones. Anyway, out of nowhere I was contacted and asked if I would be the 'face' of Irish incontinence. How did they know????? However, I turned down this golden opportunity. (Did you see that Freudian 'golden' there? Isn't the subconscious gas?) It's not that I am ashamed of my faulty bladder, no. Not ashamed. I must love my body in all its imperfection. But at the same time I don't want to appear on the telly in an ad break, wearing a navy suit and smiling strangely and saying, 'Terrible trouble holding on to your wees? Me too! But help is available!' Or 'Hello, I'm Marian Keyes and my bladder is banjaxed!'

Now, 'shifting gears', last month I mentioned that Himself's team, Watford, are doing tremendously well this season, so well in fact that they have qualified for the play-offs – where they have to play other contenders to see if they get promoted to the Premeer Division. An occasion of great joy but my heart is quite heavy.

If they lose, Himself will be devvo, but if they get promoted, frankly it'll be worse. Next season will be a fecking bloodbath, with Himself coming home in a fouler every Saturday and me having to hide all the figurines.

Although it was a very work-filled month, I haven't too many entertaining stories for you. It's no fun to hear that this journalist came to the house, then that journalist, then I went and signed books, then I went on the radio. It's tedious to listen to, I'm sure.

Right then, I must go! I am off to Canada, then the US for me tour there.

Previously unpublished.

May

Canada!

US!

Crackers!

Cripes, busy, busy month. I'll attempt to do it justice for you. Spent two days in London before going to Toronto – Watford were playing in the first leg of the play-off semi-finals, where they bate the tar out of Crystal Palace. Hurray!

Suzanne called over and we had a great laugh, but then she had to go because approx twenty people had arrived to style me and take my photo. I'm not sure for what. At this stage, I'm so used to people turning up with make-up brushes and camera equipment and suitcases of strange clothes that I meekly and unquestioningly stand still so they can 'do' me.

On Sunday, I arrived in lovely Toronto and spent several days in passport checks – three different times! When did the Canadians get so suspicious? They are such a kindly people that I was surprised!

Monday was spent doing lady-bits wear-and-tear – I got waxed to kingdom come, pedicured, had my eyebrows and eyelashes tinted, my hair blow-dried, all of me fake-tanned (yes, I know you're not meant to do it the same day as waxing, but I'm not made of time). All set for work! Time-consuming, though. I bet Philip Roth doesn't have these worries.

Tuesday: a big important day – Watford are playing the second leg of the Crystal Palace match. Himself has made great friends with Manuela, the legendary concierge of Four Seasons Toronto who has tracked down the location of a bar in Toronto where we can watch the match.

So at 2.15 we get a taxi to Scallywags Sports Bar in downtown Toronto, where the kindly barkeep Sheryl makes both of our days by a) giving the Watford match precedence over the Roy Keane testimonial, which is on at the same time, then b) recognizing me. ('You are the image of Marian Keyes!')

Watford get a result! Which means they are in the final against Leeds in two weeks' time! Himself will be abandoning me mid-tour to see it in Cardiff.

That night, we go to see *Lord of the Rings*, the musical. I must admit, I agreed to go to it because I thought it would be hilarious, then I discovered it was three and a half hours long and thought, '*Nothing's* that funny.'

But we went and it was hugely impressive. An AMAZING set – a forest extends right out into the audience and the floor changes levels and the lighting is magnificent and there are times when the wind starts gusting and is blowing right out into the audience and then bits of black ash (except they're only bits of non-ashy paper, it's just the lighting that makes them look like ash) start flying at us and it's all very involving.

Gandalf was bad, though – he had that stupid beard-and-no-tash combo that I find so baffling. Also his hood kept falling off. But worst of all, he had all the gravitas and other-worldly wisdom of a geography teacher with discipline problems. Very, very UNCONVINCING. Also, the music was not the Middle Earth experience they promised. Indeed, there were one or two Andrew Lloyd Webber moments. However, it was a great spectacle.

Thursday, Montréal. God, what a FABULOUS city. Not like

anywhere I've ever been before, sort of French, but not exactly, sort of Canadian, but not that either, but some amazing exotic mix. LOVED it. Also, incredibly warm welcome. Wonderful readers' event on Friday night. Just before the reading, I popped into Lululemon (Canadian yoga wear, even though I only do yoga once a decade, but the leggings and T-shirts and mini-hoodies are lovely).

Saturday, Boston! Meeting Caitríona, Seán and Anne Marie, who have come from New York, Eileen, who has come from Dublin, and Suzanne from London! Thrilling! All of us together. Terrible rain in Boston. We are Irish, we know about rain, but our jaws are hanging open. Dangerous rain, which could concuss you.

We spent our time shuttling between the hotel and Au Bon Pain. In fact, we calculated that all during the weekend, at least one of us was either *at* Au Bon Pain, *on the way to* Au Bon Pain, *returning from* Au Bon Pain or *eating something purchased at* Au Bon Pain.

Au Bon Pain took on a mythological air, like the 108-minutes computer in *Lost*. We needed someone on the Au Bon Pain shift at all times.

We attempted to go out for dinner on Saturday night, but the combination of it being Mother's Day weekend, plus graduation weekend, meant everywhere was booked out, and with Seán's friends Danny and Kristen there were nine of us and so everyone laughed in our face when we showed up looking for a table, so we ended up in some place called Chili's, which was very enjoyable in a cheap, dirty-floored sort of way. Shur, it's all about the people!

On Sunday morning we woke up to discover that the governor of Massachusetts had declared a state of emergency because of the rain! I've never before been in a place where there's a 'state of emergency'. For a moment I was quite thrilled! Then I realized that many, many poor divils have had their houses flooded and it's not thrilling at all. Merely wet and miserable.

Caitríona and Suzanne brave the flood waters to go shopping, and the rest of us sit in my hotel room, eating our stuff from Au Bon Pain, and the whole thing is like a very slow play. Now and again Anne Marie looks out at the stormy sky and says, 'Look at it.' Then she shrieks, 'LOOK AT IT!!!!'

Next, Himself wanders over and stares out the window and says, 'The flood waters are still rising,' and Seán says, 'Try the phone again, are the lines still down?' Great fun!

Monday, they all go home and I do Bostonian work. Brookline Books hosts a FABLISS reading for me on the Monday night, where I have a full house, despite the rain.

Wednesday, New York! Where I have a mini-meltdown (I have one on every tour): when getting ready for the Bryant Square reading, I discover I've lost my foundation. I become hysterical, yelling, 'I have twenty lip glosses! Three mascaras! Even two Touche Éclats! Why couldn't I have lost one of them???' Then I discover the missing foundation in Himself's washbag and all is well.

Excellent events in NYC, sponsored by Clarins – people were THRILLED with their goodie bags. In fact, even Michael Morrison, very important person in William Morrow/HarperCollins, was spotted disappearing with a bronzer.

Friday, Washington DC. BEA – a GINORMOUS book fair. Everyone from US publishing there. On Saturday afternoon, Himself says goodbye – he's leaving for Cardiff for the Watford play-off final against Leeds, with a promise to meet me on Monday in Seattle. Everyone is very concerned about me being left on my own, as if I'm a half-wit. 'I am a grown woman,' I assure them, 'I am forty-two and a half.'

'Yes, but . . .' they say.

'I'm fine,' I insist, getting quite narky. 'I'm fine, okay? FINE!!!'

Then I return to the hotel, to get ready for the HarperCollins party, and when I leave, I lock my key in my room . . .

Mortified.

Even though it was a party, it was actually extremely nice. It was held at the Smithsonian Castle, which has a garden, and I got there early and bagsied a seat, a sort of park bench. I was very happy to have a seat, even though the anxiety that the hotel wouldn't let me back into my room was gnawing at me like a toothache.

A buffet was set up, and I hopped out of my bench and quickly got a plate of food – mostly cheese and crackers – and CRAMMED it into me because it's impossible to eat at these things: as soon as you put a mouthful of food into your clob, someone asks you a question requiring a long, detailed, food-free answer.

I was eating at high speed, covered with cracker crumbs – on my skirt, my face, in my hair. Then! I espy Dennis Lehane! I'm a big fan. Lovely Debbie Stiers (head of publicity at HC) says, 'Oh, Marian, you wanted to meet Dennis, didn't you. Dennis! Dennis! Over here.' And I was frantically waving my hands to indicate that no, I didn't want to meet Dennis Lehane, not while my mouth was filled with food and I was covered with cracker crumbs, but too late, he had arrived and I had to extend a crackery hand and mumble through a clobful of cheese that I'm his biggest fan. (He was v. gracious.)

Also, John Connolly shows up (excellent Irish thriller writer, for those who don't know him, but I presume everyone does) and it was very nice to see another Irish person and we laughed Irishly together, making jokes about potatoes and rainfall, then we linked arms and danced a jig. John knows Dennis. Maybe he might mention to Dennis that I'm not always covered in cracker crumbs.

Because of Himself not being there, everyone was kindly and solicitous. Even big cheeses (pun) at HC kept checking in with me, including Michael Morrison. At one stage he says, 'Notice anything different about me?' and does that sweep with his hands that people do when they are proud of their new look.

Although Michael is always friendly to me, he is a vay, vay powerful person and it is important to get this right. 'You did something to your hair?' I suggest weakly, and he says, 'No! I'm BRONZED. I'm wearing the Clarins bronzer!' And, of course, once he'd said it, I could indeed see that he was looking very sunkissed.

Sunday, Seattle. (Hotel in DC *did* let me back into the room after I'd produced photo ID.) News reaches me: Watford have won the match! They are now officially Going Up. Everyone is THRILLED and I really must stop being a doom-mongrel. Next season will be *wonderful*, they won't have the shit kicked out of them every Saturday and most Tuesdays, and they *won't* be relegated.

Monday, Himself reappears and has a present for me: a yellow memorial shirt of the match.

Five fantastic events in Seattle, including one at Starbucks HQ, and at Third Place Books the woman who came from Hawaii officially wins the Person Who Travelled Furthest To See Me prize.

Then back to Canada, to BEAUTIFUL Vancouver and BEAUTIFUL Vancouver Island, where CBC Book Club and Munro's Books do fantastic events and I'm on telly four times in twenty hours.

Then we go home.

Previously unpublished.

June

Writing!

Except I'm not!

Let's see. I got back home at the start of month and since then I've been trying to get back into a writing routine, which is not going well and is going, in fact, very, very badly.

I had loads of articles to write, which was good, because it eased the terror of switching on the computer after a long time away from it. But eventually I ran out of deflection mechanisms and I had to face the horror of the novel.

I tried to follow the advice which I give to other authors: put one word in front of another; do a small amount every day; ignore your crapness. I'm trying to be positive, to do my best, but the default setting in my brain is Negative, and the arrow always sneaks back there, no matter how hard I try to send it to Positive.

Now and then I stand at the top of the stairs in my nightdress, my hair askew, and shriek at Himself, 'I am creatively bankrupt!' Then a gardener comes thumping in through the front door (yes, they're still here, they will always be here, I've accepted it now), pushing a wheelbarrow of bark (or something), and I howl at him, 'I am a spent force, a torn docket, a busted flush!' (He puts his head down and hurries past with his burden, dying to get home that evening to tell his wife and family about what a lunatic I am.)

Next I ring up all my friends and family and screech at them that the gig is up, that the game is over, that my career as a writer

401

is at an end and do they know of any jobs I could do? Then everyone tells me to shut up, that I'm always saying that and that maybe I should take a little break and read some books and do something mindless. But I tell them not to be so silly, how can I take time to read books when I'm supposed to be WRITING one!

(Although the garden still isn't finished, it no longer looks like the Battle of the Somme; now it looks more like the foundations of a multistorey car park. The house – because we are terraced and all gardeners and their 'stuff' must come through our hall – looks like a building site. Filth everywhere.)

Anyway, *Big Brother* is on – THANK GOD. It is a marvellous diversion. This has been the evening routine for the past month. 7.30–8.00: the lovely, lovely Dermot O'Leary (more of which, later). Then 8.00–9.00: Himself watches football between two bizarre nations (for example Upper Volta versus Luxembourg, because the World Cup is on) and I Do Other Things (not really sure what, remove make-up, sing tunelessly, that sort of thing. Also I do meditation, most days anyway, except – disaster! I time myself using Shaunie the Sheep kitchen timer (Shaunie from *Wallace and Gromit*). I put Shaunie in the bathroom so his relentless ticking doesn't distract me from meditation – I'm perfectly capable of extreme distraction, left to my own devices. Anyway, one night I was sitting there and sitting there and sitting there and thinking, 'Christ alive, this meditation lark is as boring as all get out! Will it ever end? Well, the short answer is no, not if I was depending on Shaunie to alert me to Time's Up. For poor Shaunie was injured – his neck was stuck at thirteen minutes. Just stopped dead. It transpired I had been meditating for about six hours, and hadn't known when to stop because Shaunie didn't brrrrrring and let me know. (Like in *What's Eating Gilbert Grape*, when Leonardo DiCaprio stayed in the freezing bath because Johnny Depp went off with a woman and forgot to tell him to get out.) He hasn't repeat offended (Shaunie the sheep, not Johnny Depp), but I am nervous around him now. The trust is gone.)

Then at nine o'clock I fight my way through the rubble of the hall, the muck, the filth, the abandoned bananas and tabloids and two-litre bottles of Lilt, and return to The Room, where we watch *Big Brother*, until ten o'clock. When that ends we watch Russell Brand until 10.30. (Funny how everyone has radically rethought their opinion of Russell Brand just because a rumour did the rounds that he'd rode Kate Moss. Everyone now insists that he's sexy, but many people pretend that 'Oh, I *always* fancied him.' I'll be honest. I didn't always fancy him. But I sort of do now.)

At this point I go to bed and Himself watches the second half of the match (taped from earlier). A routine is nice. I've tried making a few new dinners – the Goan beef curry was a success, the hot Thai salad less so. But we must take risks in order to find out what works and what doesn't, is that not so? When a risk fails – as it occasionally must, for then it would not be a risk – we must not be hard on ourselves. We must simply get a pizza out of the freezer and live to fight another day.

What else? Well, you know the way me and Caitríona are bridesmaids for Rita-Anne, and you know the way I came up with a cunning plan to dress us in Missoni coats? As a way of justifying purchase of Missoni coats? Well, plan has gone awry. But not in a bad way.

Rita-Anne saw some lovely coats in Brown Thomas which she thought would do for us. The only thing wrong was that they weren't Missoni coats. But they were the right colour and had detailing which echoed the detailing on her dress (I can say no more, I'm sworn to secrecy about her dress, I can say NOTHING which might give the game away). So I visited said coat and found it to be perfect. Immediately I informed Caitríona in New York, who did her best to track it down, and after many setbacks she located it, tried it on and pronounced it to be excellent, if slightly short in the sleeves. Done deal! Coats bought for a November wedding and it is still only June! I am *such* a swotty Virgo!

I've only one slight gripe: they are excellent coats, but are from Moschino's Cheap & Chic range, and while there is no denying that they are chic – no one could dispute that, *mes amies* – they were several light years from cheap. But beautiful, undeniably beautiful, and if we like we can sell them on eBay after the wedding. 'For far more than we paid for them,' according to Himself, who is an optimist. (And can be delusional on occasion.)

My mammy has tried to book an appointment with a personal shopper in House of Fraser for her mother-of-the-bride outfit but they told her to get lost and try again in mid-October, that right now is way too early for autumn clothing.

Frankly, I do not know how her nerves can stand it. If it was my daughter I would have had the mother-of-the-bride outfit bought before my daughter had even met her prospective husband. My mother waited until a mere six weeks before my wedding before deciding on her outfit. How can she do it? Clearly, she is a daredevil, a risk-taker, a knows-no-fear-and-laughs-in-the-face-of-danger-etc. kind of person. That's Pisceans for you. (When she gets her appointment we are all going to go along. I will report.)

Highlight of the month: I touched the flesh of Dermot O'Leary! (Only his hand, but all the same.) I was on *Big Brother's Little Brother* on Friday 23 June. Thrilling! Himself and Suzanne came too, and as it was eviction day all the friends and family of the potential evictees were in the green room. Suzanne made many friends (that is her way, she is gregarious). She moved and shook her way through the friends and family.

June

I had to maintain a dignified distance because I was about to slag off some of their nearest and dearest on national telly. Awkward, undeniably awkward. I saw Davina from a distance. I opened the window and shouted out, 'I LOVE YOU, DAVINA-AAAAAAAAAAAAAAAAA!' I don't know if she heard me.

On the final day of June everything broke. Himself's back – it 'goes' on him occasionally, but will he go to the doctor? No. Indeed no. He simply suffers through – you'd swear they had never invented painkillers. That's men for you. My dad is exactly the same. Then the SkyPlus broke. Then the computer got a virus and had to be carted away – terrifying. We don't know how bad the damage is, it's very scary. Then *I* broke.

I'd been wallowing in UNPRECEDENTED good health and hadn't had a virus/ear infection et al in MONTHS. But this all came to an abrupt end on 30 June and now I'm enjoying balmy temperatures, aching limbs, cotton-wool brain and a conviction that an invisible person is hanging around me and jabbing a hat-pin into my ear at irregular intervals.

Previously unpublished.

July

A good month!
Despite being made to go to the opera!

A *much* better month than last month. To start with, my writer's block has lifted and I was able to write a fair bit of the new book, which is v. v. heartening because I always feel worthless when I'm not being productive.

I've been writing about a character called Lola Daly and I've come to a natural stopping point with her and now have to get into the mindset of a new character who was to be called Sive but is no longer called Sive because non-Irish people don't know how to pronounce her name (when I tested subjects, some were calling her 'Siv-ee' and others were calling her 'Sieve' (small round things with many holes, used in cooking), when the actual pronunciation is Syve, sort of like Scythe (Grim Reaper's tool) but with a *v* instead of a *th*.

And let me tell you something funny, if I gave Sive her Irish spelling, she would be spelt Sadhbh, which would REALLY pose problems).

The thing is, I find when I'm reading that if I don't know how to pronounce a character's name, I can't really bond with her. Clearly Sive will not do. So now I am experimenting with Kate and Grace to see if either of those names will 'take'.

So what else? Went to England early July because my parents-in-law John and Shirley were celebrating their fiftieth wedding anniversary. Fifty years! Fair play. Cousins and old friends and the original best man and bridesmaids descended in droves upon Warwickshire, and Himself was the person in charge of organizing the celebratory lunch, which was for eighty people, and he was a nervous wreck.

At one stage I turned and asked him how he was, and he was sitting bolt upright, his food untouched, a sheen of perspiration on his pale forehead, and he muttered through bloodless lips, 'I just want it to be all over and for it to have gone smoothly.' (Which instantly became our catchphrase – we are now saying on the slightest of pretexts, 'I just want it to be all over and for it to have gone smoothly.')

For the most part, the anniversary party DID go smoothly, despite the shadow hanging over all of us (which I'll get to).

The day after the knees-up, we went with John and Shirley to Glyndebourne (place in south of England where opera goes on). Now, I will openly admit to not being an opera person. I'm just not. I just don't get it. And at least I'm being honest about it and not faking being cultured and at the end I don't lepp to my feet and bellow, 'Oh bravo, Diva most fair, bravo, bravo! Tour de force!' Instead I clap politely and eye the exit.

This particular opera was *Così fan tutte* and it has the most stupid plot ever – two blokes decide (egged on by a friend who is a definite bad influence) to check if their girls were faithful/ unfaithful, so they announce they are going off to war (as you do) and come back wearing very bad moustaches and pretending to be Albanians. Duped by the moustaches, the two girls don't recognize their old boyfriends, and after a fair amount of shilly-shallying get off with the 'Albanians'. Moral: women are stupid and duplicitous.

Frankly, I was annoyed. No wonder the world is so weighted

against women if this sort of propaganda is doing the rounds. And yes, I know, it's all about the singing really and I shouldn't get caught up in the plot, because all opera plots are shit, but still, I was annoyed!

The day after the sexist opera, lovely Shirley went into hospital and had a mastectomy. She'd been diagnosed with breast cancer in June and the doctors allowed her to have her party before the operation.

She was a superstar about it all. She came out of hospital thirty-six hours later and her only painkillers were paracetamol! If it was me, I'd have been on a morphine drip. Then the wait started for the results, to see if the cancer had spread. Two full weeks of a wait. A very tense, anxious time.

Meanwhile, the war in Lebanon started and her doctor managed to get trapped there and it seemed she wouldn't be able to get the results on the appointed day and things got even tenser. Anyway, we've just heard the news and it's all pretty hopeful, so thank Christ. But she's been totally, totally amazing. It's incredible to me that she was so calm about it all and that there was no song-and-dance, no post-operation infections, no allergy to the hospital food, no catching of MRSA, no reaction to the painkillers, no demanding of strong opiates – all of which would happen to any member of my family who had an operation. She is a complete trooper and an example to us all.

Himself and myself went to London for a day and a half that week and managed to get bridesmaids' boots – with me and Caitríona being bridesmaids at Rita-Anne's wedding and wearing coats instead of meringuey dresses? Yes, well, we needed brown suede knee boots to go with the coats. And it was a real boon to track down the only size 35 brown suede knee boots in London (just in!), and my cup overfloweth when I managed to drag them up to my knees! Joy abounded! A second pair was bought for Caitríona and despatched to New York and yes – hers fitted her too!

We're going gangbusters on the wedding! Great progress is being made. Ema is flower girl and her dress has been bought, and Luka is ring-bearer and he's getting kitted out for his morning suit etc. when he arrives in Ireland on 3 August! I CAN'T WAIT!!!!!!!!!!!!

Then, on the Friday of that week, me, Himself and Suzanne went to the *Big Brother* eviction. It was so great, despite the fact that Nikki (my favourite) was evicted. And you should see Davina (McCall) in real life – she's even more beautiful, if you can possibly imagine such a thing. Her skin and her hair and her eyes GLOW, and although she is pregnant she still looks really chic (that is, of course, because she is half-French).

Suzanne is very, very funny and even though it is puerile, every time an unattractive man walked past, she would nudge me or I would nudge her and say, 'You gave him a blowjob in a hedge' and 'You had anal sex with him, then he broke it off with you and you called round to his house in the middle of the night, begging him to take you back' just like we used to do in our twenties.

Oh yes! The garden is finished!! It's very nice and it hasn't got a blade of grass (Himself's stipulation, that mossy grass was killing him). It's all gravelly and decky and granitey and that sort of thing. Plants though, also, just not grass. Pleased, yes, extremely pleased. Definitely worth all the mud and upset.

What else? I made vegetarian moussaka – Christ alive, what a song-and-dance! I made it because Shirley (beloved mother-in-law) made it for us the night before the big party and it was delicious. (Even though it includes lentils. Mind you, I'm a big fan of lentils, I'm prepared to defend them because I think they get a very bad press.) I asked (like a lick-arsey daughter-in-law) for the recipe and although she warned me it was 'a bit fiddly', nothing prepared me for the hour-and-three-quarter marathon in the kitchen. Aubergines – yes, aubergines! Putting salt on them, them draining them and whatnot. Then the lentils – two different types – took ages. And when all that stuff was done, I had to make a topping with flour and eggs and ricotta cheese. Came out nice though.

Mam and Dad went to Canada on their holiers, and Dad was in mortal fear of losing his luggage, and in fairness he is right to be afraid because he is related to me, who has the worst luggage karma in the world. I lose my bags so often that I don't bother going to the belt any more (honest to God). I go straight to the desk and start filling in the forms.

Part of their trip included a cruise to Alaska. (When they got back they complained to me about the cold – it's Alaska, for the love of God! What were they expecting? Balmy sunshine?) However, when they got on the ship, Dad's bag had gone missing! Yes, Mam's two bags turned up but Dad's was in the wind. He created 'merry hell' (good phrase) by all accounts, kicking up a right fuss at reception, demanding to see the captain, no less, and threatening to get an injunction to stop the ship from sailing until his bag was located.

Sadly, the bag turned up before he got a chance to put his words into actions, but in fairness, is it any wonder *I'm* anxious, considering what my parents are like?

Meanwhile, my rude good health continues. Apart from a small spell of cystitis I'm in top-notch condition, which is as it should be considering the ENORMOUS AMOUNT of supplements I take every day – so many I'm actually ashamed to list them, but anyway: magnesium (to stave off sugar cravings); spirulina (TONS of it, on

Vilma's advice); vitamin B6; vitamin B5; calcium (to guard against osteoporosis); omega 3s (because you have to, you are no one if you don't, all the fashionable people will laugh at you); acidophilus (to keep digestion in tip-top condition).

And there's more, but I don't want to seem neurotic, which of course I am, but no one wants to look it.

Previously unpublished.

August

The universe is wrong!
Pinkness!

As I write, I'm just after breaking my laptop and I am typing this at Himself's office computer. I'd just switched off the laptop after a morning's work and accidentally dropped it on the floor. Now, I am always dropping things, I am clumsy and careless, but I didn't expect it to be BROKEN, because if I broke everything I dropped I would have nothing left at all! But yes, I DID break the fecker. A lump fell off it and the battery fell out and even Himself, who can fix everything, couldn't fix it.

He has just ferried it off to the people in Cabinteely, who fixed the main computer when it pure crashed a couple of months ago. He thinks it will be at least a week before it's fixed, and to be quite honest, I'm upset. Clearly I regard the computer as an extension of myself and the work has been going well – slow but well – and I am really getting into my new character Marnie and now is not a good time to have to stop. Really, it's not.

Some might take the view that perhaps the universe is telling me it's time to take a break, but no, the universe is *wrong*.

Ontra noo, I suspect the universe hasn't a clue. Everyone thinks the universe is this wise old yoke, who knows everything, but I reckon it is a con job. The universe probably has Alzheimer's, because this is not a good time for me to stop work, *at all*.

Then I went upstairs to do my meditation, in the hope that I might 'centre' myself (I'm not sure if I'm making fun of myself or not. In a way I am, but in another way I take it all quite seriously).

I went to set my Shaunie the Sheep kitchen timer – I've stuck with him even after he let me down that other time – but to my alarm his head was on back to front. (How?!) I set it, but held out little hope, and sure enough, Shaunie didn't brrrringg in twenty-five minutes but clicked to sixty and stared at me in shame, his head once more back to front. I'll have to get another timer, but I can't bring myself to throw Shaunie out. I will put him on a shelf with some other broken things, as a reward for long service.

So what else has been happening? Well, it's been a busy time – months can be long things, can they not? – and I have much to report, which I'll try to do as quickly as possible before Himself comes back and ousts me from his chair.

(Speaking of Himself, the football season has started, and as you know at the end of last season Himself's team (Watford) got promoted to the Premeer Division and I wasn't happy, suspecting that they were in over their heads. They've played three matches since the season began, they have lost two and drawn one, and I have a knot in my stomach every time they play. Himself is being quite bullish and gung-ho, but I'm not enjoying it one bit.)

We've been awash – yes, AWASH – with visitors. Ljiljana arrived from Prague, with Ema (six), Luka (four) and Zaga (sixty-five). (Zaga is Ljiljana's mother. When I was at the Belgrade book fair she fed me so much on two successive nights that I nearly wept from fullness. This was my chance to get revenge.)

God, how weird! Ljiljana has just rung. And me just writing about her! It is funny being in Himself's office, in the hub, with phones ringing, etc. Normally I wouldn't know about anything until I came downstairs at the end of the day. I told her the sorry story of my smithereened laptop and how upset I was, and she said the next stage would be denial, then anger, then I would say, 'Feck this for a game of soldiers, I'm going shopping!' (Acceptance, I believe that stage is called.)

So, in instalments, we went to Lahinch. First Tadhg, Susan, Lilers and Luka. Then Rita-Anne, Jimmy, Ema and Zaga, then, bringing up the rear, Himself and me. Lovely, lovely time, except a consignment of them went out in the boat to see the Cliffs of Moher and nearly drowned. Honest to God! I stayed back in the house, working, and the next thing I heard a helicopter clattering overhead, which I just thought was some smug, fat golfer in a visor and hideous clothes, getting choppered into the Lahinch golf course. But no! It was the Air and Sea Rescue Helicopter, and it flew so close to the window that myself and a rescue man in a red jumpsuit made *actual eye-contact*, then he winked – yes, WINKED, at my age! – at me.

It eventually transpired that it wasn't Lilers/Zaga/Himself et al who needed rescuing, but it was bad enough. Huge waves had their boat almost on its side. Zaga puked, Lilers, Ema and Luka went to bed as soon as they got back, and even Himself, who has a cast-iron constitution, needed a pint of stout and a plate of chips to settle his stomach.

There had been bold talk of going to Inisheer the following day, but these plans were abruptly abandoned with Zaga stating she was never again getting on a boat for as long as she lived.

After a week we came back to Dublin and there wasn't enough room for me in the car so I had to get the train, which I was v. excited about, as I was hoping for 'local colour', entertaining anecdotes, etc. Sadly, the only thing that happened was that I and another woman were sitting on a bench at Ennis station, eating a scone (me), and the next thing a man in a hat emerged from the stationmaster's office (possibly the stationmaster) with a yellow measuring tape (one of the ones that can stand by themselves, fyi). 'Girls,' he said, 'would you mind getting up. I want to measure the bench.' We duly got up and he duly measured the bench (four foot six) and I would love, love, *love* to pretend that this was just his hobby, something to do to pass the time when he'd finished the sudoku in the paper, but then he said, 'We're getting more benches for the platform, I needed to see how long it was.'

Once I got on the train, no one addressed a single word to me for the three and a half hours it took to get to Dublin. I was quite bitter about this because Anne Marie once got a bus to Donegal and sat beside a woman who opened the conversation by saying loudly, 'Suck my dick! Yes! Suck my dick! That's what they sprayed on my fence, the local gurriers. Suck my dick!'

However, I did have a TREMENJUSSLY chatty taxi driver from the station, and we complained at length about the Irish Government and the Gardaí and their swizziness in extracting millions in speeding fines from the poor people of Ireland for doing 43ks in a 40k zone. We were in firm agreement that there are only seven roads in Ireland where it is ever possible to do above 40, because the rest of the time we are stuck in gridlock and crawling along at 8ks an hour, and that the coppers position themselves with their cruel little machines on these seven roads. Then the taxi driver changed the conversation to mackerel fishing, which I did not enjoy half as much.

Now, if I may talk a little about Ema and Luka – I love them hugely, they're very beautiful, inside and also outside, with gorgeous skin and eyes and hair and everything, legs and all, that sort of stuff. Ema is a girl's girl and I had a lovely time with her. I had a lovely time with Luka too, but every time I tried to kiss him he made a face and ran away, whereas Ema hung around with me and made me put down the roof on the car and drive around listening to Sister Sledge and wearing pink sunglasses. She said frequently, 'We have the same taste, Mariana.' (That's what she calls me – Mariana. Is that not gorgeous?) Then, when we were washing our hands in the loo in Roly's, the soap was pink and she said, 'Pink! It's our colour!'

I missed Ema very much when she went back. I would love to share a flat with her and I've decided that if Himself leaves me, that is precisely what I will do. She's brilliant company, and we could sit around all day long, watching *Bounding* (seminal line: 'Pink, pink, what's wrong with pink?') and swapping pink lip gloss and trying on pink shoes. Now and again, we would don our pink fairy wings and put lovely spells on each other with our lovely pink wands. (I think the child has a gift: she put a spell on Susan so that she would pass her driving test – and she did!) We would eat only pink foods – cranberries (and thereby keep cystitis at bay – mind you, she is only six, she mightn't be in as much danger as I am), ham, smoked salmon and strawberry-flavoured Starbursts. (I don't like strawberries, but I like things with fake strawberry flavouring.)

Speaking of cystitis and thereby moving the conversation to matters gynaecological, my monthly visitor was very late, so late that I wondered if I was pregnant and actually did a test (there were a couple in the drawer left over from more hopeful days), but I wasn't, then I decided I must be starting the menopause. Then I discovered that I had my dates wrong by a week.

No sooner had the Praguers returned home than Himself's parents arrived. Shirley is doing very well, she says she feels better than she has in years, which is a massive relief to hear.

Then I gammied my back. I tried on my new baggy-sleeved top that I got in London, and it's sort of Russiany looking, and I was so overcome with its lovely newness and Russianness that I decided to try a little Cossacky dancing, as you do. Inevitably it ended in tears with me falling over and damaging my back. I have pulled a muscle, which keeps spasming like a jack-in-the-box.

Culinary news this month: I did an Introduction to Vietnamese cookery class and an Introduction to Indian cooking one. And I made a risotto, the first one I ever made, and it turned out very well – God, it's scary though, isn't it. I read Alastair Little's cookbook and it said for risotto you must adopt 'a rigid and unwavering methodology' or some such and I thought, 'For God's sake, it's only a bit of rice!' However, I DID adopt the rigid and unwavering methodology and it was v. nice – Himself said it was 'a triumph'. He is a tremendously easy man to please, thank Christ.

Oh God, he's back and he wants his computer, he needs it to do the tax return. I have to go. I'm going to France on 10 Sept for a walking holiday – this time in the Loire Valley. I will report. Also, on 10 Sept I will be forty-three and I love, love, *love* getting older. My only regret is that I am not fifty-seven. Or ninety-two.

Previously unpublished.

September

La Belle France!
Birthday passes 'peacefully'!

I had *un visit merveilleux* in France. Much fancier this year (in the Loire Valley). Staying in chateaus (or chateaux, if we want to be correct about it, and why not?) that have been turned into *les hôtels* and dining like kings *chaque* evening on 28-course dinners. Despite walking up to fifteen miles a day, it was not enough to cancel out all the grub and I am now in familiar territory where I hate looking in the mirror, hate having to get dressed and am terrified to weigh myself. But it was worth it!

Now, in an abrupt change of subject, I've had an idea for a retro, 1970s-style sitcom. You know I said that I'd love to move into a flat with Ema (six-year-old niece) and surround ourselves with pink? Well, Himself said one evening in France when he had a fair bit of drink on him that if I was moving in with Ema he was going to 'throw his lot in' with Luka (five) and Milinko (seventy). (Milinko is Luka and Ema's granddad, is father to Ljiljana, father-in-law to my brother Niall and husband of Zaga (sixty-five).) The thing about both Luka and Milinko is that they are very good-looking. When me and Himself were in Belgrade, we looked through old photo albums and there were loads of Milinko looking like Errol Flynn, and even now he has a roguish twinkle in his eye.

But Himself said he'd miss me and that was when the whole

sitcom thing arose. We said we'd live next door to each other – and that's the name of the crappy sitcom – *THE BOYS NEXT DOOR*!

We spent most of our *temps en France* detailing it. Right, in one EXTREMELY PINK flat live me, Ema and Zaga. We have three single beds in a very pink bedroom. Zaga speaks no English (except for her catchphrase) and does an awful lot of cleaning. Her catchphrase is 'You STUPID boy' accompanied by a cuff to the head of the offender. Zaga has an amazing cleaning cupboard, a bit like a Batcave, and when she touches a special mop, a bed leaps from the wall, all made up with lovely pink bedclothes. She sleeps in there if me or Ema have visitors. (More of which later.)

Zaga is the most popular of all the characters and the live studio audience goes wild, clapping and cheering, whenever she comes on. Also, 'You STUPID boy' becomes a worldwide catchphrase, with politicians and everyone saying it.

Right, Ema (six). Very, very pink and her catchphrase is 'Is it pink?'

Me (forty-three). I have no catchphrase yet. Myself and Himself decided on one for me one night over dinner in the Château de Pray but we've forgotten it. Himself had a fair bit of drink on him, but I've no excuse. I've suggested that my temporary catchphrase be 'One day we'll all be dead and none of this will matter', as I *do* say it a lot, but Himself thinks it lacks catchiness.

Okay, then, the boys' flat. It is moodily lit, with low sofas, shag-pile carpets, a Scalextric race track and an actual bar, stocked only with brandy. The brandy is Milinko's, because when we were in Belgrade he offered it to Himself in such a great accent that we've been saying it ever since. It's impossible to recreate on the page, but I'll try: 'Brrrrrrennndy?' Accompanied, of course, by a roguish twinkle. That is Milinko's catchphrase.

Luka's catchphrase is 'My trousers . . .' Said sort of dismally. This is because he has lost them. Again. He is standing there in his jocks, indicating his trouserless state with a fatalistic hand gesture which implies that trousers are unpredictable beasts, faithless characters, liable to leave you at a moment's notice, regardless of the embarrassment and heartache their departure causes you. This relates back to his visit to Ireland in August 2005 (he was four). He had a long anorak, which came to mid-thigh, and his jeans were a bit too loose for him and we'd be walking around Lahinch and every now and then he'd stop and say sadly to Himself, 'Himself, my trousers . . .' and Himself would look down and Luka's anorak would still be on, protecting his modesty, but his jeans would be down around his ankles.

In *THE BOYS NEXT DOOR*, Luka will lose his trousers every episode: he might have to leave them behind when departing from a lady's boudoir at short notice (her husband came home or she asked Luka when they were getting engaged); he might get them caught on barbed wire while sneaking over a back wall; he might lose them in a poker game; he might get mugged for them . . . The list is endless.

And then there's Himself. He is the voice of reason in the boys' flat. His catchphrase is, 'Ah lads, have sense.' To which Luka usually replies, 'You're not mines daddy!' (As happened, in actual real life, on his last visit to Ireland), then they leap up and have a Darth Vader/Luke Skywalker battle recreation.

We have put together a synopsis of the first six episodes, to pitch to TV companies:

Episode one. Himself gets locked out of his flat and the other two boys are too 'busy' within to hear him knocking, so he has to come and spend the night in the girls' flat, sleeping in Zaga's bed

(Zaga stays in the mop-cave). Unfortunately for Himself, Ema and I are doing (pink, of course) face masks and other 1970s-style girlish things, and Himself is obliged to do them too. Much laughter.

Episode two. Exactly the same as episode one, except it is Milinko who is locked out and has to do the pink face masks.

Episode three. Luka has to go to ground for a while as he has had a paternity suit slapped on him. While everyone else is out and about, he has to spend the day cleaning with Zaga. She says 'You STUPID boy' a lot because he is not a dab hand with the dusters.

Episode four. New pink strawberry-flavoured cigarettes have been introduced to the marketplace, aimed at children (not so unlikely). Ema, who up until then had been vehemently anti-smoking, is charmed and immediately develops a forty-a-day habit. ('How can they be bad if they're pink?')Worse, she falls into roguish company as Zaga and I insist she does her smoking on the balcony, which we share with THE BOYS NEXT DOOR, and she spends a lot of time with Milinko, who offers her 'Brrrrrrreeendy?' which she declines as it is not pink.

Episode five. Zaga, who is very protective of my non-drinking status, goes bananas when Milinko offers me a 'Brrrrrrreeendy'. She rants on and on and on in Serbian for a least five minutes and I get Ema to listen and translate. She nods and says 'Uh-huh' and 'Hmmm' and 'O-kaay' and when Zaga finally finishes I say to Ema, 'What did she say?' And Ema thinks hard and says, very slowly, 'She said – "You STUPID BOY!"' Uproarious laughter.

Episode six. We did have an episode six, but neither of us can remember, now that we're home. I know we thrashed it out over dinner in the Château de Noizay. In fairness, Himself can't be held accountable because he had a fair bit to drink, but once again, I have no excuse.

So what do you think? Is it a runner? We also have great ideas for guest appearances from other family members, including Caitríona, who will ring from New York every time she sees Spiderman. Her catchphrase is: 'A hot meal at a fair price.' (From a terrible weekend we spend in Tijuana. Well, I say weekend, we were meant to stay the weekend, but we went on Friday night and came back to LA on Saturday morning because it was so awful, where I was nearly thrown in the slammer at the border by accidentally trying to bring a Mexican apple back into the US of A, and I wouldn't mind but it wasn't actually a Mexican apple, it was an American one which I'd brought along but hadn't eaten.)

We came back from France on the car ferry and the weather was so terrifying that I was genuinely worried that I might be about to die. Himself felt seasick, but then again he'd had a fair amount to drink. In fact, usually that journey is very pleasant. You get on, have your dinner, take a turn around the souvenir shop (much leprechaun merchandise), then retire to bed.

My birthday passed without incident. I moved from forty-two to forty-three without drama. Good presents. A BEAUTIFUL powder-blue casserole dish from John and Shirley, a juicer from Himself, also products from Bliss and Sisley anti-age gear from Rita-Anne and Jimmy.

Best present of all was a painting by Tadhg. Tadhg is an immensely talented artist but has the low self-esteem that I have and is afraid to engage with his talent. It was shark-subduingly uplifting to get a painting that he had done and it is really brilliant.

Now I'm back from France and keen to get on with the book, which was going vair, vair well before leaving, but I've been asked to do all kinds of publicity things and I would rather poke myself in the eye with a rusty compass than do any of them, but I am obliged because of favours owed, or a sense of guilt, or because the person will end up in penury, or the well-grounded expectation that the journalist will shaft me further down the line if I don't.

I would just like to live a quiet life, writing my books and my newsletter and meeting people who read my books and cooking nice dinners in my powder-blue casserole dish (indeed, cooking nice dinners FOR the people who read my books).

It feels like nearly every interview I do, I'm misquoted badly enough to sound like a half-wit and I'm finding it wearing. Perhaps if I faked my own death . . .

Anyway, changing the subject to backs. Mine is better, and also my computer is fixed, thanks be to Christ! Himself, however, has come a cropper. A day or so after we got back, he did his back in – brace yourself, you simply will not BELEEEEEVE this – *while cutting his fingernails!*

Honest to God! Is no pursuit safe! There are traps every which way we turn! He is in bad pain and I'm begging him to see a back person but he keeps repeating, like a robot, 'Nothing you can do for a bad back.' Surely that can't be so? What are osteopaths? Are they not back experts? At least we should go and see one and pay an extortionate sum of money to be told that bed rest is all that will fix him. At least then, protocol will have been observed.

Yes, then my mother went deaf. The thing is that she's always had a 'bad ear'. In fact, so have I. And Caitríona. And Tadhg.

Mam is pretty much deaf in her 'bad ear' and has to have a hearing aid in it. Me, Caitríona and Tadhg aren't deaf in our 'bad ears', we just get lots of infections in them, but I'd say we'll go deaf at some stage, if Mam is our template. But anyway, didn't she get an infection and go deaf IN HER GOOD EAR!!! Isn't that terrible? How unfair is that? She's had two 'goes' of antibiotics and still isn't right. She will have to go and see an 'ear man'.

I have been to see an 'ear man'. Oh yes. Three years ago, or it might have been two, when I had several very bad ears in a row and had three 'goes' of antibiotics without it making a difference. It took ages before I got to see my 'ear man' because he was so in demand, and the minute I walked through his door he took one look at me and said, 'There's nothing wrong with your ear. It's your jaw. You need to see a "jaw man"!' (So I did and he diagnosed TMJ and as a result I have to wear an attractive rugby-player-style jaw guard to bed.)

So anyway, yes, poor Mam. And God knows I was impatient enough with her before, what with having to repeat everything to her twice, but I'm ten times worse now.

Example of one of our conversations:

'Mam, do you remember the night of your birthday?'

'What?'

'OH, FOR GOD'S SAKE!!! I SAID, DO YOU REMEMBER THE NIGHT OF YOUR BIRTHDAY?'

'No.'

'No? You don't? That great night?'

'What?'

'CHRIST ALIVE, NOT ONLY ARE YOU DEAF BUT YOU ARE SENILE TOO!!'

'What?'

Poor Mam. I am horrible. And it's all ahead of me.

Also, Rita-Anne has had an eye infection necessitating a trip to the Eye and Ear Hospital. And Susan has injured her neck, but details are sketchy because she's in Spain. Some sources say it happened on a surfing lesson. Others say it occurred in the gym. Truly we are the sickest family in the entire province of Leinster.

Meanwhile I've started Pilates. Yes, myself and Himself have started getting lessons. It looks easy, it looks like you're doing nearly nothing, but in fact is as tricky as bejaysus, but we are looking forward to having 'strong cores'. So on that happier note, so ends September. Much occurring in October. Kicking off with a visit to London, Himself's birthday, Rita-Anne's hen weekend and a promotional trip to Madrid and Barcelona, where we are assured that we will be mugged for our shoes. Perhaps we could set an episode of *THE BOYS NEXT DOOR* there and Luka could be mugged for his trousers.

Previously unpublished.

October

Wedding plans

Arrangements concerning R-A's wedding are taking up much of my time, in particular trying to find my mammy a make-up artist who would come to her house the morning of the wedding and do top-notch make-up for a pittance.

I found her a lovely woman who has 'done' me on occasion, but she (my mammy) baulked at the cost, chastising me for my extravagance, saying that when she got her make-up done at a saloon for my wedding, it was nothing like as expensive. I reminded her that my wedding was a) eleven years ago, and b) in a different currency, and that c) this woman was coming to her house to do it so that Mam didn't have to travel to Dún Laoghaire for it and get the 46A home wearing her wedding face.

But she was not to be persuaded and I had to suffer the embarrassment of cancelling the lovely woman and I stomped around the house for a while, complaining that as far as my mammy was concerned I could do 'nothing fucking right'.

October also saw us celebrate Himself's birthday. Also, I went to the cinema three times in October. Normally I'm lucky if I go three times a year, and I don't know why the sudden spate.

Also, television and the return of *Strictly Come Dancing*! God, I love that programme. The return of *SCD* means that I've moved from my summer crush on Davina McCall to my autumn crush on Claudia Winkleman.

Yes, so then, off to Spain for the book tour. I'd never been to

Barcelona before and everyone said, 'Jesus, don't go there! You'll be mugged!' Like, *everyone* said it! My friend Judy said her husband Fergal was 'nearly' pickpocketed on the Ramblas. My hairdresser said I'd be mugged for my shoes and handbag. Even Mam had her take on the matter. I said to her, 'Mam, I'm going to Spain on a book tour.' Normally, whenever I tell her I'm going away on a book tour, she affects a total lack of interest, in case I might think I'm getting 'above myself'.

I could say to her, 'Mam, I'm going to Mars on a book tour,' and she'd say, 'So does that mean you won't be here for your dinner on Thursday?'

But when I said, 'Mam, I'm going to Spain on a book tour,' she visibly started and said, 'Where in Spain?' And I said, 'Madrid and Barcelona,' and she said, 'Barcelona? What are you going there for?' And I said, 'I just shagging told you! A book tour.' (Relations were still slightly strained after the make-up artist fiasco.) And she said, 'A book tour? In Barcelona? But you'll be mugged. People at bridge went to Barcelona and they were mugged!'

But we had the most AMAZING time in Barcelona – have you been? It's beautiful and interesting and full of charm and history and character and fabliss inexpensive handbags. We stayed at the Hotel Arts, which is glamorous and beautiful and efficient. We had a room overlooking the sea and woke up every morning to glorious sunny light, which was so cheering as it's already wintery in Irlanda.

I'm not saying I didn't love Madrid too, because I did and do, it's just that I've already been to Madrid and this was my first time in Barcelona and I spent all my time in Madrid working and only had to do one interview in Barcelona, then the rest of the time was mine, and apart from a mild but unshakeable dread that I'd be mugged for my jeans and have to make my way back to the hotel in my knickers I had a great time.

Yes, Gaudí! Why aren't all buildings like his? They're fun and magical and exquisite. Also, Barcelona – I couldn't help noticing – has more chemists per square inch than anywhere else I've ever been. My kind of town, without a doubt. (Recently I met a woman who, like me, likes to browse in chemists. I think I might set up a club for 'our kind'.)

I was very glad about the many hours I'd spent watching *Dora the Explorer*, because all the Spanish I know has come from that. *Hola. Adiós. Gracias. De nada.* It is an excellent programme and I'm so sad that Ema and Luka have outgrown it and now scorn it.

We went to the football in Barcelona; they were playing some poor crowd called Recreativo. And one of my favourite footballers, Ronaldinho, was playing. He is always skipping about and kicking up his heels and chatting to the grass and grinning from ear to ear. No matter what happens, he smiles away like a happy, happy person, even if someone kicks him in the head, which must happen from time to time in his line of work. I find such positivity mucho charming. *Muy bueno*.

As we took our seats in the stadium, Himself and myself really wanted Barcelona to win but we were afraid that if we supported them, even secretly, we'd ruin their chances. We feel we are the kiss of death on any team we support. (Watford, Ireland.) So we decided to have a little competition to see which of us is the most 'kiss of death'; he supported Barcelona while I was 'up' for Recreativo. Within moments it was clear that I was the runaway winner – Himself has started addressing me as Beso de Muerto (sort of Spanish for 'Kiss of Death') as Barcelona were 'all over' Recreativo and beat them 3–0 and I'd say they were not a happy bunch of lads on the bus back.

Previously unpublished.

November

Wedding!
Cat cake!

Yes, it finally happened, on 11 Nov the little sister got married. Lovely so it was, yes, lovely. And by then of course the worst was over, as I had survived the hen night – they made me go to a nightclub, at my age! I ask you! It was Lillie's Bordello and they were extremely nice to us, so very nice, and it made Rita-Anne very happy.

Then everyone went on to a casino as Rita-Anne is lucky at that sort of thing (cards, winning money) but I scarpered.

I should also mention the cat cake. Or The Cat Cake, to give it its proper title. Rita-Anne had been insistent that she didn't want anything vulgar for her hen night – no policemen getting their lad out, no chocolate mickeys, etc. – so, because she loves cats, I got a special cake for her, made in the shape of a cat. It was a chocolate biscuit cake. Remember this because it becomes important later.

So yes, hen night survived, the last week was counting down, family members were arriving from far-flung parts, then a) Seán Ferguson got a bout of bad sinuses; b) Rita-Anne complained of feeling 'fluey'; c) Caitríona got an ear infection necessitating a trip to Dr Murphy for antibiotics; d) the minute Luka set foot from Prague into my parents' house, he too started bellyaching with a terrible sore ear; e) Ljiljana puked the night before the wedding; and f) Heather, the mother of the groom, got so sick at

429

the actual wedding that a doctor had to be called (sadly not Dr Murphy as the wedding was in Wicklow and Dr Murphy lives many miles away in Blackrock).

(At the wedding I was sitting beside poor Heather and we bonded very strongly over bad health. I commiserated on her bad stomach and she said sadly that she often became ill on big occasions and I, sensing a kindred spirit, cried out, 'So do I!'

'Do you?' she asked hopefully, also (I'd say) sensing a kindred spirit.

'And I bet you feel really guilty?' I said.

'Yes!'

'And you feel that no one understands!'

'Yes!'

'And you suspect that half the time they think you're faking it!'

'Yes! And I'm not!'

'I know you're not! It's exactly the same for me.'

Beautiful, so it was.)

So yes, rehearsals, dinners, airport trips, purchase of fizzy vitamin C, the week went by in a blur. And at one stage I found myself in my parents' dining room, where the remains of the cat cake had been deposited and all of a sudden, *mes amies*, it was like being possessed. Before I knew what I was doing, I was 'at' the cat cake, shovelling it into my clob, a chocolate biscuit frenzy, with pieces of cake flying around the room and on my face and in my hair and on the walls and me supposed to be off the sugar, but obviously the high emotion of the week was getting to me and it was better to eat cat cake than to drink.

I ate LOADS. I am very ashamed, also frightened. I have tentatively, with trembling limbs, climbed back up on to the sugar-free horse and hope I manage to stay there, but Christ almighty, I am such an addict.

November

Then the morning of the actual wedding arrived and it was weird because we've talked about it and prepared for it for so long and there it was – upon us! It was a very girly morning. Rita-Anne, Caitríona, Ema and Mam came to my house to have their hair and make-up done, then Rita-Anne got into her dress and she looked so beautiful, and her dress was utterly amazing, then we had pink champagne, except for me and Ema, who shared a modest bottle of raspberry smoothie (pink – oh, but of *course* – in fact the pink champagne was her idea. Himself had gone out fully intending to buy *non*-pink champagne, but Ema rang him and gently talked him round. Please bear in mind she is six).

Then we went to the church, and Himself was the chauffeur for Rita-Anne and Dad, and he'd bought a special chauffeur's hat off eBay which made him look disconcertingly like a male stripper.

All went well in the church, Luka (the ring-bearer) didn't drop the rings, and him and Ema walked very slowly up the aisle, *just like they were told to*, they are such good children. Me and Caitríona, walking behind them, weren't half as slow and were nearly passing them out by the time we got to the altar.

Meanwhile, Dad, who has been a nervous wreck for the past month and who had been pacing, *actually pacing*, like a caged lion for the week before the wedding, nearly trampled us all into the ground, racing up the aisle, dragging Rita-Anne with him. (Sad but true story about Dad. He was so nervous about who he had to collect from the airport and when he had to do it and when he had to deposit them back there that he woke in the middle of the night shouting, 'What time do I have to be at the airport at?' It would take a heart of stone not to laugh . . . The Airport Bus was an alternative to Dad providing a taxi service – but the Airport Bus is only handy if you've about a week to spare. Very long route, the 746. Very, very long, but it'll get you there in the end.

However, bring sandwiches. Also water, it wouldn't do to get dehydrated. Also perhaps one of those neck-cushion yokes. And a book of crosswords. And, to be on safe side, malaria tablets – probably no need really, it's just that the route does enter hyperspace for a while and God knows what you might pick up in there. Hyperspace is *riddled* with germs.)

Then vows, kiss the bride, clapping, communion, register signing, organ, back down the aisle, porch, coldness, shaking hands, photos, cheery comments about coldness of day, car, drive to Wicklow, more photos, more photos, more coldness, more cold photos, extra coldness, just one more cold photo, in you go, just this one last one, yes, know you're cold, just this last shot, dinner, speeches, book opened on how long speeches would last, a fiver a bet, I bet twenty-three minutes, only out by four minutes, but the winner was Ema (six –yes, only six), who put her winnings behind the bar for everyone to have a drink on her. Very generous spirit.

Much dancing, which I sadly missed as I had sneaked up to the room to check who had been evicted in *Strictly Come Dancing*, then discovered that I was vay tired and that everyone else was vay drunk, so decided to go to bed. Plan foiled when Caitríona, Suzanne, Seán Ferguson and Himself knocked on door, also wanting to know who had been evicted. Alas, I could not tell them as the results show had (perplexingly) been on an hour earlier than usual. However, my friend Judy saved the day by texting the result. Then they left to spread the news.

On Friday 24th I went to London to report on Behind the Scenes for self-same *Strictly Come Dancing*!

Other news this month – have been watching *I'm a Celebrity*. Gas. I'm not boasting but they asked me to be on it. Christ alive, I've never been so glad that I said no. Kangaroo's bits. God, no.

Also, I am a judge on the Orange Prize. I've known for ages but have been sworn to secrecy but announcement was made on Weds night. Dragged my rotting carcass to meeting, awash with Lemsip. Am thrilled, thrilled, thrilled to be a judge, very, very honoured. Also will get many free books. Naturally, my joy will be corrupted by snobby types complaining that if a chick-lit author is judging the Orange Prize, then the barbarians are at the gate, my dears. But my response will be a mature and dignified one. Yes. TOUGH SHITE, SNOBBY AMIGOS! THEY ASKED ME AND THEY DIDN'T ASK YOU!!!!!!

Now, Baxter. Baxter is a small pink toy dog which Caitríona bought for me in New York. However, Caitríona does not trust the post and the only time we ever get anything from her is when either she or a good friend is coming to Ireland. About two months ago Danielle came, bringing my birthday present from Cait (lovely things from Bliss), also Baxter. However, I didn't know that Baxter was called Baxter. Danielle said he looked like her mother's dog Dessie, and I thought, 'What a fine name. I shall call you Dessie, little pink dog.'

I immediately became very fond of Dessie and foresaw a long happy life with him.

THEN! A message from New York. Caitríona said she had heard rumours that I had been hitting 'Baxter' with a big stick and that she was very concerned. She and Seán had apparently employed quite a different method of discipline with 'Baxter'. She admitted that she was sorely missing 'Baxter', that although she had taken the decision to send him overseas to a wealthy family in order to give him opportunities that he wouldn't have got had he stayed 'Stateside' she was regretting her altruism. Between the Big Stick rumours and the 'name change', she was considering reapplying for custody.

Naturally I wasn't hitting Dessie with a big stick. It was quite a small stick, more of a ruler than a stick, and it wasn't so much to cause him pain as to remind him of things like erect posture, etc.

When Cait and Seán arrived from New York for the wedding, I was concerned that they might try to kidnap Dessie and smuggle him back to New York on a false passport. Himself and myself didn't want this to happen. We have become quite fond of little Dessie and regard him as an exceptional dog. As I explained to Seán and Cait, we have invested a lot in Dessie, both financially and emotionally. We have high hopes for him. We have given that little dog everything.

She asked if she could see him and we had to say, 'Sorry, no, he is with his Mandarin tutor, Mr Lee, we want him to be fluent in Mandarin by the end of the year. So that he can start learning Arabic.' She asked if she could see him that evening, when he had finished his language class, and we had to tell her, 'Sorry, no, he does his callisthenics every evening from six until ten.'

How about *after* 10 p.m., she asked and we had to say, 'Sorry, no, that is little Dessie's "playtime" in which we structure "spontaneous creativity". This evening we are teaching him to make pancakes, then he is doing his tapestry, he is recreating a life-size copy of the Bayeux Tapestry and hopes to have it finished by month end.'

'After playtime?' she asked and we had to say, 'Sorry, no, but after playtime he has his driving lesson.'

Suddenly, in a sharp voice, she asked, 'How much sleep does Baxter get?'

'Dessie,' I said, emphasizing the word "Dessie", 'gets a full five hours. We find that five hours is the optimum time. This careful calibration is the result of lengthy experimentation, in which we cut back his sleeping time in half-hourly increments and monitored the results. We even wore white coats and carried clipboards and wore strange visor-type flashlights on our heads. Initially Dessie did well at three and a half hours, but then he started to hallucinate, so we increased it little by little to five hours a night.'

Yes, well, anyway, we enjoyed it very much. Caitríona said to tell you that I made him read *The Brothers Karamazov* in the original Russian. Also that I plan to send him to Military Academy during the school holidays. Also that she has a viral throat infection.

Interesting news from Ljiljana. On her return from Ireland after the wedding, she fell foul of a sore throat, which she parlayed into a nasty ear infection, necessitating antibiotics. She said she has never felt so much like a Keyes, not even on her wedding day.

Previously unpublished.

December

Nothing happens!
Let's be kind to ourselves

A diligent month – I worked. I wrote, I read the Orange Prize entries (which hardly counts as work) then I wrote some more.

For Christmas I went to Cambridge to Chris, Caron and Jude. Also present were Himself's parents, John and Shirley, and Caron's mother, Bobbi. It was a very nice day and I didn't have a repeat of The Cat-Cake Incident – see, I was worried about how I'd fare around the orgy of chocolate that constitutes Christmas, but I've come through and am 'in the clear'. Christ alive, it was hard though. Funnily enough, I've no interest in drink, none at all, but to see a chocolate truffle going into a mouth that isn't mine gives me a pain of longing in my stomach.

Wait till I tell you something funny: a few days after Christmas, Himself comes up the stairs and says, 'Do you want to go on *Celebrity Big Brother*?' And I said, 'When? We'll be in London around the 9th of Jan, won't we?' And he says, 'NO! You big thick! Not on Dermot, but on *Celebrity Big Brother*. The show! All of it!'

Well, *mes amies*, I was dumbfounded. I am a GINORMOUS fan of the show, but decided that it might be disastrous to be on it. Just in case I was getting too big for my boots, Himself said, 'Someone's dropped out at the last minute, they're desperate, they'll take anyone. When I told them you probably wouldn't do it, they asked me if *I'd* be interested.'

Then, a few days later, the front page of the *Star* was all about how 'a number of A-list stars have pulled out' of *Celeb BB* and how the bosses 'are in crisis talks'. So as a result I do not think I am 'It'.

So how did I spend New Year's Eve? Despite many invitations to glitterin' events (well, Mam and Dad invited me to a do in the golf club because the pal that was meant to be going with them was in hospital and the tickets had been paid for and for one lapse-y, insane moment I actually considered it and then I thought, 'Christ alive, are things so bad that I would consider going a) to a do in the golf club where they serve the soup in the same kind of metal bowls that doctors use to put removed gall-stones into; b) with my parents; c) and all their mates (except for the one who was in hospital, obviously); and d) on New Year's Eve!!!!!!!!!!!!!!!!!!!!!!!!!!').

In the end was in bed by 9 p.m. I mean, I hate New Year's Eve – I'm famous for it. In my humble opinion, New Year's Eve is the worst night of the year, even though many people think it's the best.

However, if you did go out on that dreadful night, I hope you had a wonderful time and a) that you didn't lose one of your shoes; b) that you didn't spend the chimes weeping alone in a corner; c) that you didn't try to get off with your friend's boy-friend; d) that you didn't have your phone stolen; e) that as you wandered the streets in search of a non-existent party, you didn't fall and cut your knee; f) that you didn't pay more than a hundred euro for your taxi home; and g) that you didn't wake up this morning in a strange bed, in a strange part of the city, with your coat

MIA. (These have been some of the ways I have 'celebrated' NYE in the past, so you will see why I prefer to go to bed at 9 p.m. on the evening in question and park myself out of harm's way until the whole wretched business is over.)

And I'll tell you something else – no resolutions! No, not one! I never make them because life is hard enough and I genuinely believe we all do our best all of the time. We are HUGELY imperfect and we always will be and the last thing we should be doing is making our already hard lives even harder by trying to achieve a load of things that we are SIMPLY NOT CAPABLE OF.

We will inevitably fail (because we over-aspire) and then we feel like wretched failures and *even worse* than before we began trying to run six miles a day, or live on a tenner a week in order to clear the credit cards, or imbibe only spinach juice.

No resolutions. Repeat it with me. No resolutions! No resolutions! NO RESOLUTIONS! (Unless you are trying to stop smoking, and the only reason I will support you is because life is made hell for smokers, you are practically stoned in the streets, you poor things, and I suppose things would be marginally more pleasant for you if you were free of it.)

So repeat after me: 'There is no need for me to make New Year's resolutions because every day I try my best. I may live a messy, lapse-ridden, imperfect life but it's the best life I can live. If I fail in some small way (chocolate, wine, over-spending, laziness – pick your poison), it's not because I'm a bad person, it's because it was all I was able to do on that particular day. I'm a human being and that means it's a waste of time, striving to be perfect.'

Even those people with shiny, happy, perfect Facebook posts aren't shiny and happy and perfect all of the time – they're just

showing us the parts they want us to see and we shouldn't lacer-
ate ourselves with self-hatred for not being as thin and tanned
and going on as many holidays as them. You might find it hard to
believe, but they too get strange nameless fears and pangs of
bleakness and bouts of peculiar sadness – despite having spent
New Year's Eve in Mauritius wearing a Missoni bikini with their
photogenic spouse and children.

Come on, let's say it together:

'Just for today I will go easy on myself, I'll let up on the con-
stant demands I make of myself and I'll allow myself to be
mediocre.

'Just for today, the world won't end if I don't achieve anything –
if I even regress.

'Just for today, I'll forgive myself for all the pain I cause myself
by virtue of being human.

'Just for today, I won't speak harshly to myself.

'Just for today, I'll treat myself with all the compassion that I
deserve.'

And off we go, living our lives.

Previously unpublished.